The Rough G

Surviving the End of the World

by Paul Parsons

www.roughguides.com

Credits

The Rough Guide to Surviving the End of the World

Editing: Matthew Milton
Layout: Matthew Milton & Tom Cabot
Proofreading: Jason Freeman
Production: Gemma Sharpe

Rough Guides Reference

Editors: Kate Berens, Ian Blenkinsop, Tom Cabot, Tracy Hopkins, Matthew Milton, Joe Staines
Director: Andrew Lockett

Publishing information

This first edition published August 2012 by
Rough Guides Ltd, 80 Strand, London WC2R 0RL
11 Community Centre, Panchsheel Park, New Delhi 110017, India
Email: mail@roughguides.com

Distributed by the Penguin Group:
Penguin Books Ltd, 80 Strand, London WC2R 0RL
Penguin Group (USA), 375 Hudson Street, NY 10014, USA
Penguin Group (Australia), 250 Camberwell Road, Camberwell, Victoria 3124, Australia
Penguin Group (New Zealand), 67 Apollo Drive, Mairangi Bay, Auckland 1310, New Zealand

Rough Guides is represented in Canada by Tourmaline Editions Inc.,
662 King Street West, Suite 304, Toronto

Printed in Singapore by Toppan Security Printing Pte. Ltd.

304 pages; includes index

A catalogue record for this book is available from the British Library

ISBN: 978-1-40538-596-1

1 3 5 7 9 8 6 4 2

Contents

Part 3
Saving us from ourselves

Part 4
Rage of the machines

Part 5
Death stars, missiles and threats from space

Part 6
Planet Titanic

Introduction

Armageddon. Doomsday. The end of the world as we know it. Call it what you want, the notion that some cataclysmic event will one day befall us and our planet – and perhaps even the rest of the universe too – has existed in our consciousness since the dawn of recorded history.

Tales abound in the Bible: Noah's flood, the destruction of Sodom and Gomorrah, not to mention the ominous warnings concerning Judgment Day. Other religions, including Islam, Hinduism and Buddhism, as well as Norse and Ancient Greek faiths, all put forward their own particular visions of how the world will ultimately end. In Buddhism, it is predicted that the teachings of Buddha will be lost, leading to a breakdown of civilization. In Norse mythology, a great battle between the gods, called Ragnarok, brings disasters and devastation to Earth.

The Hindu religion offers perhaps the most interesting interpretation, in which the universe does not end but undergoes cycles, each lasting many billions of years. Between each cycle is an era of timelessness, in which matter is regenerated by the Hindu god Brahma. This, as it happens, resonates with modern theories in physics, one of which says that our universe undergoes cycles of expansion and contraction, each separated by a new Big Bang in which time itself briefly vanishes. This is known as the "ekpyrotic theory". It is supported by ideas in string theory, a branch of subatomic particle physics, which states that particles of matter are made from tiny vibrating strings of energy (you can read more about this in **Part 6** of this book).

Religious scriptures are not the only texts that foretold prophecies of doom. Self-proclaimed prophets have long been making their own forecasts of the trials and tribulations that fate has lined up for the world. Foremost among these was the sixteenth-century French physician Nostradamus who, during his later life, made well in excess of six thousand predictions – ranging from the Great Fire of London to, some say, the 9/11 terror attacks. Nostradamus's predictions took the form of abstruse four-line verses, making it hard to ascertain their exact meaning. At least, that's the excuse proffered by Nostradamus scholars when asked what happened to his predictions about the world ending in 1984, 1999 and 2000. Mercifully, the next of Nostradamus's Armageddons isn't due until the year 3797 – which should give a little more time to get the translations right.

Our age has its own new breed of science expert: the futurologists. Think of them as Nostradamuses with PhDs. By using modern scientific knowledge, along with an understanding of historical precedents, futurologists try to make reasoned deductions about how the future of our world might unfold, and then make recommendations as to how we should act now.

Professor Nick Bostrom is a futurologist working at the Future of Humanity Institute, a think-tank based at the University of Oxford that tries to identify the big issues that the human species will face over the decades to come. One of Bostrom's pet interests are what he calls "existential risks", or threats to humanity's continued existence – in other words, Armageddon scenarios. Bostrom is concerned by the paucity of research into existential risks, their consequences and how human beings can mitigate them.

Particularly alarming is our neglect of low-probability but high-impact scenarios. These are events that don't happen very often, but when they do, they cause so much damage that there's a chance they could snuff out the human race altogether. Giant asteroids colliding with the Earth – the kind of calamity that wiped out the dinosaurs – are a prime example. An asteroid of this size might only strike the Earth once in ten million years, but when it does it could kill pretty much everyone on the planet – seven billion people at the latest count. This means that, even though asteroids only strike once in a geological age, they kill an average of seven hundred people per year – and thus really ought to merit our attention.

The human species has a habit of learning from its mistakes. That's no bad thing, when the mistakes are minor – or even not so minor, in the case of world wars and the global banking crisis. We are able to learn our lesson and, hopefully, move on. But when the mistake is something that can annihilate us all in one fell swoop, we're not going to get a second chance. Instead, we need to exercise some foresight and act in advance – rather than waiting for experience's bitter lesson.

Bostrom says that unless we take the danger posed by these wildcard existential risks more seriously, we could be done for. It's a sentiment shared by many other futurologists. Richard Gott, a physicist by trade at Princeton University, has calculated that there's a 95% chance the human race will be extinct in less than ten thousand years. In his calculation, Gott considers all the humans that have or ever will exist. He argues that a random individual from any point in time could find themselves anywhere in this sequence of people with equal probability.

It is, therefore, 95 percent likely that we are among the final 95 percent of humans who will live. Estimates suggest that 60 billion humans have been born already. If these people constitute the first five percent of humans to be born, then the total number of humans that will ever exist is, with 95 percent probability, around 1.2 trillion. Assuming the world's population levels out at around 10 billion, with average life expectancy at 80 years, this gives humanity about 9120 years. Gott's thesis is known as the Doomsday Argument. Its big weakness is its dependence on human life expectency not rising above eighty years. Many biological technologies – not to mention electrical and mechanical devices – now promise to extend human life even longer than that.

This book brings together the best scientific speculation about how life on planet Earth, in particular the human variety, will ultimately draw to a close – and it surveys the ideas that scientists and engineers are now working on to prolong our time here. There are also tips aplenty for the hapless citizen caught up in the mayhem.

Humans are now changing more rapidly than at any point in our history, both through evolution and as a result of deliberate modifications made to their bodies through the emerging field of "transhumanism" (covered in **Part 6** of this book). But as the Earth eventually reaches the end of its natural life, humans will need to take in their stride perhaps the biggest change of all – migrating away from our home world, and striking out to establish a new civilization in space.

Armageddon could be the end of life, or it could just be the end of life as we know it – for even those who survive will never be able to return to the existence they once knew. Society's landscape will have been forever reshaped by the upheaval. But perhaps that's a good thing. Charles Darwin, in his theory of evolution, showed that change – and the ability to adapt to it – is the secret to a species' success.

Watching from a safe distance an older, wiser humanity will then truly be able to claim that they, by the power of their ingenuity – and not in spite of it – have survived the end of the world.

Paul Parsons, 2012

To Callum, who in two years has managed to destroy many things, but not yet the planet.

What's in this book

Science fiction has certainly not been idle in speculating about all the various ways we humans might bite the dust. **Part 1: The end is nigh... isn't it?**, delves into the colourful imaginings of cinema and literature, to assess just how likely alien invasions, zombie plagues and attacks by mutant carnivorous plants might be. It also investigates the claims of Nostradamus and his followers, while taking a look at the Mayan prophecies, 2012 scare stories and other doomsday predictions.

Real-world science has its own share of horror stories too, of course. Scientists are increasingly putting forward a host of scenarios which they believe pose serious threats to the continued existence of humanity on Earth. The really bad news is that these prophets of doom actually know what they're talking about. Their theories are based not on runes and crystal balls, but sound knowledge and evidence.

As the poor old dinosaurs discovered to their cost 65 million years ago, Earth is regularly pelted by comets and asteroids from outer space. Scientists have found plenty of evidence that regions of the world have been afflicted by megatsunamis – tidal waves that can be hundreds of metres in height – and which were probably caused by catastrophic landslides. Recent outbreaks of deadly viruses such as swine flu, bird flu and sudden acute respiratory syndrome (SARS) have put the world on alert to the threat posed by biological pathogens. Throw in a few death rays from space (particles and radiation flung out by distant stars) and you'll begin to appreciate just how many hazards are obligingly provided by our home planet and solar system. All are investigated in detail in **Part 2: Savage Earth** and **Part 5: Death stars, missiles and threats from space**.

But we are also a danger to ourselves, it seems. Thanks to our evolutionary success as a species, we are now faced with the problem of over-population: could the human race be outstripping its natural means of sustaining itself on Earth? Weapons of mass destruction are another self-inflicted hazard – nuclear, chemical and biological armaments that give terrorists and rogue states truly terrifying destructive capability. And there is, of course, the huge great elephant in the room that is climate change – the steady increase in global temperatures we're facing, together with the rising sea levels that accompany it. To find out more about how we are fast becoming our own worst enemies, head for **Part 3: Saving us from ourselves**.

If we're to believe the scientific pundits, some of the technological advancements we are most proud of carry high risks of turning against us. Nanotechnology is one example – tiny robots, smaller than biological cells. Some scientists have speculated that these devices could run amok, converting all the matter in the world into more nano-robots – a scenario known as a "grey goo" catastrophe. Another, more widespread notion is that robots of a more standard size will rise up and take over the Earth. Extrapolating the current exponential rise in the power of computers, the idea predicts that one day computers will be able to outthink the human brain, a scenario that's become known as the "technological singularity".

And it's not all about microchips and metal – the new field of synthetic biology is allowing scientists to literally build new life forms from the ground up, by designing custom DNA in the lab. Sceptics are concerned that bringing new species into existence this way could have unintended consequences which we would be foolish to ignore. If you want to scare yourself with some machine-inspired techno terror, turn to **Part 4: Rage of the machines**.

Nothing lasts for ever, of course, and no matter how ingenious we might be, sooner or later the Earth and the sun will reach the end of their lifespans. **Part 6: Planet Titanic**, takes the long view, looking at what life for the human race might be like thousands of years from now and whether we might have an extra-terrestrial future. Not to mention what wriggle room we – or any other species that might be out there – might have if the entire universe were to come to an end.

The end is nigh... isn't it?

It seems mankind has been anticipating his end – and the end of the planet he lives on – for almost as long as he has existed. In this section of the book, we take a look at all the many doomsayers that have predicted the end of the world (sometimes even, helpfully, giving specific dates) and their wild ideas about how that end might come about. Not to be outdone by previous millennia, we give plenty of space to the even wackier depictions of cinema and sci-fi, too.

Nostradamus and co

prophets of the apocalypse

On 29 April 1987, smart-aleck children all around the world had an excellent excuse for not having done their homework: "sorry sir, but the world is going to end today." A much-publicized doomsday prophecy had been put about by the American cult leader Leland Jensen who, in the early 1970s, had founded a religious sect of the Bahá'í Faith, named Bahá'ís Under the Provisions of the Covenant. He predicted that, on 29 April 1986, Halley's Comet would enter orbit around the Earth and would collide with the planet a year later. Jensen didn't exactly have a great track record in apocalyptic predictions: he had previously garnered national attention in 1980, when he led a group of followers into fallout shelters, convinced the US was about to suffer a nuclear holocaust. Needless to say, both the 1980 holocaust and the predicted appearance of Halley's Comet had no basis in any kind of evidence whatsoever. That evening, those cheeky school-children were working late in detention – this author included.

Jensen is but one of thousands who have made grand predictions of calamitous world events. Perhaps the most famous doomsayer of them all was Michel de Nostredame – better known by the Latinized form of his surname, Nostradamus. He was born in 1503, in a small town in southern France called Saint-Rémy-de-Provence. He was an apothecary and medical-school dropout,

Portrait of Michel de Nostredame (Nostradamus), from the frontispiece of a collection of his prophecies.

who grew interested in the occult following a visit to Italy. In 1550, he set himself up as a seer, publishing the first of the almanacs containing his predictions, which in 1555 he condensed into a book called *Les propheties*.

Harbinger of doom

Nostradamus made his prophecies in the form of four-line verses known as quatrains. Those who have analysed the cryptic prose in the quatrains have found what they claim to be predictions of the Great Fire of London, the rise of Hitler, the atomic bomb and even the 9/11 terrorist attacks – to name just a few. However, the quatrains are so abstruse that there is much ambiguity in their meaning and they can be interpreted to mean pretty much anything anyone liked. In addition, Nostradamus often wrote in an obscure form of French, making it hard to translate his text into plain English. So much so that even Nostradamus's advocates are still arguing as to some of the quatrains' specific meanings.

One quatrain makes reference to a great battle against "Hister" – widely regarded among the hardcore Nostradamus devotees to

Predicting the future, twenty-first century style

Mark Twain once said: "prediction is difficult – especially of the future". When it comes to making prophecies today, the most informed predictions come from a scientific field of study known as futurology. Futurologists are savvy in many areas of science, technology and sociological development – and they combine these areas of expertise to spot trends that they think will shape the future.

Nick Bostrom, of the Future of Humanity Institute at Oxford University, is working to identify what he calls "existential risks" – future events that could threaten the very existence of the human species. These include climate change, the development of nanotechnology and emerging fields in bioscience. But existential risks can also result from wildcard events – low-probability but high-consequence occurrences that befall the Earth every now and again. Examples of wildcards might include massive asteroid impacts, pandemics of virulent diseases and ice ages. These are all discussed later in this book.

The techniques used by futurologists are wide and varied. Some rely on individual analysis, using their own expertise and research; others use consultation with panels of experts. Some do away with expert analysis entirely – asking non-experts to vote on what they think is the most likely future course of events. The resulting aggregate view – sometimes termed the "wisdom of crowds" effect (after a popular book of the same name) – has been remarkably accurate in other contexts with assessable outcomes.

For instance, the Iowa Electronic Market (a betting market run by the University of Iowa) has been more accurate than the opinion polls in predicting the outcome of US presidential elections 74 percent of the time, and predicted Barack Obama's victory in 2008. (The same phenomenon is probably the reason why "ask the audience" is by far the most effective lifeline on the TV quiz show *Who Wants to Be a Millionaire*, yielding the correct answer 91 percent of the time – compared to just 65 percent for "phone a friend".)

prophesize the rise of Hitler and World War II. However, others have questioned this conclusion, arguing that when the quatrain was written Hister was the French name for the lower Danube. Nostradamus made his own prediction for when the world will end – at least, that's what his devout interpreters decided. Unfortunately for all concerned, it was to have kicked off in July 1999. The rational men of science shouldn't smirk too smugly though: even the great physicist Sir Isaac Newton dabbled as a seer, predicting that the biblical events foretold in the Book of Revelation would come to pass in the year 2000.

And there were occasions when Nostradamus appeared to have got it unequivocally right. Michel predicted that "London will burn up suddenly in the year '66" – and the Great Fire of London did indeed take place in 1666. But you can't help suspect it's just a statistical fluke. Anyone could make the occasional fortuitous prediction given enough tries – and Nostradamus's prophecies number in excess of 6400.

In this respect, Nostradamus was like a lottery player with several million tickets. The odds of winning might be millions-to-one, but every week millions of people play the lottery; so it isn't surprising that someone usually wins. Human beings seem to have a weakness for finding patterns in randomness, which can often lead us astray in our judgements. Our innate fondness for the inexplicable explains the fascination that some people have for Nostradamus and his predictions, as well as other unscientific forms of divination such as numerology, palmistry and astrology.

The Mayan prophecies
just why is 2012 so special?

If ancient prophecies foretelling of the end of days are ten a penny, perhaps we shouldn't be too mortified to read about the most topical one, which says that human civilization is due to draw its last breath on 21 December 2012. You've probably heard of the 2012 apocalypse prediction already – perhaps via the disaster movie of the same name. For some reason, this prophecy seems to be bigger

Roland Emmerich's 2009 movie *2012* was a CGI-heavy depiction of how civilization might collapse if the Mayan prophecies turned out to be true.

than all the others – and has got an awful lot of people believing in it. Of course, you might be reading this book after the fateful day has passed. But if not, and you think there might be something to it, then be sure to read on before you cancel your pension plan, cash in your mortgage and embark upon the mother of all holidays.

The idea that the world could end in 2012 all stems from a calendar that was used by the ancient Mayan civilization, which occupied the Yucatán region of South America from around 2000 BC until the Spanish conquests of the sixteenth century. During the golden age, from AD 250–900, the Mayans were known for their considerable knowledge of science and mathematics, agriculture and for their architectural achievements – notably the many spectacular stepped pyramids that can still be found across the Yucatán today.

As well as all this, the Mayans were highly adept at tracking the passage of time. They used two short-term date systems – the 260-day Tzolk'in calendar and the 365-day Haab' calendar. The fact that they had a calendar based on a 365-day cycle (equal to the time taken for the Earth to complete one orbit around the sun) demonstrates how advanced for the time their astronomical knowledge really was. And perhaps that's partly why people are so spooked about 2012.

Close-up detail of a Mayan calendar, carved in stone.

These two Mayan calendar systems were combined to form the Calendar Round, a cycle lasting 52 years, after which the dates on both calendars simultaneously would return to zero, and the cycle could begin once again. A 52-year calendar is fine for recording short-term dates, but not so useful when it comes to logging events in the history books – or for making future predictions. For this purpose, the Mayans also came up with what is called the Long Count Calendar.

Mayan maths

Our system of counting is known as base-ten: it is centred around ten basic digits (0–9). The Mayan mathematicians, however, favoured base-twenty and base-eighteen, in which there are twenty digits (0–19) and eighteen digits (0–17), respectively. Each date in the Long Count Calendar is then specified by four base-twenty numbers and a base-eighteen number, each separated by a dot. So a typical Long Count date might look something like 1.5.10.7.3. (The base-eighteen number is the second from the right.)

Working in from the right: the first number counts individual days; the second number counts increments of 20 days; the third number

360 days; the fourth 7200 days; and the fifth and final number counts in giant increments of 144,000 days. Each of these 144,000-day increments were known to the ancient Maya as a *b'ak'tun*. The date we've given as an example thus corresponds to 183,743 days from the calendar's zero-point. The Mayan timekeepers took as their zero-point 11 August, in the year 3114 BC.

If you've managed to follow all that, you'll be in a position to see what all the fuss is about over 2012. The Mayans attached great significance to the number thirteen and, accordingly, the Long Count date 13.0.0.0.0 – the end of the thirteenth *b'ak'tun* – is generally regarded as the end date in the Long Count Calendar. This occurs 1,872,000 days (13 x 144,000) from 11 August 3114 BC. Which, if you translate it into our own date system – the Gregorian calendar – and factor in all the quirks such as leap years, brings you to 21 December 2012.

End of the world as *who* knows it?

The trouble is – as most Mayan scholars today will tell you – that the Mayans themselves saw this as anything *but* the end of the world. Instead, they believed such a turning point in the calendar would mark the beginning of a new age of enlightenment, and thus would be cause for a considerable celebration (marking 5128 New Years, no less).

So where did the idea that the world is going to end come from? It seems to have sprung from the work of the American archaeologist Michael Coe. In his 1966 book *The Maya*, he put forward an interpretation of ancient Mayan scripts, suggesting that the Mayans believed the passing of the thirteenth *b'ak'tun* would correspond to Armageddon. That now seems to be very far from the truth. The world is not going to be destroyed when the Mayan calendar ends, any more than it will be destroyed when the calendar hanging on your wall ends – we get to 31 December and then start again at 1 January. Similarly, the Mayans will just begin a new *b'ak'tun*.

But, of course, everyone loves a good yarn and so the stories of 2012 being the end of the world have stuck – and since become amplified further by the Internet (not to mention that pesky movie).

B'ak'tun up the wrong tree

Those who continue to cling to the notion of the 2012 apocalypse have put forward various theories for the cause of Armageddon – though none of them are based on sound science.

Perhaps the most common of these says that a rogue planet, called Nibiru (which is meant to have been discovered by the ancient Middle Eastern Sumerian civilization) is going to crash into the Earth. This is, of course, impossible. I'm writing this in 2011 and, given the size of planets and the speeds at which they move through the solar system, any planets near enough to hit us in late 2012 would already be very visible in the night sky – to anyone looking with the naked eye. Astronomers, with the aid of powerful telescopes, would most likely have been tracking the thing for the past decade.

Another idea is that a powerful solar flare is going to trigger a geo-magnetic field reversal, wherein the Earth's magnetic field changes polarity and potentially exposes us to harmful radiation from space in the process. Geomagnetic reversals do happen (see p.239). And solar activity is indeed due to reach a peak in 2012 (as it does every eleven years). But the coming peak looks set to be no more tempestuous than any other.

Furthermore, the suggestion that the magnetic fluctuations accompanying a solar flare might tip the Earth's core enough to trigger a field reversal clearly hasn't been thought through. The core, after all, is twice the size of our moon, yet its magnetic field is less than one percent the strength of a humble fridge magnet. This is like trying to move a boulder using a stick made of balsa wood.

Other mooted perpetrators of Armageddon 2012 include: celestial alignments of the Earth and the sun with the supermassive black hole at the centre of our galaxy; alien invasions; and impacts of comets and asteroids with the Earth. Of the three, only the last has any remote kind of likelihood. But such a collision is no more likely to occur on 21 December 2012 than on any other day of the calendar that you might care to choose.

The hunt for Nibiru

Ever since the discovery of the sun's eighth planet, Neptune, in 1846, astronomers have been searching for Planet X – a new member of the solar system whose gravity was supposed to explain strange kinks observed in the orbit of Uranus. Could Nibiru, the hypothetical planet predicted to collide with the Earth by 2012 doomsayers, be the same Planet X that the astronomers have long been seeking?

The name Planet X was first used by the American astronomer Percival Lowell in 1906. He believed that there must be another planet orbiting beyond Neptune and began combing the skies using the Lowell Observatory (built with his own money), looking for objects that were changing their position from night to night. Such rapidly moving celestial bodies could only be orbiting around the sun – anything further away would appear static, like the stars.

But Lowell's search drew a blank. Other astronomers, meanwhile, scoured the solar system at the other end, looking for a planet close to the sun – believing that it could account for anomalies in the orbit of Mercury. So convinced were they that they jumped the gun and pre-named this world Vulcan. However, Albert Einstein's theory of general relativity, published in 1916, explained Mercury's bad behaviour with no need for extra worlds, and the hunt for Vulcan was soon after abandoned.

In 1930, Clyde Tombaugh, a young astronomer from Kansas, discovered Pluto – a small icy body plying the outer solar system beyond Uranus (and, for some of its orbit, beyond Neptune too). However, studies of the motion of Pluto's moon, Charon, made it clear that Pluto wasn't nearly massive enough to be influencing Uranus.

The final blow for the Planet X theory came in 1989, when the *Voyager 2* probe flew past Neptune. Its measurements provided a revised estimate of the planet's mass. Using this new mass, Neptune's gravity then explained the anomalies in the orbit of Uranus.

The final twist in the story came in 2006. The discovery of numerous Pluto-like objects in the outer solar system – one of them bigger than Pluto itself – led the International Astronomical Union to reclassify Pluto and these new worlds as "dwarf planets". Astronomers are now sure that the eight remaining planets – Mercury, Venus, Earth, Mars, Jupiter, Saturn, Uranus and Neptune – are the only planets in our solar system.

Strange alignments

astrologers' hunches

Throughout history, astrologers have offered prognostications of woe based on the positions of the planets in our solar system. Of key importance, they said, are alignments between the planets – that is, when two or more planets form an approximate straight line that passes through the Earth. In the 1680s, Sir Isaac Newton formulated his law of universal gravitation, revealing that the planets do indeed exert a force on the Earth, and that these forces from the moon and sun are responsible for raising ocean tides.

For reasons best known to themselves, astrologers then began to speculate as to whether these same forces might also have a bearing on whether the king was about to die, whether war with other nations might be brewing, and indeed whether the world was soon going to end.

Most of astrology's predictions are based on pseudoscientific reasoning and subjective interpretations – as any comparison of a range of daily horoscopes for the same star sign will reveal. The movements of the planets have about as much influence on world affairs as the colour of your curtains.

Still, it's reasonable to ask whether we might have anything to worry about from the kinds of forces that planets really do exert, which we know about thanks to Newton. After all, the oceans are a force to be reckoned with: anything that's capable of controlling them (to raise the tides) must pack quite a punch. Sure enough, in 1974 scientists John Gribbin and Stephen Plagemann published their "Jupiter effect" theory, claiming that the gravitational effects of planetary alignments will alter the Earth's orbit around the sun, could trigger earthquakes and, in extreme circumstances, even tear the planet in half.

Tidal force

A planet's gravity makes itself felt in two quite different ways. First of all, there is a basic force of gravitational attraction between all massive objects. In our solar system, the dominant force any planet experiences is that pulling it towards the sun. This is what keeps the planets orbiting, and stops them flying off into space. And it's the same force that keeps the moons, including our own, circling around their host planets.

Newtonian gravity is what's known as an inverse square law, which means that its strength diminishes in proportion to the square of the distance from the source. So a planet orbiting four times further away from the sun only feels one-sixteenth as much gravitational force.

But gravity has a second effect, known as tidal force. Let's say an astronaut in space was falling feet first towards a planet. Because of the inverse square law, gravity is stronger closer to the planet, and so the astronaut's feet feel a slightly greater force than his head does – the net effect is a small force that tries to stretch him out lengthways. Also, because gravity is a radial force there is also a small inwards component to the force that tries to squash the astronaut ever so slightly around his waist.

These phenomena together are known as tidal forces. Their magnitude increases with the size of the object being stretched and squashed. Our hypothetical astronaut would experience only mild tidal forces (unless they were falling towards an especially strong source of gravity, like a black hole – see p.214). For an object the size of a planet, however, the tidal forces are strong enough to raise the ocean tides. Whereas ordinary gravitational attraction diminishes in proportion to the square of the distance from the source, tidal forces diminish with the distance cubed – so a planet four times as far away from the sun experiences just one sixty-fourth as much tidal force.

Spring and neap

Earth's ocean tides are raised by a combination of the gravitational tidal forces from the sun and the moon. The force exerted by the moon is roughly double that of the sun – its relatively small mass is more than compensated for by the fact that it's nearly four hundred times closer to us.

When the sun and moon line up, during new moon or full moon for example, then high tides are especially high. These are sometimes known as spring tides (though their name has nothing to do with the season). Conversely, when they're positioned so you could plot a line from the sun to the Earth to the moon and form a right angle, their tidal forces partially cancel one another out. The result is a high tide that's lower than usual – known as a neap tide.

The Jupiter Effect

In their 1974 book *The Jupiter Effect*, two Cambridge University astronomers – John Gribbin and Stephen Plagemann – proposed that an alignment of the planets due to occur in 1982 would trigger major earthquakes around the world.

Although the direct gravitational effects of the planets on the Earth during an alignment are negligible, the pair's theory suggested a seemingly convincing indirect method – via the effects this alignment might have on our star, the sun.

The alignment they described wasn't really an alignment in the strictest sense – more of a loose grouping, with all the planets lying within an arc spanning a 98-degree sector of the solar system. Their idea was that, in this configuration, the combined gravity of all the planets would be sufficient to alter the sun's surface activity. This increases the number of sunspots and solar eruptions and thus ramps up the volume of particles streaming from the sun's surface – what's known as the solar wind.

The solar wind is made up of electrically charged particles that are occasionally drawn down onto the Earth's poles by the planet's magnetic field, causing aurorae. The Jupiter Effect theory supposed that the extra volume of particles now drumming down from space would stir up the Earth's atmosphere and that this atmospheric disturbance would in turn alter the planet's rotation rate.

This would then change the shape of the Earth's crust. Because the planet is spinning (doing so once every 24 hours) it is deformed from a spherical into a flattened spheroidal shape by the centrifugal force of this spin. Any changes to the rotation rate alters the centrifugal force, causing the planet's shape to become either more or less flattened – depending on whether it spins faster or slower. And this additional deformation would cause the crust to crack and shift along existing tectonic fault lines, leading to devastating earthquakes.

The theory was controversial. And, of course, 1982 came and went with absolutely nothing along these lines happening. John Gribbin, who went on to become a highly successful popular science author, has since expressed regret at his involvement with the theory.

These tides themselves vary in height. That's because the moon's orbit isn't quite circular, but varies in distance from the Earth. If its closest approach, known as perigee, coincides with the spring tide alignment then the result is an especially high – perigean – spring tide. If a perigean tide happens at the same time as a violent ocean storm, it can lead to serious flooding.

These are instances when alignments of celestial objects can, and do, affect events on Earth. Though, as we'll see, they're about the only credible examples there are!

Planetary portents

So if the gravity of the moon and sun are able to influence the Earth then could the forces from the other planets in the solar system ever do the same? The simple answer is no. The biggest planet in the solar system is Jupiter, but even its mighty gravitational pull is just one percent what we feel from the moon. Meanwhile, the tidal force it exerts is even smaller, just 0.0006 percent of the moon's. In fact, of all the planets, Venus exerts the biggest tidal force – because it's the closest planet to Earth – but even this only amounts to just 0.005 percent of the moon's influence.

Even if all the planets were to align in the sky, their combined gravitational pull could muster no more than 1.7 percent of what we already experience from the moon, while the tidal forces they create could not exceed 0.006 percent of the lunar value. It's also worth remembering that, although planetary alignments are rare, over the course of the 4.5 billion years since the solar system's formation, Earth has experienced many such events and appears to have survived unscathed.

Doom-mongers have even suggested possible alignments between other celestial objects in our galaxy, the Milky Way. One theory for how the world might end in 2012 centres around an alignment between the Earth, the sun and the supermassive black hole at the Milky Way's centre. Even if such a thing were to happen – and there's nothing in the sky that suggests it might – the magnitude of the gravitational and tidal forces would be smaller than those exerted by any of the planets – even the tiny, far-away dwarf world Pluto. In short, it's nothing to lose any sleep over.

Monstrous visions

this is the way the world ends: not with a bang, but a Godzilla

Hollywood, of course, has always pictured the world ending in many more imaginative, terrifying and splendidly ridiculous ways than astrological planetary alignments. Try this one for size. A 200m-high prehistoric monster clambers out of the Atlantic and goes to work on New York City – flattening buildings, eating the population, and generally making matchwood of anything and everything that gets in its path.

It's a scenario that's done the rounds in many a Hollywood movie – most recently the 2008 mockumentary *Cloverfield*. Most of these films portray the monster wreaking localized devastation. But, unless authorities can figure out a way to halt the advance of such a creature, there's nothing stopping it, and others like it, from devouring the planet – making this a potentially global threat. So what's the best way to deal with a giant sea monster? And is this, ahem, really something we need to worry about?

What's the plan?

Evacuate, evacuate, evacuate! Those would be the first, second and third things on the mayor of NYC's lengthy and hurriedly scribbled to-do list. Chances are he would just have received a phone call from the near-hysterical police commissioner. The police are invariably the first to respond in any emergency situation. But when several squad cars and countless officers become Godzilla's elevenses, it's time to call back-up. After notifying the secretary of defense, the mayor probably has about an hour to get as many people out as possible before the military start shooting.

Roughly 1.7 million people commute in and out of Manhattan every day, over the course of some three hours. If the authorities commandeered public transport and set up contraflows on what are normally inbound routes, then it would perhaps be possible to get a million people out within the hour. However, with NYC's population currently at over eight million, there will inevitably be civilians in the way when the bullets start flying.

One hell of a bang!

It's fair to say any remaining Manhattanites will be attempting to dodge far worse things than bullets – if, that is, the armed forces have done their homework. That's because a creature 200m high will have metres-thick skin. And this means that bullets, and even anti-tank rockets, will inflict little more damage on Godzilla than small needles might do to you or me.

Sadly, we have no purpose-developed munitions for dealing with renegade prehistoric beasties. But perhaps the most promising weapons we do have might be those designed for dealing with extremely well-protected targets: munitions such as bunker-busting bombs, or shells and missiles designed to knock out heavily armoured battleships.

Bunker-busting bombs currently in service are able to penetrate

That giant, fire-breathing lizard attacks the citizens of Tokyo once more, in 1971's *Godzilla Versus the Smog Monster*.

A prototype Massive Ordnance Penetrator – the mother of all bunker-busters – is carefully unloaded in preparation for testing.

through six metres of reinforced concrete before exploding. And the silver bullet in this corner of the arsenal would be the Massive Ordnance Penetrator – a new bunker-buster that the US Air Force developed, which first emerged in 2011. It is said to be capable of punching through over 60m of reinforced concrete (or equivalent) before detonating a massive 2.5 tons of high explosive.

If that failed, then use of even more destructive weapons would have to be sanctioned. This would, inevitably, include the nuclear option. Governments won't – one hopes – want to destroy an entire city if they can help it, and so it's likely that tactical nuclear weapons (smaller devices, designed for battlefield use) would be used first to try and minimize collateral damage. The USAF B61 tactical nuclear bomb has a variable explosive yield from 0.3 to 170 kilotons (that is, it's measured by the equivalent amount of TNT needed to produce the same blast). By comparison, the bomb that destroyed Hiroshima exploded with a yield of around 15kt. Still, that much TNT going off in downtown Manhattan is going to make quite a mess.

Another option without the residual radioactivity of a nuclear explosion, might be a thermobaric weapon – a device that scatters fuel into the air and then ignites the mixture to create an especially violent detonation. In 2007, the Russian air force demonstrated its thermobaric weapon – its "Father of all Bombs". This packs seven tons of high explosive as fuel which, when mixed with the air, yields a blast equivalent to 44 tons of TNT.

So just how big could Godzilla feasibly be?

A thermobaric weapon could probably put paid to the biggest of prehistoric creatures. But what about Godzilla, a gargantuan lizard bigger than anything ever discovered by palaeontologists?

The biggest dinosaurs were the herbivorous sauropods that lived in the Earth's Jurassic and Cretaceous periods many millions of years ago. The largest of these, the brachiosaurus, is thought to have measured up to 30m in length and weighed over 70,000kg (seventy tons). Modern-day blue whales are much heavier than this (weighing in at around 180 tons). However, they have the buoyancy of ocean water to help support this great weight. Land animals must support their entire bodyweight on their own legs – and this sets a limit to how big they can get, based on simple physics.

To see how, imagine a cube. We'll call its side-length r. The cube's total weight increases in proportion to its volume, as you'd expect, which is r cubed (r x r x r). However, its ability to support that weight depends on its cross-sectional area, which only increases in proportion to r squared (r x r). Because r cubed grows faster than r squared as r increases, there comes a point at which the cube becomes too heavy to support itself. Concrete is a material with a compressive strength of 2 million kg per square metre and a density of 2400 kg per cubic metre. So, if our cube were made of concrete, the maximum value of its side-length, r, would be 833m (the point at which the weight equals the compressive strength), beyond which the cube collapses.

Those are the principles. In 1985, physicist Jyrki Hokkanen of the University of Helsinki, Finland, applied them to muscle and bone in order to calculate the maximum possible mass that a four-legged land animal could theoretically have – finding it to be around 100,000kg (one hundred tons). This would make for an animal some 40m in length. Hokkanen didn't (unsurprisingly!) examine the case of an upright bipedal monster like Godzilla, or the creature from the sci-fi movie *Cloverfield*. But, with half as many legs, these beasts would have a considerably smaller cross-section with which to support themselves – limiting them to perhaps fifty tons in total mass, and a height of around 20m.

Promotional material from the original 1933 RKO movie *King Kong* cited the giant ape's height as 50ft (15m) – which is well within the range that both physics and biology permit. But true Leviathans such as Godzilla seem somewhat unlikely – without even considering the odds of prehistoric creatures actually surviving somewhere in the world today. Needless to say, given the degree to which the planet's surface, skies and oceans have all been scoured by scientific exploration, the chances of finding such a monster are extremely small.

Spinosaurus was the largest of the bipedal dinosaurs (yes, even larger than *Tyrannosaurus rex*).

It came from outer space

UFOs, green men and hostile E.T.s

Flying saucers fill the skies, full with little green men packing ray guns. Ever since H.G. Wells's 1898 novel *War of the Worlds*, many people have wondered about the possibility of intelligent life on other worlds – and what might happen if that intelligent life turned out to be not altogether friendly.

The first and most obvious question to ask is what the statistical likelihood is of aliens even existing at all. Until 1995, the possibility seemed so unlikely as to be nonexistent. Up to that time, our sun was the only star that we knew to harbour planets. Then the first extra-solar planets were detected: planets in orbit around other stars. Now there are well over five hundred known extra-solar planets. One of these, Gliese 581 g, has a similar mass to the Earth and lies at sufficient distance from its host star for liquid water to exist on its surface. The search is now on for more of these Earth-like extra-solar worlds.

Now that we know there really are planets like our own orbiting other stars, the chance that life exists on one of them becomes much greater. It may still be that life is a hyper-rare occurrence on these planets. But, even so, with three hundred billion stars in the Milky Way galaxy, it would have to be a very rare phenomenon indeed for there not to be other inhabited planets out there somewhere. Radio astronomer Frank Drake, of the University of California, Santa Cruz, has estimated that our galaxy could be home to as many as ten thousand advanced extraterrestrial civilizations.

Why come here?

The next thing we might ask is what motivation they would have in coming to Earth – let alone attacking it. Science-fiction movies have put forward ideas such as food, resources, living space, slaves and even sport (as was the case in the *Predator* film franchise).

But do these ideas really stand up to scrutiny? Take the question of resources, for example. Let's assume, as many a sci-fi film and novel has, that the aliens' home planet might be running low on minerals that are essential for their industry. But if, as seems to be the case, uninhabited worlds are more common than not – there are thousands of them – then why would a species go to all the trouble of attacking a planet where there are aggressive natives that must be overcome? The aliens could simply settle down on the nearest barren rock and mine away to their heart's content, uninterrupted – and without wasting a single beam from their laser pistols.

Equally, how likely is it that they would come to Earth for extra living space? We know from experience that populations typically

The stop-motion aliens in Tim Burton's *Mars Attacks* (1996) paid homage to the aliens of classic B-movies from the 1940s and 1950s – not to mention comic-strip green men such as Dan Dare's adversary, the Mekon.

double every forty years – as recently as 1960 the human population on Earth was a "mere" three billion, whereas it's now nearly seven billion. So, while elbow room might indeed be a considerable problem, colonizing a new planet is only going to buy you another forty years or so before you have to attack and colonize yet another one. Any intelligent alien life would have surely concluded that their time and energy would be better spent settling on the large number of uninhabited worlds – perhaps utilizing some kind of terra-forming technology, engineering the planet's environment to make it a suitable home for your species. After all, even we lowly humans are already coming up with ingenious ideas in geoengineering – altering our environment in order to counter global warming, as discussed on p.89.

We come in peace?

On a similar note, biological scientists have argued that warlike species have a habit of eventually wiping themselves out. "Survival of the fittest" notwithstanding, the aggressive tendencies of such species eventually lead them to pick a fight with a species tougher and fiercer than they are. And so we might reasonably hope that advanced extraterrestrial civilizations that are old enough to have developed the technology needed to cross the gulf between the stars would have learned the virtues of a peaceful existence.

Not everyone takes this view though. For instance, British physicist Professor Stephen Hawking argues there's no reason at all to suppose aliens would behave any differently to human civilizations upon discovering and subsequently occupying new lands throughout history – whether these lands be inhabited or not. Aliens would see us the way colonies in the US saw the Native Americans, looking at our blue planet the way the British Empire looked at the Indian subcontinent.

For this reason, Hawking cautions against trying to make contact with alien races. The fact is, we may already have. For the last fifty to sixty years, our television and radio signals have been travelling out through space at the speed of light. That means that any intelligent aliens within fifty light years of Earth – and there are some 1400 star systems within this range – may already have gotten wind of our presence.

Of course, it's one thing to have the desire to travel to other star systems, but possessing the means is another matter entirely. That may one day become possible: there have been numerous theoretical schemes put forward for travelling across space at close to, or even faster than, the speed of light.

Are they here already?

Some people are convinced that aliens have arrived on planet Earth already. Every year, a multitude of UFO sightings are reported to authorities. Most of these can be explained away as overexcited spottings of ordinary aircraft or weather phenomena. But a small number continue to defy explanation. The key point to bear in mind is that, as yet, there's no conclusive evidence that these sightings are of extraterrestrial origin – the U stands for unidentified, and right now that's how they remain.

Perhaps the most infamous UFO report of all was the Roswell

Afghanistan and Vietnam: the home advantage

"Bows and arrows against the lightning." That's how H.G. Wells, in his 1898 novel *War of the Worlds,* described the difference between the military technology at humanity's disposal and that of an invading extraterrestrial race.

The universe has been in existence for around fourteen billion years. On the other hand, the first modern humans appeared on Earth just a few hundred thousand years ago. Given the current status of our interstellar space-travel capabilities, any invading aliens entering Earth's atmosphere are likely to be billions of years more technologically advanced than we are. Their weapons will vastly outstrip anything we are capable of. We would effectively be trying to fight off stealth bombers with World War I biplanes. In the face of such overpowering might, any conventional military response to the invasion is likely to be crushed instantly. Indeed, science fiction has often imagined world governments adopting a cravenly pragmatic approach, officially surrendering to the aliens within hours. Invariably, however, there'll be an underground resistance movement duly formed, waging war on the off-worlders using guerrilla tactics.

This form of warfare has proven especially effective in theatres of war such as Vietnam and Afghanistan – where small groups of fighters have proven superior to more technologically advanced adversaries. That's because these fighters had the home advantage – they knew the battleground and were better adapted to it than their attackers. The Viet Cong, for example, stuck to a policy of avoiding pitched battle. Instead, they used hit-and-run techniques, and dug out extensive systems of concealed tunnels. These weren't just shelters, but supply bases, headquarters and transportation passages: even when villages were under US control, there might be a tunnel network beneath it, continuing the offensive. The Viet Cong also adapted the weapons of their enemy: in one year, American bombs would leave some twenty thousand tons of explosives scattered around the Vietnamese countryside, which the Viet Cong would attempt to use themselves.

Human beings would need to be similarly ingenious in combating an alien enemy, but they would have the same advantages that the Vietnamese had. We are the product of millions of years of evolution here on Earth. So our biological design is optimized to Earth's gravity, to Earth's atmospheric composition, to the temperatures here and to surviving in the wild using the natural resources that our planet has to offer.

H.G. Wells's aliens were ultimately destroyed by the fortuitous microbiological happenstance of microbes – Earth-based bugs to which we have evolved an immunity. Likewise we might triumph over a real alien invader simply because this is our home, where we have lived and evolved as a species for umpteen millennia.

One of hundreds of photographs of unidentified flying objects taken by the American public in the 1950s and 60s, and kept on file by the CIA.

incident. The story goes that in 1947 an alien spacecraft crashed in Roswell, New Mexico. The American government supposedly stashed the remains of the craft at Area 51 – a military base in the Nevada desert, known to be used for testing and development of experimental weapons, where the technology was then dissected and incorporated into various US military and space projects.

It's highly unlikely that's the case. If the US government has had access to interstellar space-travel technology for several decades – even if such craft were damaged – how come NASA currently has no way of launching astronauts into space? Since the retirement of the space shuttle in June 2011, the US has had to buy seats on Russian Soyuz missions. Indeed, the US manned space programme is currently in its worst state since the 1970s – not exactly what you would expect from an organization in possession of a super-advanced spacecraft.

Independence day?

So should we be worried about the threat from alien invasion? Probably not. While alien contact is a possibility, the idea of wave after wave of aggressive aliens descending on the Earth is surely quite a long shot. Even if interstellar war does break out, the human race might not be doomed. While the aliens would almost certainly have superior technology that would severely outgun us, we would have the home advantage – which we could exploit to wage an effective guerrilla war against the invaders.

Albert Harrison, a psychologist at the University of California, Davis, and author of the book *After Contact* (1997), believes an alien invasion could actually serve to unite our fractured world. He cites historical precedents, such as the alliance that Britain and the US were able to establish with the Soviet Union during World War II against Nazi Germany. Though it's worth noting that the Soviet Union only sided with the Allies after Adolf Hitler broke his pact with Russia, invading Soviet territory. It's not inconceivable

Chain of command: who's in charge on doomsday?

When Godzilla hauls his scaly body out of the ocean, when the skies fill with alien battle groups, when an asteroid is spotted on a collision course with Earth or, indeed, when any other existential threat to life on our planet emerges – who will make the decisions regarding our response?

In fact, there's already a precedent for this kind of thing – well, sort of. In February 2009, the first meeting took place of the United Nations Working Group on Near Earth Objects, an international scientific panel to try and coordinate the world's response to the threat from comets and asteroids colliding with the Earth.

However, the UN has no governing power over nations. It can only make recommendations for world leaders to either act on or – as has been the case with the existential risk posed by climate change – largely ignore. In reality, we can probably expect specially negotiated coalitions between nations to form the backbone of our response to existential risks – at least in the near term. That's certainly been the case with other world crises, via organizations such as the G8 and NATO. And so, given that the United States will almost certainly be the major player in such an alliance, it seems likely that the US president will be the one to have the casting vote on how the world handles Armageddon.

that nations might even attempt to cut a deal with an invading alien force.

This brings us to the possibility of peaceful cooperation with aliens, or indeed surrender to them. It's possible to imagine the potential benefits it might bring in terms of medicine, technology, knowledge and overall quality of living. But the idea of humanity relinquishing its sovereignty is unappealing enough to explain why sci-fi writers have rarely explored this idea.

Zombie plagues
life ain't easy when you're dead

Here's a recipe for a really bad day. You wake up to find that all your neighbours – and, it transpires, a good deal of the population – have been transformed into walking corpses. Worse still, they all seem quite peckish, with human flesh – and brains in particular – topping the menu. As if that weren't bad enough, a single bite from one of these living cadavers is all it takes for you to join the party. Zombie plagues are a horror staple that refuses to die, fittingly enough. From the writings of H.P. Lovecraft in the 1920s, through George A. Romero's *Living Dead* movies, right up to *28 Days Later* (2002), zombies have been terrorizing us for generations.

In the real world, zombies are, thankfully, a lot less common. In 1985, Canadian anthropologist Wade Davis published *The Serpent and the Rainbow*, an account of his research into zombies in Haitian voodoo culture. In it, he explains how voodoo witch doctors place victims into a kind of zombified state through the use of neurotoxins and hallucinogenic drugs. Two special powders are introduced into the bloodstream (usually via a wound): the first includes tetrodotoxin (TTX), a powerful and frequently fatal neurotoxin found in the flesh of the pufferfish; the second powder consists of dissociative drugs such as datura. Together, these powders are said to induce a death-like state in which the will of the victim is entirely subjected to the control of the witch doctor.

Traumatic as that sounds, it's still a far cry from the rabid undead plagues of the movies. Zombies are usually portrayed as the result of some strange infection that's transmitted by bite, which

What's worse than a plague of zombies? A plague of zombies with rudimentary vestiges of intelligence. In George A. Romero's *Land of the Dead* (2005), some members of the zombie hordes are able to perform some of the basic tasks of their former lives: a truly terrifying prospect.

transforms healthy humans into a walking corpse over the space of a few hours. The basic idea behind this isn't *entirely* alien to the natural world. The rabies virus, for example, is carried in the saliva of infected animals and is transmitted through bite wounds. Once inside a new host, it heads for the central nervous system and attacks the brain, causing the host to become delirious and aggressive.

There are also organisms known to invade the brains of animals, radically altering their behaviour: take the *Toxoplasma gondii* parasite, for instance, which infects mice and rats. However, it can only actually breed inside the intestinal tract of a cat. This can only happen if the host mouse or rat gets eaten. To this end, the parasite has evolved to alter the behaviour of infected rats, making them attracted to the smell of cat's urine: while the parasite does not literally brainwash rats into wanting to be devoured, it can lead rats by the nose into suicidally perilous situations.

New viruses and infections are continually evolving – as we

Zombie survival guide

Essential zombie escape kit:

Car, van or other form of enclosed transport

GPS (assuming the satellites are still functioning)

Mobile phone (assuming the networks are still up)

Food for several days

Bottled water

First-aid kit

Flashlight

Sleeping bag

Shotgun(s)

Ammunition (lots of)

Crowbar (or baseball bat)

One or more companions

A plan

Not so essential, but great if you can get them:

Night vision goggles

Laptop and mobile Internet

Body armour (including full-face helmet and neck guard)

Kangaroo bars

Baby monitor cameras (for watching doors and windows)

Signal flares

Backup handgun

Grenades

AA-12 full-auto shotgun

Things to avoid:

Incendiary weapons

Taking prisoners

And remember...

Always aim for the head!

Always watch your back!

Always have an escape plan!

discuss with relation to SARS and swine flu in Part 2. So perhaps we shouldn't be too surprised if one emerges that turns people into shambling maniacs. What then?

Undead outbreak

Dr Robert Smith? (the question mark is actually part of his surname), at the University of Ottawa, Canada, has a pretty good idea. In 2009, he and his colleagues published a scientific study into a hypothetical outbreak of a zombie plague. They used a mathematical disease model to quantify both the spread of the infection through the popu-

Hollywood and reality

The end of the world has been portrayed many times in Hollywood movies. But how many of them have got their science right?

Far-fetched

Core dump

In *The Core* (2003), the Earth's core stops spinning, leading to a shutdown of the planet's magnetic field, which lets in harmful radiation from space. In order to get the core spinning again, a team of scientists drill down to the centre of the Earth to detonate a nuclear payload. Forget it: temperatures at the Earth's core are hotter than the sun's surface.

Instant ice age

Unless something is done about man-made climate change, the planet may well be heading for environmental meltdown. What is certain, however, is that we aren't going to see floods and ice ages wracking the planet overnight, as portrayed in 2004 eco-howler *The Day After Tomorrow*. It takes huge quantities of energy to influence Earth's climate systems, which in turn take at least decades to dissipate or accumulate.

Renegade neutrinos

The movie *2012* treats us to the spectacle of a flood of neutrino particles from the overactive sun boiling the Earth's core, creating turbulence in the planet's interior, which proves bad news for the outer crust and all on it. This is all wrong. Neutrinos hardly interact with ordinary matter – billions of them are streaming through you every second as you read this – and so could never deliver that much energy to the planet's 1200km-diameter inner core.

Far-sighted

Stellar caprice

In the 1951 film *When Worlds Collide*, a renegade star named Bellus is on a collision course with the Earth. While a direct collision of a star with the Earth is unlikely, it has since been discovered that close brushes do occur and can be hazardous, rattling comets from the outer solar system and sending them plunging in towards our planet.

lace and the effectiveness of different strategies for dealing with it.

They took as the theatre for their model a mid-size city, with a population of five hundred thousand people – about the size of Washington, DC, or Bristol. First of all the researchers ran a basic model to find out what would happen to the people if no action was taken at all. Never mind 28 Days Later – everyone in the city was either dead or a zombie after just four days.

Pigs in space

The first scientists to take seriously the idea that major pandemics could be caused by pathogenic bugs drifting to Earth from space were Cardiff University's Chandra Wickramasinghe and the late Sir Fred Hoyle in 1979. But the atmospheric 1955 movie *The Quatermass Xperiment* got there first, telling the tale of an astronaut who returns to Earth with an alien infection.

Igor, it's alive!

Concerns over the dangers of genetic tinkering and biologists cooking up creations that threaten the future of humanity are ten a penny. But in 1818, Mary Shelley penned the original bio-disaster story with her novel *Frankenstein*. It was first adapted into a movie in 1910. *Frankenstein* remains today the enduring moral fable of biotech gone wrong.

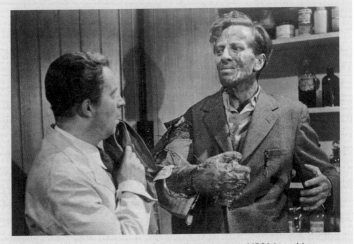

You can catch some nasty colds up there in outer space: MRSA is nothing compared to the deadly disease an unwitting astronaut brings back to Earth in *The Quatermass Xperiment* (1955).

Next they looked at three different intervention strategies: quarantining the zombies; trying to cure them; and all-out attack. The first strategy failed dismally. For it to work, authorities would need to capture not just every zombie, but every infected human who's yet to turn into a zombie. And this is virtually impossible. Instead, the strategy resulted in a mere handful of zombies in quarantine, while all the rest of the city was, again, either dead or zombified.

Trying to cure the disease fared little better. Dr Smith? and his team modelled this upon already existing medical treatments – perhaps a potent antiviral injection – that could be administered to captured zombies, turning them back into humans who were then released. In this case, the model resulted in an interesting result: two coexisting populations of humans and zombies. Yet the odds were still stacked heavily in favour of zombies: the human component of this end state was tiny, a handful of survivors trying to face down an overwhelming undead horde.

The most effective strategy, the researchers found, was simply to launch wave after wave of physical attacks – destroying the zombies over and over again, each time with increasing force, until the creatures and their infection is exterminated.

Search and destroy

This course of action would be a job for the military. If the zombies were massed in one place, out in the open, heavy machine guns and autocannons would cut them down in no time. And with armoured vehicles to protect the troops it would be a relatively risk-free operation. However, if the undead had gone to ground and the city had to be cleared, one building at a time, by soldiers on foot carrying handheld rifles, then casualties could start to mount.

In this case, there could be a difficult decision ahead. With its home turf already compromised and the army being essential for maintaining order, the government would be reluctant to risk valuable soldiers and equipment on a fruitless task. And with the risk of the infection spreading as time goes on, nuclear attack could well be the most effective way to contain the problem and avoid greater loss of life later on.

Home security and zombies

While the armed forces are busy liberating the streets from zombie rule, what's the best advice for the individual citizen confronted by the living dead?

Assuming you already have enough food in the cupboards for a few days, the thing you're really going to need is weaponry. Handguns and rifles are all well and good, but in the heat of combat delivering that all-important headshot could be tough – as the movies are fond of telling us, the attackers can only be stopped by removing the head or destroying the brain. So make things easy for yourself. Get a shotgun or, better still, get several (having a spare handy is always preferable to reloading while being eaten alive). The spread of pellets in each blast will give you a much better chance of hitting your adversaries. And, naturally, be sure to grab as many cartridges as you can carry.

If you don't have a sporting arms shop in your area, then you'll have to forego the boomsticks. Get down to B&Q instead, and fill your boots with axes, chainsaws and lump hammers. Don't even think about making Molotov cocktails though – it takes time for fire to destroy the brain and in the meantime you'll have walking bonfires coming at you.

The next task is to turn your home into a bunker. Use any heavy objects you can find to blockade weak points like doors and windows – but remember to leave yourself an escape route. You'll also benefit from someone to watch your back, so if you're alone get on the phone – assuming the networks are still running – and find out if any of your friends are still alive. Obviously, a thorough inspection for bite marks will be mandatory before you let any of your mates through the door.

If the zombies begin to overrun your house then don't hang about: cut and run. If you can, get to your car. Lock the doors, fasten your seat belt. You may not own an armoured Range Rover but even a Nissan Micra going at speed will be more than a match for the average squashy zombie.

If you can't get to a vehicle then you'll have to rely on your feet – you'll need to move fast and so travel light. Recommended kit to carry in this situation must surely include the humble but highly effective crowbar: excellent for dealing with any locked doors that block your path, and readily repurposed for busting skulls should you find yourself cornered.

Invasion of the killer tomatoes
evil weeds

From John Wyndham's mobile, human-stinging triffids to Audrey Jr, the insatiable, bloodthirsty alien shrub in *The Little Shop of Horrors*, (1960) imaginative authors have long wondered whether the greenery might one day rise up against us. But could a plant ever acquire animal-like traits such as intelligence and mobility?

Scientists have long known that plants – far from being the passive entities we might think – are masters over their environment, and capable of many complex behaviours that we would call intelligent.

The begonia never forgets

Perhaps the best-known example of an active plant is the Venus flytrap. Its cage-like jaws can snap shut on hapless insects – which are then gradually digested and absorbed by the plant. The trap mechanism is activated by tiny hairs, which act like tripwires. However, in order to spring the trap, each hair must be tripped not once but twice, in quick succession. This is to prevent the traps (which have a limited lifespan) being triggered by random events such as falling raindrops. But for this to work the plant must be able to remember which hairs have been triggered recently – in other words, it has a very primitive form of memory.

The flytrap isn't the only plant with a capacity for remembering. Vines and other climbers also exhibit impressive powers of recall. For a vine to curl one of its tendrils around a support, it must feel that the support is there and also sense sunlight falling on its leaves. But experiments have shown that these two stimuli don't necessarily have to happen together. Researchers have found that the vines can remember the sense of support for as long as two hours before the second sense – sunlight – is registered.

Plant intelligence

Many plant biologists are now taking the view that plants don't just demonstrate memory, but many other facets of intelligence too – they are able to sense their environment, defend themselves against threats, communicate with their fellow plants, and compete for food.

Some plants employ devious strategies to fend off grazing animals. Acacia trees can tell when a herbivore is stuffing its face at their expense and give off bitter-tasting tannin in response. Not only that, but nearby acacia trees can sense the odour of chewed leaves on the air and give off tannin of their own before a hungry acacia-chewing herd of mammals even arrives. Some plants can remember such a herbivore attack for many months, and appear to learn from the experience. If the plant gets attacked again within this time, it releases its tannins much more quickly.

It's not just about foliage – plants are equally canny below ground, in how they deploy their root systems. Professor Brian Forde, at the University of Lancaster, has found that plant roots are able to sense very low concentrations of glutamate, an indicator

A Venus flytrap munches on a mealworm.

of nutrient-rich patches of soil. Human beings are also sensitive to glutamate – it's how we recognize foods rich in protein. So it's almost as if the plant roots are tasting glutamate in the soil and then growing towards it.

Most amazingly of all, researchers at Ben Gurion University of the Negev, in Israel, have shown that plant roots are capable of self recognition. When two specimens of the same species are planted side by side, their roots grow aggressively towards one another – as they compete for the resources in the soil. But when each specimen is grown from the same parent – making them genetically identical – the opposite happens. The roots grow away from each other, as each plant tries to avoid wasting energy competing with "itself".

Nerves of wood

How do plants achieve these incredible feats of cognition? Humans and other animals have a brain and nervous system which gather signals from the senses, store them, and process them to make decisions. But plants have neither brain nor nerves.

One theory is that plant intelligence arises through a network of chemical signals that mimics the problem-solving power of animal brains. Plants have very many cells, which are able to pass chemical signals between each other – just as neurons exchange electrical signals inside a brain.

Several methods at the plant's disposal can then turn these "thoughts" into actions. One way a plant can make such movements is by the transfer of fluids within the plant. For example, shifting liquid away from one side of a stem makes it wilt, causing the stem to bend in that direction. Venus flytraps use rapid changes in acidity to alter the size of the cells in their traps and make them snap shut.

Triffid power

In John Wyndham's 1951 novel, *Day of the Triffids*, a species of (possibly bioengineered) plant has infested Earth: one that can move and which has a nasty habit of stinging humans with a fatal toxin. Could plants ever become this mobile – shuffling around like Wyndham's

In *The Day of the Triffids* (1962), giant, mobile stinging plants terrorize a world in which the majority of mankind has been blinded by a spectacular meteor storm. Humanity regresses to tribalism, with different factions banding together in safe enclaves. Or not-so-safe enclaves, as this picture shows.

vicious flora? Luckily for us, it seems unlikely.

Plants generate the bulk of their energy from photosynthesis – using special green pigments in their leaves to convert sunlight, carbon dioxide and water into carbohydrates, upon which they then feed. A calculation carried out by Seth Shostak of the Search for Extraterrestrial Intelligence Institute, California, and Margaret Turnbull, of Washington's Carnegie Institution, has shown just how unsuitable photosynthesis is for powering a man-size creature.

The light from the sun reaching a square metre of the Earth's surface amounts to around a hundred watts of power – enough to illuminate a standard lightbulb. However, only about 35 percent of that – 35 watts – gets absorbed by the plant. And, of that, only about a quarter – so around nine watts – makes it into plant food. If we assumed that the surface area of a human-sized plant were roughly three square metres, that means they'd be receiving about 27 watts of energy from photosynthesis. Furthermore, if it's assumed that the plant requires about the same amount of energy per day as a human being – two thousand calories – then it would need to receive about one hundred watts throughout the day. In other words, sunlight falls short by a factor of almost four (and that assumes the sun shines all day, which obviously it doesn't). Mind you, these calculations are based on the presumption that the plants aren't – like the Venus fly-trap – supplementing their diet with tasty morsels of meat.

Weed control

If John Wyndham's triffids were to ever exist, they would most likely be animal-plant hybrids. Indeed, such hybrids already exist. The con-voluta worm (aka *Symsagittifera roscoffensis*) has green algae cells living under its skin. These generate sugars via photosynthesis, upon which the worm then feeds. It's just about possible – albeit extremely far-fetched – that bioengineering could accidentally produce a new animal-plant hybrid life form with the mobility and killer instincts of a predatory animal. Wyndham's novel implies that the triffids were accidentally released, bioengineered life forms of Soviet origin. They became so widespread only because they were a valuable source of oil.

As for weaponry to take out a triffid, forget weedkiller – or even shotguns. Machetes would be a good bet for close combat, and of course they don't need reloading, but close range isn't advisable in triffid combat – they have those pesky stingers to contend with. Out in the open there's no match for a good old flamethrower. It's no kind of permanent solution, of course. That would have to come from the biochemists who unleashed these renegade organisms in the first place – assuming they have survived the green menace.

Savage Earth: our deadly planet

Planet Earth can be a dangerous place to live. With volcanic eruptions, earthquakes, extreme weather and worse, it sometimes seems amazing that human beings have managed to survive here at all. This section of the book takes a look at some of the big natural phenomena that can at any moment wreak massive destruction: phenomena such as supervolcanoes and megatsunamis (tidal waves that could dwarf the ones that struck Japan in 2011 and Sumatra in 2004). We begin with some of the most terrifying natural phenomena of all: earthquakes and volcanoes.

The Earth shook

perilous plates

One of the perennial dangers we face as dwellers upon the Earth's surface is the violence of an earthquake. Our planet's crust is a jigsaw of interlocking tectonic plates that float upon a mass of viscous molten rock, known as Earth's mantle. The mantle itself is rather like a pot of thick soup on a hot stove, bubbling and churning with the heat from below – in this case, the planet's hot core. This roiling mantle sticks to the overlying crust, pulling it this way and that. Plates jostle and scrape together as they move across one another. The rock is usually rough and so this movement generates a friction that inhibits the plates' movement. They lock together until enough pressure has accumulated to part them – at which point there's an abrupt jolt as the plates suddenly move. And this jolt can be powerful enough to flatten buildings, knock down bridges and wreck whole civilizations. This is an earthquake.

The strength of an earthquake is measured on the "moment magnitude" scale. This is the measure developed in the 1970s to replace the better-known, but outdated, Richter scale from the 1930s. The magnitude is calculated as being equal to the rigidity of the Earth's crust (a measure of the crust's resistance to movement) multiplied by the size of the area that slipped (bigger quakes can move larger areas of crust) and the average amount of slip on the fault (literally how far the plates have moved past one another).

Smaller quakes are extremely common – it's estimated that every year there are well over a million quakes of magnitude 2–2.9 around the world. These quakes are harmless. Anything above magnitude 7 is very bad news though – there are around fifteen such quakes annually, and usually at least one in excess of magnitude 8. The tsunami that devastated Japan in 2011 was triggered by an undersea earthquake

An illustration from Voltaire's *Candide* depicts the devastating earthquake in Lisbon, Portugal, of 1 November 1755. "The sea rose boiling in the harbour and broke up all the craft that harboured there," wrote Voltaire. "The city burst into flames, and ashes covered the streets and squares; the houses came crashing down, roofs piling up on foundations, and even the foundations were smashed into pieces. Thirty-thousand inhabitants of both sexes and all ages were crushed to death under the ruins."

which measured a 9 on the moment magnitude scale.

While earthquakes can have global repercussions, in terms of economic impacts and human misery, they are not the sort of event that could lead to physical devastation on a global scale – and certainly not a mass extinction. But they can cause substantial loss of life at a local and regional level. The deadliest earthquake of the twentieth century was the quake which took place in Tangshan, an industrial city in China with approximately one million inhabitants, in 1976. The 25-mile-long Tangshan Fault, which runs near the city, ruptured due to tectonic forces caused by the Okhotsk Plate sliding past the Eurasian Plate: the exact number of casualties caused by the earthquake is not known, but it's estimated that between a quarter and three-quarters of a million people lost their lives.

Earthquake engineering

Many earthquake deaths result from people being trapped inside collapsing buildings. This has led to a new branch of technology called earthquake engineering, in which scientific knowledge is applied in order to build structures that are quake-proof. In fact, the ancient Inca civilization of Peru had a pretty good idea how to go about this. They used no mortar in their construction – their buildings were made by fitting precisely cut stone blocks next to one another as snugly as possible. When an earthquake struck, this gave their buildings the ability to flex and sway rather than crack and crumble under the force of the tremor.

Nobody today would want to live in a house with no mortar. Nevertheless, modern-day earthquake engineers have taken the Incas' philosophy on board, and employ measures such as shock absorbers in a building's foundations to give the flexibility needed to soak up vibrations. Another common feature incorporated into many modern skyscrapers is known as a tuned mass damper – essentially a long, massive pendulum weighing hundreds of tons. Taipei 101, the third-largest skyscraper in the world, is equipped with one: as the building sways during an earthquake, the pendulum swings in the opposite direction to counter the movement.

Earthquake engineering is now so advanced that it's often not so much the magnitude of an earthquake that dictates numbers of

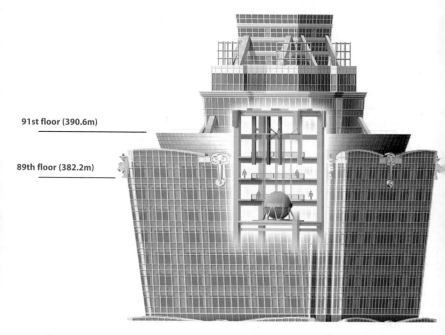

91st floor (390.6m)

89th floor (382.2m)

Illustration of Taipei 101, one of the tallest skyscrapers in the world, with its pendulum-like tuned mass damper in the centre, protecting it from earthquakes.

casualties, but its location: technologically advanced nations, who are able to take advantage of sophisticated earthquake engineering, fare much better than developing areas.

Coastal regions often suffer much worse damage. If an earthquake takes place beneath the sea floor, then the sudden displacement of the Earth's crust can be transferred to the ocean water, creating a tidal wave, or tsunami, that rears up tens of metres above normal sea level and can sweep many kilometres inland, claiming lives and washing away property. For more on tsunami threats see p.47.

Fire from below

Earth's crust gets rubbed up the wrong way

Boundaries between tectonic plates are not just sites of earthquake activity – the weakness of the Earth's crust in these areas often gives rise to volcanoes too. The weaknesses allow hot molten rock, called magma, to rise up from the Earth's interior and burst forth as a volcanic eruption.

Volcanoes can also form above what are known as hotspots – locations of anomalously hot currents in the magma within the mantle layer. Hotspots often reveal their presence via chains of volcanoes on the landscape where, over millions of years, tectonic motion has brought fresh regions of crust to the surface.

The Deccan Traps

Another kind of volcanic event, which is less violent than volcano eruptions or earthquakes, is a basalt-flooding incident. Basalt flooding occurs when a huge volume of molten magma from the Earth's interior oozes up through breaches in the crust, floods the landscape and then solidifies. Areas of the planet's crust that have been resurfaced in this way are known to geologists as "large igneous provinces".

Some of these events may have happened on vast continental scales during the Earth's prehistory. These rock formations are known colloquially as traps. This name comes from the Swedish word for stairs, *trappa*, because successive flooding events create stacked up layers of basalt which give the terrain a step-like, terraced appearance.

Perhaps the most famous large igneous province is the Deccan Traps formation in western India. The Traps cover an area of five hundred thousand square kilometres and are more than 2km thick. It's believed that the processes creating traps like this would have had a marked effect on the global climate. That's because the huge volume of magma would have been accompanied by a sizeable release of volcanic gases, such as sulphur dioxide. This gas is known to block the sun's rays, leading to a planet-wide cooling effect.

This effect cooled the world by an estimated 2°C during the formation of the Deccan Traps, between 60 and 68 million years ago. And this has led some palaeontologists to speculate that the formation of the Traps could have been a contributory factor in the demise of the dinosaurs.

Other examples of large igneous provinces are the Siberian Traps in Russia and the Emeishan Traps in western China. Another spectacular example can also be seen on our nearest planetary neighbour, the moon, where the dark lunar plains known as "maria'" (which, among other things, make up the facial features of the "Man in the moon") were created by ancient basalt-flooding incidents.

Magma is a mixture of different rock types, such as silicon, sodium and iron. It is ejected from a volcano at an extremely high temperature – typically 750–1400°C. The rising up of magma is an essential process in the formation of new crust at divergent fault lines – where tectonic plates are moving apart. This often occurs beneath the ocean, at sea-floor spreading sites. (The latter being where hot magma is bubbling up at an undersea fault line and solidifying on contact with the water to create new ocean floor, which then moves outwards, allowing the process to repeat.) At a volcano, the release of magma is a little more violent. A volcanic eruption usually occurs when the pressure of magma from below overpowers the rock lying above it – a solidified crust at the top of the volcano known as the caldera – and the volcano blows its stack.The magma released then either forms molten lava that oozes from the caldera, or flying frag-ments that solidify in mid-air, known as volcanic bombs.

By far the most devastating kind of volcanic eruption is known as a pyroclastic flow – a cloud of gas, ash and lava fragments at a temperature of more than 1000°C. The cloud cascades down the flanks of the volcano and up to 200km across the surrounding land, at hundreds of kilometres per hour. Whereas it's possible to evacu-ate populated areas threatened by slow-moving lava flows, staying ahead of a rapidly spreading pyroclastic flow is extremely difficult.

Like earthquakes, volcanoes generally cause localized devasta-tion (for a very notable exception, see p.45). The most deadly vol-canic eruption was that of Mount Tambora, Indonesia, in April 1815, which killed in excess of seventy thousand people. Many of these died from starvation in the famine that followed, resulting from the destruction of livestock and farmland.

The volcanic leviathan: supervolcanoes

On 18 May 1980, just after 8.30am, the Mount St Helens volcano in America's Washington State blew its top – flinging ash and lava nearly 25km into the air. The blast, which released energy estimated as being nearly five hundred times that put out by the Hiroshima bomb, devastated hundreds of square kilometres of land, killed 57 people and caused over $1bn in damage.

Now imagine a volcanic eruption packing thirty times the explo-

Volcanic Explosivity Index

How do you define what constitutes a supervolcano eruption? In 1982, Chris Newhall, of the US Geological Survey, and Stephen Self, of the University of Hawaii, came up with a magnitude scale for categorizing volcanic blasts, known as the Volcanic Explosivity Index (or VEI for short). Anything mustering a VEI of 8 qualifies as a supervolcano.

VEI	Ejected volume	Plume height	Frequency of occurrence	Example
0	<0.00001km^3	<100m	continual	Mono-Inyo Craters, California
1	>0.00001km^3	100–1000m	daily	Mono-Inyo Craters, California
2	>0.001km^3	1–5km	weekly	Mono-Inyo Craters, California
3	>0.01km^3	3–15km	yearly	Mono-Inyo Craters, California
4	>0.1km^3	10–25km	>=10 yrs	Eyjafjallajökull, Iceland (2010)
5	>1km^3	>25km	>=50 yrs	Mount St Helens, Washington State (2010)
6	>10km^3	>25km	>=100 yrs	Krakatoa, Indonesia (1883)
7	>100km^3	>25km	>=1000 yrs	Mount Tambora, Indonesia (1815)
8	>1000km^3	>25km	>=10,000 yrs	Lake Toba, Indonesia (74,000 years ago)

sive force of Mount St Helens. This is the kind of explosion produced by a phenomenon known as a supervolcano – eruptions with apocalyptic consequences, which have punctuated the Earth's prehistory. A supervolcanic eruption is one in which the volume of lava, ash and debris ejected exceeds one thousand cubic kilometres. They are eruptions achieving a Volcanic Explosivity Index (VEI) of 8 (see box above). By comparison, the 1980 eruption of Mount St Helens ejected a single cubic kilometre of material and was classed as a VEI5 event.

Supervolcanoes are formed above hotspots where molten magma rises up from the Earth's interior and presses against the planet's overlying crust. Ordinarily, the weight of the rock making up the crust is sufficient to hold the magma down, but eventually the pressure becomes too great and the crust literally explodes – flinging debris up to 50km into the air (halfway to the edge of space) and smothering entire continents in volcanic ash.

Supervolcanoes are difficult to spot on the landscape. Ordinary volcanoes like Mount St Helens form a distinctive cone shape as debris ejected during successive eruptions piles up around them. But the chamber of molten magma beneath a supervolcano is often tens of kilometres across. When the volcano erupts, much of the ground directly above is blasted away, and once the eruption finishes any ground that is left (and which might have had debris piled up upon it) sags downwards as the entire region is resurfaced by residual magma.

Nevertheless, there are a number of supervolcanoes known to exist in the world today. One is situated beneath Lake Taupo on the North Island of New Zealand. This was the site of the most recent supervolcano eruption, thought to have taken place around 26,500 years ago. Others can be found at Lake Toba in Sumatra and on the island of Kyushu, in Japan.

But one of the most talked-about supervolcanoes in the world today lies beneath Yellowstone National Park, in Wyoming. This volcano measures 45km by 85km – so big that it takes up much of the area of the park, and it can only be seen clearly when the whole area is imaged by satellite.

The Yellowstone supervolcano has been a cause for concern in recent years. Observations made between 2004 and 2008 showed that the caldera had risen by 20cm in this time, the biggest increase since seismological measurements at the park began in 1923. While 20cm might not seem like much, it is quite a significant rise, given that the caldera has risen by a total of 74cm since the 1920s. Happily, the rate of its rise was seen to slow again in 2009. However, there is much speculation that Yellowstone could be due for another eruption. Geological studies of past eruptions suggest that they occur roughly once every 650,000 years; the last one took place 640,000 years ago.

The coming storm

How might we know when a supervolcanic eruption is imminent? The first giveaway would take the form of earthquake activity. Yellowstone is already extremely active seismically – in January

2010, more than 250 small quakes were detected over the course of just a two-day period. Prior to an eruption, these quakes would become more violent, as the caldera heaves and strains against the enormous pressure pushing it upwards. Finally, the caldera cracks and gives way in a gigantic explosion.

The force of the blast and the hot burning lava would mean instant death for anything within a few hundred kilometres – and probably out to around a thousand – from the eruption. Hot ash would soon begin raining down, coating the land with a layer metres thick – in which people, and any other life forms unfortunate enough to be caught, would suffocate. Even at distances of up to 2500km away, ash deposits would still be likely to reach 35cm thick. When Yellowstone erupts it's likely the resulting ash cloud would coat the entire continental US.

While this thinner ash covering would be incapable of killing people directly, it would be quite sufficient to wipe out plant life, including food crops, leading to widespread famine. It's estimated that during a typical eruption of the Yellowstone supervolcano, 75 percent of plant life in the northern hemisphere could be exterminated. Meanwhile, the vast quantities of sulphur dioxide and ash flung into the atmosphere would cause acid rain and trigger a volcanic winter, blocking out the sun and causing global temperatures to drop by as much as 20°C for many years after the event.

During one of the world's last supervolcano eruptions (a caldera beneath Lake Toba, on Sumatra, 74,000 years ago) the resulting volcanic winter is believed by some experts to have triggered a minor ice age, estimated to have wiped out around sixty percent of the entire human race, creating a population concentration in central eastern Africa and India that affected the genetic inheritance of all humans today. Supervolcano eruptions are indeed a savage and unstoppable force of nature – and one that no amount of modern technology can prevent.

Volcanic winters

In 1991, Mount Pinatubo – a large volcano in the Philippines which had lain dormant for almost five hundred years – blew its top spectacularly, flinging an estimated ten cubic kilometres of ash, lava and debris into the atmosphere, giving it a rating of 6 on the Volcanic Explosivity Index – the same destructiveness category as Krakatoa's legendary 1883 outburst.

The massive quantity of ash and volcanic gas cast up into the stratosphere by Pinatubo lingered for several years. At its peak, it blocked out roughly ten percent of the light from the sun, producing a sustained drop in global temperatures of approximately 0.4°C. On this occasion the effect was small, and short-lived enough, not to have any major implications for life on Earth – at least, not when compared with the volcano's other, more immediate consequences in terms of destruction of agricultural resources, buildings and infrastructure and nearly one thousand fatalities.

What Pinatubo had caused was a very mild case of what's known as a volcanic winter. History and prehistory are littered with far worse examples. The 1883 Krakatoa eruption was followed by four years of extreme cold and record snowfalls around the world. The year after the 1815 eruption of Indonesian volcano Mount Tambora became known as the "year without a summer" as the atmospheric pollutants from the eruption literally turned summer into winter – with some northern hemisphere locations experiencing frost and snow in June.

A huge cloud of hot, volcanic ash is thrown into the air by the erupting Mount Pinatubo, Philippines, June 1991.

The black cloud

A mind-boggling forty thousand tons of space dust falls to Earth every single year. The dust consists mainly of remnant particles of the cloud from which the sun and planets originally formed 4.5 billion years ago. Other dust comes from the evaporation of comets – lumps of dirt and ice – as they get closer to the sun. The Earth experiences many regular meteor showers throughout the year, as it passes through the dust streams left behind by comets and these tiny particles burn up spectacularly in the planet's atmosphere.

Ordinarily, though, this cosmic dust is diffuse enough not to have any noticeable effect on the amount of sunlight reaching the planet's surface. But in a few thousand years, that could all change rather dramatically. Astronomical surveys reveal that our solar system's natural orbit around the galaxy is carrying it towards a dense cloud of gas and dust, the edge of which is currently just four light years away. This cloud is a thousand times denser than the dust in the solar system today.

Not only could this blot out much of the light from our star, it could also diminish the solar wind – the stream of electrically charged particles from the sun that helps to protect the entire solar system from galactic radiation. To make matters worse, some even believe the dust will eat away the Earth's atmosphere. The cloud will probably harbour a quantity of hydrogen (the most abundant element in the universe) as well as dust. If this came into contact with our atmosphere it would tend to react with the oxygen therein to form oxygen-hydrogen compounds, robbing us (and all other aerobic life on Earth) of the gas needed to breathe.

Volcanic winters are caused because the extra gas and dust in the atmosphere makes the planet more reflective, and thus bounces the sun's rays away into space. The prime contributors to this effect are volcanic ash and droplets of sulphuric acid, formed from volcanic sulphur dioxide gas which has reacted chemically with oxygen and hydrogen in the atmosphere.

Nemesis from the sea

terrible tsunamis

At 2.45pm on Friday, 11 March 2011, a magnitude-9 earthquake shook the eastern coast of Japan. The quake's epicentre was located a little over 70km offshore. Just minutes later, a giant wave of water – in places almost 40m high – struck the coast. The water washed inland, inundating some 470 square kilometres. As of February 2012 the confirmed death toll was 15,846 – with over 3320 people still missing. The wave destroyed buildings and property to the value of $34bn, according to some estimates. It ignited fires, toppled bridges (and one dam) and crippled the cooling system at the Fukushima nuclear power plant, causing three of its reactors to explode, scattering radioactive material across the surrounding area. The total financial impact of the disaster was $235bn, making it the costliest natural disaster on record.

This freak wave came just seven years after a similar event was triggered by an earthquake off the coast of Sumatra. A staggering 230,000 people died as the waves from this quake raced across the Indian Ocean to devastate regions of Indonesia, Thailand, Sri Lanka and India. Japan has experienced so many of these devastating ocean waves (with almost two hundred on record) that they have a special name for them – tsunami, meaning "harbour wave". Scientists all over the world have now adopted the word, preferring it to the colloquial term "tidal wave" as these waves have nothing to do with the regular tides – which are caused by the gravity of the sun and the moon.

Tsunamis have been recorded throughout history. Greek historian Thucydides wrote about them in the fifth century BC. However, the 2004 Indian Ocean event which, together with the earthquake that caused it, released energy equivalent to a 26-megaton nuclear explosion, remains the worst tsunami disaster on record.

Tsunamis do their damage by virtue of the sheer volume of water rushing across the land during the initial surge, and they cause further destruction as it then recedes back again. Water is extremely heavy. With a density of one kilogram per litre, a cubic metre of the stuff weighs a ton. Imagine the many tons of water in a tsunami wave, rushing towards you at speeds of anything up to 100kph on land – and carrying with it solid debris that it has swept up along the way. You'll then get some idea of how the carnage of the 2011 tsunami – seen in video footage washing away cars, houses, bridges and aircraft (as it tore through Sendai Airport) – was inevitable.

What causes them?

The most common cause of tsunamis is undersea earthquakes, which can suddenly catapult the sea floor upwards by many tens of metres. This sets up a large disturbance in the water that travels out from the earthquake's epicentre at speeds of up to 800kph. And yet, while in deep ocean water, the passage of a tsunami is practically imperceptible. The amplitude (the height of the wave) in deep ocean is usually just a few tens of centimetres, while the wavelength (the distance between successive wave crests) can be hundreds of kilometres. Standard ocean waves have wavelengths of between just 30 and 40m.

When a tsunami reaches the shallow water near to the coast, however, it becomes a lot more evident. In a phenomenon known as wave shoaling, the rising sea floor pushes the wave upwards, causing the amplitude to increase from tens of centimetres to, typically, tens of metres: a wall of water rears up out of the sea. The speed of the waves

How do you escape a tsunami?

There are various methods to get a brief warning that a tsunami is coming, giving a few short minutes in which to head for higher ground. Detection of the seismic waves from an offshore earthquake is one such indicator – although not all undersea earthquakes cause tsunamis, so this can lead to false alarms. A more reliable system is to use underwater sensors that can detect the brief rise in ocean pressure which accompanies a passing tsunami. This is the method used in the DART (Deep-ocean Assessment and Reporting of Tsunamis) system sensors. These consist of a pressure sensor on the ocean floor, linked to a buoy which can then transmit data by satellite. The United States now has 39 DART sensors dotted around the Pacific, Atlantic and Caribbean.

There is one very reliable way to tell if a tsunami is on the way – though you need to be on the beach to see it. The first part of a tsunami wave to reach the shore isn't a wave peak but a wave trough. And this means that, for a few minutes before the first wave peak arrives, the sea level will appear abnormally low. In fact, the water can go out by hundreds of metres, in a phenomenon known as drawback. During the 2004 tsunami, ten-year-old Tilly Smith, who was on holiday with her parents in Phuket, Thailand, saved many lives on Maikhao Beach when she saw the drawback effect in action and sounded the alarm. She had learned about tsunamis in a geography lesson just a few weeks earlier.

drops to between 50 and 100kph and their wavelength shortens to around 20km. This means that, were a particular tsunami wave to slow to 60kph at the shore, it would take ten minutes for the half-wavelength containing the wave's peak to pass by – and during this time, the water just keeps coming and coming. And there's no guarantee that the first wave will be the only wave – or that it will be the biggest.

Megatsunamis

The tsunamis that struck in 2004 and 2011 were a few tens of metres in height and caused massive amounts of destruction. But tsunamis can get much, much bigger than this. In 1958, a wave ripped through Lituya Bay, Alaska, that had an estimated maximum amplitude of 524m – half a kilometre high. The force of the wave was sufficient to break off two-metre-thick spruce trees on the shores of the bay as if they were matchsticks.

This was a phenomenon known as a megatsunami – a wave with an amplitude exceeding 100m. In Japan, they are known as *iminami* ("purification waves"). The Lituya Bay tsunami was caused by a gigantic landslide in the bay's Gilbert Inlet, itself triggered by a magnitude-eight earthquake. The mass of rock fell into the water and, like a cinder block tossed into a pond, triggered a massive wave. Amazingly, two boats in the bay were able to ride the wave, and their occupants survived – a third, however, wasn't so lucky and its two-person crew perished. The wave soon dissipated upon reaching open ocean.

There are fears that there could be an even bigger megatsunami in store. A volcanic ridge called Cumbre Vieja on La Palma, one of the Canary Islands, off the west coast of Africa, is believed to be slowly cracking in half. A long fissure has opened on its eastern side. Some geologists believe that the next time Cumbre Vieja erupts, the volcano's entire western flank will slip into the sea, generating a megatsunami a kilometre in height. This would tear across the Atlantic in around eight hours, and would still be around 50m high when it arrived at the eastern seaboard of the United States and the Caribbean.

Worst-case scenarios predict that cities along the coast would be devastated and tens of millions of people would lose their lives.

Megathrust earthquakes

Both the 2004 Indian Ocean tsunami and the wave that struck Japan in 2011 were caused by megathrust earthquakes beneath the ocean floor. The Earth's crust is made up of a network of interlocking slabs of rock, known as tectonic plates. These plates are gradually replaced over time. New crust wells up in the form of hot magma at sites known as sea-floor trenches. This pushes the old crust outwards until it's eventually forced beneath the tectonic plate next to it, in a process called subduction. It's at these subduction sites where mega-thrust earthquakes can occur.

The plate that's slipping down into the Earth's interior doesn't move smoothly, but sticks against the plate above it. The force deforms the overlying plate, bending it downward until suddenly the pressure becomes too great and the top plate suddenly snaps back into position – usually by several tens of metres. This mass of crust springing back acts like an enormous paddle displacing a huge volume of water upwards, which then propagates out in all directions as a tsunami.

The 2004 Indian Ocean tsunami was the result of a megathrust quake caused by the India tectonic plate subducting beneath the

The diagrams below, showing a cross-section of two tectonic plates, illustrate the process that shapes a megathrust earthquake and causes a tsunami.

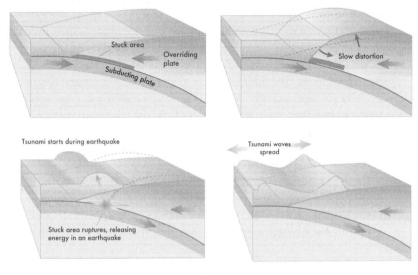

Burma Plate. Similarly, the 2011 tsunami that struck Japan was thrown up by a quake caused by the Pacific Plate sliding beneath the Okhotsk Plate. Around eighty percent of all tsunamis occur in the Pacific Ocean, due to the area's large network of subduction zones (known collectively as the Pacific Ring of Fire).

There is concern that the same scenario could soon play out off the Pacific coast of America. Here, a subduction zone runs 80km offshore, where the Juan de Fuca plate slips beneath the North American continental plate. Known as the Cascadia subduction zone, it is quite capable of producing magnitude-nine earthquakes – the same force that caused the 2004 and 2011 tsunamis. The last quake struck Cascadia in AD 1700, and geologists believe their frequency to be once every four hundred to six hundred years. The next one could bring devastation to California, Oregon, Washington and British Columbia.

Hurricanes: Katrina and her sisters
ill winds blowing no one any good

Hurricanes are the most devastating variety of thunderstorm. Whipped up over warm, tropical seas, they blow inland bringing heavy rain, winds of more than 250kph (155mph), and ocean storm surges in excess of 10m high. An angry hurricane can span more than 2000km across and crank out energy at a rate equivalent to a ten-megaton nuclear explosion every twenty minutes. It's hardly surprising, then, that these monster storms are believed to have claimed more lives in the past fifty years than any other kind of natural disaster. And yet meteorologists believe hurricanes can and will get very much worse. They say that the effect of climate change in warming the oceans – as well as other one-off violent events, such as asteroid impacts – may in future generate hurricanes bigger and more powerful than anything we've seen so far.

The worst hurricane this century was Katrina, which killed over 1800 people, and caused damage totalling over $100bn, when it made landfall on the southern United States in August 2005. Though even this terrible storm isn't the most devastating on record. That

Hurricane Katrina took a heavy toll on New Orleans and its residents.

was the Bhola cyclone which struck the Indian subcontinent during November 1970, and claimed half a million lives.

The most powerful hurricane we know of was Typhoon Tip, which swept through the Pacific in 1979. Its wind speeds exceeded 300kph, and it measured 2220km across. Miraculously, fewer than one hundred people were killed when it tore across Japan and the Micronesian island state of Guam.

Hurricane, cyclone or typhoon?

What's the difference between a hurricane, a cyclone and a typhoon? Physically, nothing; geographically, everything. The fundamental physical phenomenon is known as a cyclone, a rotating weather system formed by warm, moist air rising up from the sea. By convention, a cyclone that forms in either the eastern side of the Pacific Ocean, or in the Atlantic Ocean, is known as a hurricane – whereas one blowing up in the Western Pacific is called a typhoon.

It takes a number of processes to give rise to a cyclone. The first is convection. Gases expand as they are heated, which makes them less dense and causes them to rise upwards. It's the reason why hot-air balloons fly. In tropical seas, convection causes warm air to rise to high altitude, as far as 15km up. Here, where the ambient temperature is much cooler, moisture that was carried up in the warm air condenses back into liquid water and falls as rain. The now cooled air drops back down too, and so a cycle is set up – of warm air rising, and cool air falling.

The warm air creates a region of low pressure. Think of the upward air current as being rather like a vacuum cleaner, sucking water vapour up from the ocean surface. This low pressure also tends to suck in nearby air from sea level to form a central rising column with air from the surroundings flowing radially in towards it. This central column is known as the eye of the hurricane.

The convection cycle is then stirred round by a process known as the Coriolis effect. It's named after the French scientist Gustav Coriolis, who was the first to correctly explain it. The Coriolis effect is caused by the Earth's rotation, and it tends to make weather systems in the northern hemisphere rotate in an anti-clockwise direction while those in the south rotate clockwise.

Why does this happen? Because of the Earth's spherical shape, the planet is wider near the equator than it is near the poles. However, the whole planet rotates in an easterly direction as one solid mass. This means that equatorial latitudes are moving east faster than polar ones. Relative to an observer in the northern hemisphere, latitudes nearer to the equator still appear to be going east. But, relative to the observer, those latitudes closer to the North Pole appear to be moving west. And this sets up a turning effect that makes northern hemisphere clouds spin in an anti-clockwise direction relative to the planet's surface.

A cyclone requires exceptionally strong convection in order to form. This means there must be a large gap in temperature between the ocean and the upper atmosphere. Specifically, the ocean tem-

How to stop a hurricane in its tracks

Hurricanes are such powerful phenomena, surely it's a fool's errand for us mere humans to even contemplate trying to stop one? And yet some scientists believe we can.

Hurricanes often run out of steam naturally. Remember, they are powered by the warm ocean – and as soon as this power source is taken away (as they make landfall), they begin to dissipate. This was demonstrated dramatically by Hurricane Katrina in 2005. The category-1 hurricane first made landfall on 25 August in Florida, and was weakened considerably, dropping to storm-force as the land sapped its power. However, upon entering the Gulf of Mexico it soon picked up strength, regaining its hurricane status and reaching category 5 in just a matter of hours.

Now there are plans to try to rob hurricanes of their ocean power source by artificial means. One scheme has been devised whereby the ocean surface would be covered with a film of biodegradable oil that locks in the water – preventing it evaporating and rising up into the air. Microsoft co-founder Bill Gates has backed another promising strategy, in which a fleet of special barges sail in front of the hurricane's anticipated path, pumping up chilly water from the deep in order to cool the ocean surface.

Of course, hurricanes form not just because the ocean is warm but because of the temperature difference between the ocean and the cool upper atmosphere. And so, an alternative way to prevent them would be by heating up the upper atmosphere. One plan suggests lofting soot into the sky. The idea is that these black particles soak up more solar radiation than ordinary air and then re-radiate it to their immediate surroundings.

An even more audacious strategy is to microwave the upper atmosphere. That idea was put forward by American meteorologist Dr Ross Hoffman. His computer simulations showed that heating high-altitude clouds by just 2–3°C can significantly weaken the convection currents driving a cyclone. Hoffman believes this could be achieved using a fleet of satellites packing microwave generators, to heat the water in the clouds in exactly the same way that your microwave oven heats the water in a bowl of soup.

perature must be at least 26°C and this is why cyclones only form over warm tropical waters, within 30 degrees latitude of the equator.

The time of year must be right too. Cyclone seasons in different areas of the tropics are simply the months in which the difference in temperature between the ocean and upper atmosphere is greatest. For hurricanes in the Atlantic, this is June to November. For typhoons,

Measuring a hurricane

The strength of a hurricane, and other cyclones, is classified on the Saffir–Simpson scale, devised in 1971 by civil engineer Herbert Saffir and meteorologist Bob Simpson.

Cat.	Windspeed (kph)	Wave height (m)	Effects	Example
1	119–153	1.2–1.5	Minimal damage – very minor flooding	Claudette (2003)
2	154–177	1.8–2.4	Moderate damage – considerable flooding	Juan (2003)
3	178–209	2.7–3.7	Extensive damage – flooding several km inland	Bertha (2008)
4	210–249	4.0–5.5	Extreme damage – massive evacuation required to escape flooding	Igor (2010)
5	≥250	≥5.5	Catastrophic damage, buildings blown away – major evacuation up to 16km inland, heavy flood damage	Felix (2007)

however, the season runs December to April. Once a hurricane or typhoon forms, it normally migrates in a westerly direction, blown by the trade winds that whip east-to-west around the planet's equator.

The hypercane

As the world gets warmer due to climate change (see p.83) so the temperature of the oceans rises, causing the number of powerful cyclones to increase dramatically. It seems as if we're seeing this already. Meteorologists warn that over the course of the last 35 years the number of strong category 4 and 5 cyclones has doubled (see box above).

In 1994, meteorologist Kerry Emanuel, of the Massachusetts Institute of Technology, speculated that when sea temperatures in the tropics reach 50°C a new kind of superpowerful cyclone will become possible – which he calls a hypercane. We're safe for the time being – the highest ocean surface temperature ever recorded so far is 35°C.

A hypercane could be big enough to engulf the whole of North America and produce sustained windspeeds up to an unimaginable 800kph (500mph). These winds would be generated by extremely low air pressure in the hurricane's eye – down to around seventy percent of normal atmospheric pressure. (The lowest pressure recorded so far in a cyclone, in the eye of Typhoon Tip, was 86 percent.) The low pressure sucks up water beneath it into a mound which, when the cyclone reaches land, washes ashore as a storm surge. It's believed the surges produced by a hypercane may be as tall as 18m. Meanwhile, the storm itself could reach high into the atmosphere, disturbing the stratosphere and destroying ozone – the molecule that protects us against harmful UV rays from the sun.

There won't be just one hypercane to deal with but many. That's because it will take a lot of heat to warm the ocean to 50°C, and dispersing this heat again isn't going to happen overnight. In the meantime, the ocean will keep spawning hypercanes until it can cool.

It's not even just global warming that could bring about the oceanic heating needed to trigger a hypercane. Extreme events such as asteroid impacts and supervolcano eruptions can raise ocean temperatures considerably too. Indeed, there is speculation among meteorologists and climate scientists that these colossal storms may have played a part in the major mass extinctions of life on Earth that have been found to punctuate the planet's fossil record throughout prehistory.

Ice ages
when snow really isn't cool

Picture the solid white crust that smothers the polar regions today. Now imagine our entire planet covered in a similarly thick sheet of ice. This is an extreme example of an ice age (a period of pronounced cold in our planet's history) that climatologists refer to as "Snowball Earth". During such a scenario, glaciers from the north and south poles would literally meet at the equator, encasing the world in an icy sarcophagus. Whether this acute scenario played out or not, there is no doubt that ice ages in which much of the planet has frozen over have been a recurrent theme in its history.

Under the ice

Palaeoclimatologists – scientists who study the climate through-out our planet's 4.5-billion-year history – tell us that, as far as we know, there have been a total of five major ice ages on Earth. These are believed to have taken place: 2.4–2.1 billion years ago; 850–630mya (million years ago); 460–430mya; 360–260mya; and between 2.53mya and 10,000 years ago. The second of these, 850–630mya, is thought to have been a case of Snowball Earth – as well as one of the longest ice ages ever to grip the planet, keeping it in the freezer for over two hundred million years.

Scientists only figured out the reality of ice ages in the nineteenth century. Swiss-American biologist Louis Agassiz is the man credited with the discovery. In the 1830s, he and several colleagues had been studying the Jura Mountains in Switzerland. They had found a number of large boulders, the geology of which seemed to be at odds with their location. These boulders turned out to be what are now known as glacial erratics – rocks scooped up by passing gla-ciers, as they oozed across the terrain, and then deposited far from their usual location when the ice eventually melted.

There are other features of the landscape that are also sure signs that glaciers have covered it in the past. Ice is extremely heavy – a cubic metre weighs almost a ton. And as this mass of material hauls itself over rock formations it leaves deep gouge marks that remain today. U-shaped valleys are another sign of glacial erosion, where the friction of a passing glacier has ground the valley floor from its normal V-shape into the more rounded form of a U. Yet another are moraines: banked-up piles of debris created by the advancing ice – as if a giant snowplough had steamed across the land, sweeping rocks and soil to one side.

Applying geological dating methods to establish the ages of rocks bearing these marks is one way in which palaeoclimatologists have figured out the timings of ice ages during the Earth's past. One alter-native technique they have used is to examine the fossil history of the region, which can reveal when animal species have migrated

The Little Ice Age

From the sixteenth to seventeenth centuries, the world experienced an era of extreme cold, during which crops failed and livestock died, leading to famine and widespread disease. In Europe, London's River Thames would regularly freeze over – and frost fairs were held on its solid surface. The sea around Iceland was frozen so thick that the country's ports and harbours were unable to operate. Meanwhile, snow fell on mountains in Ethiopia at the lowest altitudes ever recorded.

This period of global cooling has become known as the Little Ice Age. There are a number of theories as to what caused it. One blames the considerable volcanic activity during the period that the Little Ice Age gripped the world. An erupting volcano casts clouds of ash and smoke into the atmosphere, which obscure the sun and lower global temperatures.

One of the most prominent theories centres around the fact that the Little Ice Age coincided with a period of very low solar activity – known as the Maunder Minimum. This was a time when hardly any sunspots were seen crossing the solar surface. Sunspots are caused by magnetic activity on the sun, and normally accompany violent events such as solar flares and coronal mass ejections. Two other periods of diminished sunspot activity – known as the Dalton Minimum (1790–1830) and the Spörer Minimum (1460–1550) – also correspond to global cool periods.

And yet perhaps the most intriguing explanation for the Little Ice Age ascribes the drop in global temperatures to the Black Death (bubonic plague). William Ruddiman, of the University of Virginia, believes that human beings have been influencing the climate not just since the Industrial Revolution, but right from the beginning of agriculture – from around the year 6000 BC. Ever since this time, he contends, human activity has been making the world warmer. However, the Black Death pandemic of the fourteenth century caused massive loss of life in Europe – reducing the population by as much as sixty percent. And this drop in the population, says Ruddiman, temporarily reduced anthropogenic global warming, making the world cooler – and triggering the Little Ice Age.

away – perhaps in search of a warmer climate.

Cool science

What causes ice ages? Scientists have isolated a number of possible factors. Back when global warming was first discovered it was seen as useful insurance to save us all from the ravages of a Snowball

Earth scenario. And, as you'd expect, lowering atmospheric carbon dioxide is one way to bring about the opposite effect and cool the planet down. Indeed, studies of ice cores recovered from Antarctica reveal that, during most ice ages, the atmospheric CO_2 concentration was between 180 and 210 parts per million (ppm) – compared to 390 parts per million today.

Carbon dioxide can be removed from the atmosphere by large jumps in the amount of photosynthesizing plant life on the planet. This is reminiscent of what happened during the Earth's early history. When the planet was much younger, around three billion years ago, the CO_2 concentration was very much higher – many thousands of ppm. The first life forms on Earth were photosynthesizing bacteria, which functioned much like plants today. These gradually processed much of the atmosphere's carbon dioxide into oxygen – cooling the planet, and enabling oxygen-breathing animal life to evolve.

Variations in volcanic activity also alter CO_2 levels. Volcanoes

A detail from Thomas Wyke's painting of the Thames Frost Fair of 1683. During the bitterly cold period during the sixteenth and seventeenth centuries, the River Thames in London would regularly freeze over so solidly that it could be used by merchants, hawkers and entertainers.

spew out carbon dioxide, as well as stronger greenhouse gases such as methane. Changes in the level of volcanic activity throughout the Earth's history could have plunged us into ice ages – and lifted us out again. Research published by the University of Cambridge in 2010 suggested that a massive burp of carbon dioxide from the deep ocean may have ended the last ice age, ten thousand years ago.

The brightness of the sun naturally takes its toll on the Earth's climate, so it's not surprising that down-swings in solar activity are another contributor to ice ages. The Earth's own geography can have a marked effect too. The layout of the continents is changing over time thanks to movement of the tectonic plates that make up the planet's crust. Configurations of the continents that prevent the flow of warm ocean water from the equator to the polar regions cause the poles to get colder. This in turn increases their ice coverage. Ice, in turn, is white and so reflects away more of the sun's heat, leading to a runaway cooling cycle.

This can occur when land covers most of the equator, as was the case 750–1100 million years ago. It also happens when a polar sea is surrounded by land (as with the Arctic today) or when land lies at one of the planet's poles (as is the case with Antarctica).

Yet another theory, put forward by the Serbian mathematician Milutin Milankovitch, supposes that the small wobbles of the Earth's orbit (which are known to exist) introduce temperature variations on the planet's surface that may contribute to the onset of ice ages. These wobbles are happening continually and are analogous to the way the rotation axis of a child's spinning top swings around the vertical, sweeping out a cone shape as it goes (an effect called "precession") and sometimes also wobbling either side of this path (an effect called 'nutation'). Astronomical data confirm that these cycles occur. Their effects on climate would be to introduce small variations into a planet's temperature which, it was initially thought, could occasionally push it past the tipping point needed to trigger (or reverse) a mass freeze. The latest thinking, however, is that these may have the strength to take us in or out of an interglacial period (see below) – but they have little effect on the overarching ice age itself.

Life in the freezer

Ice ages present a formidable challenge to life. The frozen climate makes conditions simply too harsh for many plants and animals to survive. And with these species gone, so the pressure is transferred to creatures further up the food chain. Life becomes a bitter struggle for survival.

The landscape can be dramatically resculpted during an ice age – and not just by the force of the passing glaciers. Whereas melting polar caps today are causing sea levels to rise, freezing conditions during an ice age lock sea water away in the form of ice, making sea levels drop by 100m or more. And when the ice ultimately melts, these reclaimed lands – now inhabited – are inundated as the water returns. This was especially true of the Solent region off the south coast of England. The weight of glaciers on the northern British Isles literally tipped the country one way, like a seesaw, making the effect more pronounced.

Archaeologists have made many fascinating finds on the floor of the Solent (a strait separating the Isle of Wight from the mainland of England) including remains of creatures, such as mammoths, and signs of human agriculture and industry from during the last ice age. Officially, the last ice age ended between 8000 and 10,000 BC. However, some believe that the present clement period is merely an "interglacial": a brief respite, after which the glaciers will return. Even if that's the case though, the chill won't set in for tens of thousands of years – and that's assuming short-term global warming doesn't get us first.

We're all going to die!

a brief history of mass extinctions

Everyone knows the fate of creatures such as the woolly mammoth and the dodo – unfortunate beasts which no longer roam the Earth's surface, having become extinct long ago. It's an astonishing fact that 99 percent of all the animal species that have ever existed on Earth have gone the same way. Worryingly, many of these creatures haven't disappeared in isolated extinction events but have vanished together in calamitous group die-outs known to palaeontologists as "mass extinctions".

Dinosaur apocalypse

Probably the best known mass extinction of all – and one of the most recent – was that marking the demise of the dinosaurs 65 million years ago. Seventy-five percent of all species living on Earth were wiped out during this extinction, which is generally believed to have been caused by the impact of a 10km-wide asteroid with the Earth. The asteroid would have unleashed firestorms, monstrous tidal waves and flung clouds of ash and debris into the atmosphere that blocked out the light from the sun for many months – killing plant life, and in turn everything else further up the food chain.

The death of the dinosaurs is known to palaeontologists as the Cretaceous-Paleogene extinction (K-Pg, in geological shorthand), because it marked the end of the Cretaceous period of Earth's prehistory and the beginning of the Paleogene. Older books may refer to it as the Cretaceous-Tertiary (K-T) extinction, however Tertiary is now considered an archaic term.

Scientists discovered the K-Pg extinction by studying the fossilized remains of ancient creatures. Fossils formed from the bodies of creatures that fell to the bottom of the ocean after death, where they were compactified by layers of silt and sediment and turned to stone. The deeper an archaeologist digs down into the fossil record, the further they are looking back in time. And the fossils they find there tell them what species were living on the planet at that time. A mass extinction can be identified when the number of fossilized species at that time abruptly drops.

The Big Five

It turns out that the K-Pg event isn't the only mass extinction revealed in the fossil record. Over the course of the last 540 million years, there have been a total of five major eradications of life on Earth. There were probably earlier ones but the fossil record before this time is unreliable, as creatures with hard body parts were yet to evolve.

Before the K-Pg event, there was the Triassic-Jurassic (Tr-J) extinction, two hundred million years ago (mya). The big casualties of this extinction were the archosaurs (the ancestors of crocodiles), and this cleared the way for the rise of the dinosaurs.

Prior to this was the Permian-Triassic extinction (P-Tr), 250mya. Known as the "Great Dying", this was the biggest mass extinction that scientists have evidence for – it was responsible for the demise of seventy percent of all species on land, and 96 percent of those

Natural pollution (it's not all our fault!)

There is undisputedly far too much pollution in this world caused by human activity. Unfortunately, there's also a considerable amount of pollution on Earth that has nothing to do with the human race. Many chemicals detrimental to life and the environment are given off by natural processes, over which we have little or no control.

One example is a phenomenon known as limnic eruptions. In 1986, Lake Nyos, in Cameroon, suddenly gurgled up eighty million cubic metres of carbon dioxide gas. Because CO_2 is heavier than oxygen and nitrogen it settled into all the recesses of the landscape, driving out all the breathable air. As a result, over 1700 people and 3500 livestock in nearby towns and villages suffocated. It's thought the CO_2 could have been produced by the decay of organic material near the floor of the lake and/or the venting of volcanic gases – Lake Nyos is known to lie above a considerable magma reservoir. The CO_2 becomes mixed into the water by the high pressure at the bottom of the lake and when stirred up can be suddenly released, like a fizzy drink. The 1986 limnic eruption is thought to have been triggered by a landslide into the water. To prevent such a tragedy happening again, researchers proposed the installation of "degassing columns" – tubular pumps floating on rafts in the lake which pump up water from the bottom of the lake to the top, releasing CO_2 in safe quantities.

Limnic eruptions are localized events. But other natural pollution mechanisms can have wider-reaching consequences. One possible scenario that has climatologists worried centres around a chemical compound called methane clathrate. This is a form of water ice that has methane gas embedded within its crystal structure. It's believed that large deposits of methane clathrate could exist on the sea bed and in frozen regions of the planet's surface. The methane could be released if the clathrates ever melted – which is one possible unpleasant outcome of the rising temperatures brought about by global warming.

The big concern is that methane is itself a greenhouse gas many times more potent than CO_2. It's been estimated that if this so-called "clathrate gun" ever went off it could increase the amount of methane in the atmosphere by a factor of twelve – equivalent to doubling the amount of atmospheric CO_2, which would be sufficient to raise global temperatures by around 2°C over a timescale of just three or four decades.

in the oceans. The Late Devonian (late D) extinction happened 370mya and saw seventy percent of all species bite the dust. While the Ordovician-Silurian (O-S) event, around 450mya, was a double-whammy – two mass extinctions about a million years apart.

A mass extinction is generally defined as one in which at least fifty percent of large animal species died out – there are very many more microbial species, but they leave no readily accessible fossils to study. In addition to the Big Five, there is evidence for twenty or so smaller mass extinctions, when the extinction rate has temporarily risen significantly above the baseline death rate of between two and five biological families per million years. (A biological family is a hierarchical rank in the classification of organisms that lies above the ranks of species and genus. For example, human beings are species *H. sapiens*, genus *Homo* and family *Hominoidea* – which we share with gorillas, chimpanzees and orangutans.)

What causes them?

Mass extinctions can have a range of causes. Asteroid impacts are one, as the dinosaurs discovered to their cost. But there are a variety of others including natural global warming, ice ages, supervolcanoes and events in outer space such as nearby hypernova explosions and gamma-ray bursts. Some scientists believe that the pattern of extinction in the O-S event could be explained well by radiation from one of these violent cosmic outbursts.

Part of the problem in deducing the causes of different mass extinctions is that in many cases it's impossible to tell whether an extinction happened gradually over the course of tens of thousands of years, or was the product of a single bad weekend. Some scenarios, such as an asteroid impact, clearly fit the latter category whereas others, such as climate

The archosaur: ancestor of the dinosaur and a victim of the Triassic-Jurrasic extinction.

change, take longer. In 2008, two geologists at Hobart College, New York, suggested many extinctions could actually be a combination of both long- and short-term effects. They put forward a theory called "press-pulse", suggesting that the events are the result of life on Earth being placed under a long period of continual duress (the "press"), punctuated by sudden shock events (the "pulses").

Recovery from a mass extinction is a slow process. Indeed, it can take many millions of years for life on Earth to bounce back, as the environment first repairs itself and then new species evolve to fill the niches vacated by the ones that died. Some mass extinctions can even continue destroying organisms long after the actual extinction event has passed. For example, organisms not directly affected by the event but which are dependent on other species that were, can be thrown into a steady decline that eventually wipes them out too.

Sixth sense

In March 2011, palaeontologists at the University of California, Berkeley, announced evidence that the sixth great mass extinction of life on planet Earth may have begun. They calculated that if all the creatures classed today by the International Union for Conservation of Nature as "critically endangered", "endangered" and "threatened" – species such as the white rhino and the mountain gorilla – actually went extinct, and even if this took as long as a thousand years to happen (as seems possible), then the rate of disappearance of species would place us firmly in a mass extinction.

But it's not all doom and gloom. Mass extinctions may serve an important purpose in driving evolution. Because what doesn't kill a species quite literally makes it stronger. Every time an extinction event occurs it presents new challenges that only the strongest and fittest organisms can overcome – and this means that any species surviving the cataclysm emerge with a greatly fortified gene pool. It was the mass extinction which removed the dinosaurs from their seat of power that ultimately cleared way for the rise of us primates.

Microbiological threats

viruses, bugs and drugs

When H5N1 bird flu went global in 2005, many people feared it would be the start of a major disease pandemic. But on this occasion we got off lightly. According to estimates by the World Health Organization (WHO), only a few hundred people died. It could have been much worse. The H1N1 swine flu in 2009, for instance, claimed more than 18,000 lives worldwide between April that year and July 2010.

But even this wasn't what we'd call a real catastrophe. To see how bad things can really get you only have to look back to 1918, when Spanish flu tore around the planet, killing between fifty and one hundred million people – which was between three and six percent of the entire population and more than the total number of fatalities sustained during World War I. Going further back – to the fourteenth century – diseases could be even more catastrophic. The Black Death killed around twenty percent of the world's human population – a pandemic believed by most to have been the result of bubonic plague. Possibly the worst pandemic ever, at least in terms of the absolute number of deaths, was the gradual carnage inflicted around the world by smallpox over the course of the twentieth century, killing around three hundred million people.

Infectious diseases have preyed upon humanity throughout history. And now they seem to be getting worse. In 2008, researchers from the Zoological Society of London, the Wildlife Trusts charity and Columbia University published a report in the science journal *Nature*, in which they claimed that outbreaks of major diseases around the world have become more common during the last forty years. The question is: could such an outbreak ever wipe our species from the planet entirely?

Outbreak hotspots

The word pandemic has Greek roots: "pan" (meaning "all") and "demos" (meaning "people"). A disease pandemic is like an epidemic, only much bigger – affecting a significant portion of the world. To qualify as a pandemic, a disease must be of a new strain and it must be infectious, causing serious illness as a result. A commonly cited example of a deadly and widespread disease which is nonetheless not a pandemic is cancer – because it is not new and it's not infectious.

New diseases arise through evolution – the way organisms change and adapt to new environments. In the case of an infectious disease, this may mean adapting to the new physiology presented as it attempts to infect a new species. It's a phenomenon that has been seen many times in nature when diseases jump from animals to humans. This was certainly the case with both bird flu and swine flu. There is convincing evidence that this process was the origin of HIV, the virus that causes AIDS – which scientists believe began when SIV, a similar virus in monkeys, jumped to humans in Africa, possibly through the human consumption of bushmeat.

If that's the case then the hypothesis that there's been a recent increase in the outbreaks of major diseases starts to make sense. Forty years ago, in 1970, there were only four billion people living on the Earth – three billion fewer than there are in 2011. The increasing population has not only required humans to live in closer proximity to one another – allowing contagion to spread that much more easily – but it has also forced our civilization to encroach further and further into the habitats of many animal species. Little surprise, then, that the crossover of disease pathogens from animals to humans is on the up.

The international collaboration's research pinpointed hotspots around the world where infectious diseases are most likely to emerge. The majority were in Africa, India and China, as might be expected. Some rich nations, including Germany, England and the United States, also scored highly – although this may simply be due to the fact that these nations have invested a great deal in monitoring the spread of disease, making outbreaks more likely to be recorded in these locations than they are in the developing world.

From outbreak to pandemic

The WHO has identified six distinct phases in the outbreak of a pandemic. The first two form the inter-pandemic period: in phase

Disease control

What can we do to lessen the risk of a major pandemic decimating the human population of the Earth? To update an old adage, prevention is not only better but almost certainly cheaper than cure. This means we must do everything we can to prevent diseases jumping from animals to humans. That in turn will require minimizing the destruction and human occupation of natural wildlife habitats – one of the main reasons why humans and other wild animal species have been thrust into such close proximity with one another.

Curbing our appetite for expansion isn't going to be easy, and certainly isn't going to happen overnight. So we'll probably need some quick fixes to see us through the short term. Some researchers have suggested this could be achieved by bio-screening all travellers before they leave disease hotspot areas. Anyone testing positive for a known animal pathogen would be placed in quarantine. This wouldn't prevent localized outbreaks, but it would stop these from developing into global pandemics.

Quarantine is one of the simplest and most effective ways to stop a disease outbreak in its tracks. Quite simply, if the disease can find no new hosts to infect before existing hosts have either died, or their immune systems have overcome the infection, then the outbreak is over. The tactic proved its worth during the 2003 severe acute respiratory syndrome (SARS) outbreak, when more than 150,000 people in Taiwan were placed in isolation. This prevented the disease from becoming a major pandemic, although there was a total of 916 deaths. Quarantine can operate at a national level too. Following the 2009 swine flu outbreak in Mexico City, many airlines cancelled flights to and from the country, slowing the virus's spread.

After screening and quarantine, the next line of defence is medication. If the spread of the disease is slow enough, there may be time to develop an immune-system-boosting vaccine to inoculate the population before the pandemic reaches them. Vaccines are used for the uninfected in tandem with other drugs that slow the course of the disease in those already infected. These might include antibiotics (for bacterial diseases such as anthrax, cholera and tuberculosis) or antivirals (for diseases spread by virus particles such as influenza, smallpox and ebola).

one, there are no *major* human or animal diseases in circulation; phase two is a situation in which there are no major *human* diseases in circulation, but one or more animal diseases that merit concern. Phases three to five constitute the "alert period". In phase three, humans have been infected by an animal pathogen but as yet no human-to-human transmission has taken place.

By phase four, there are small clusters of outbreaks; human-to-human transmission has begun but it is only a localized phenomenon. In phase five, the outbreaks are larger, but human-to-human transmission remains localized. For human-to-human transmission to take place, certain biological changes must occur in the agent causing the disease – as it adapts from animal physiology to its new human hosts. But once it has become well established, we enter the pandemic period, phase six, in which human contact carries the disease to a significant proportion of the world's population.

Human-to-human transmission is a key factor in the spread of a disease pandemic. One reason is the rise of cheap air travel. An infected person can now travel from a disease hotspot to the other side of the world in a matter of hours. And if the disease they are carrying can be transmitted to others at their destination, then a localized outbreak can turn into a pandemic in a matter of days. This was the case with swine flu in 2009, which spread rapidly from its

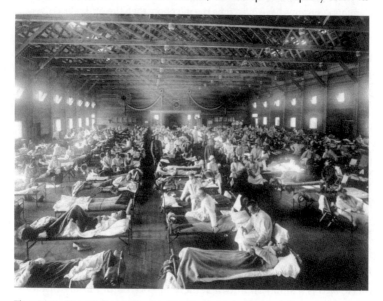

The vicious Spanish flu pandemic of 1918 spread worldwide, killing an estimated 30–100 million people. Pictured is an improvised hospital in a municipal hall in the US at the time.

Pandemic severity index

Developed by researchers at the United States Department of Health and Human Services, the pandemic severity index gives a rating of how bad a pandemic is, based on its case-fatality rate (CFR) – the percentage of people infected who ultimately succumb to their symptoms. The higher the category number, the worse the pandemic is.

Category	CFR	example
1	less than 0.1%	Seasonal flu
2	0.1% to 0.5%	Asian flu, Hong Kong flu
3	0.5% to 1%	Hepatitis B
4	1% to 2%	H1N1 swine flu
5	2% or higher	1918 Spanish flu, H5N1 bird flu

point of origin in Mexico City to the United States and then to the rest of the world.

The science governing the spread of disease is known as epidemiology. Epidemiologists construct mathematical models describing the growth of a pandemic, based on details of the area in which the outbreak has occurred, population density, local travel habits – as well as factors specific to the disease itself. These quantify effects such as how contagious the disease is – which depends on whether the pathogen particles are airborne, and can thus be spread by coughs and sneezes, as well as how easily the disease crosses natural defensive barriers such as the skin and mucous membranes.

The models also, as you might expect, take account of just how virulent the disease is – that is, how deadly it is once you become infected. This is determined by the percentage of those infected who die, and is quantified by a number known as the case fatality rate, or CFR. In 2007, the United States Department of Health and Human Services used the CFR to formulate a scale determining how severe a pandemic can be said to be (see box above).

The last virus

Contrary to what common sense would suggest, the worst pandemics aren't always the most virulent ones. This is because people who get infected by super-deadly strains don't live long enough to pass the virus or bacterium onto others. The dependence of diseases upon living carriers naturally makes it very unlikely that a pandemic could wipe out humanity entirely. The population density drops as the number of people left alive diminishes, and this puts the brakes on the rate of transmission, ultimately meaning that – however catastrophic the pandemic might be – some human beings will always outlive the disease.

The only way we could be wiped out is if a genetically modified or nanotech-engineered pathogen was deliberately developed (as a weapon, for example) to be highly contagious but initially non-virulent – until a preset trigger is activated, after which it becomes one hundred percent fatal. The initial non-virulent period would enable the disease to infect practically everyone on the planet without killing them, before suddenly switching into lethal mode, and exterminating our species overnight.

The good news is that it's extremely unlikely that such a disease could evolve naturally. But don't start the celebrations just yet. Although humanity will survive, a global pandemic wiping out ninety percent of the human population could well mean the end of civilization as we know it.

Rise of the superbugs
when bugs go really, really bad

As we have seen, epidemics and pandemics are something the human race has long had to contend with. We've accumulated a knowledge of medicine that has enabled us to fight back. And yet some diseases are now emerging that seem to have put one over on the best pharmaceutical drugs that medical science has to offer today.

These are the so-called superbugs: strains of disease-causing bacteria which have become resistant to antibiotics – the drugs

Bugs without drugs

Antibiotic resistance – the emergence of superbugs that are seemingly immune to antibiotic drugs – is a growing problem. What are the most dangerous superbugs currently known to science?

▶ MRSA

Short for "methicillin-resistant *Staphylococcus aureus*", this is one of the most widespread superbugs, and outbreaks occur frequently in hospitals. Ordinary *Staphylococcus aureus* is a common bacterium found on the skin and mucous membranes of many people. However, if it gets inside a patient it can lead to blood poisoning (sepsis) and pneumonia.

▶ C. difficile

When the natural intestinal bacteria of a patient have been destroyed – say, by a recent course of antibiotics – then the gut can become overrun by *Clostridium difficile*. This leads to diarrhoea, flu-like symptoms and in severe cases pseudomembranous colitis – a potentially life-threatening infection of the colon. *C. difficile* infections most commonly occur within healthcare establishments.

▶ NDM-1

This isn't strictly speaking a superbug. It's an enzyme which is made by some bacteria and which in turn bolsters the resistance of bacteria, such as *E. coli*, to carbapenems – one of the most powerful known antibiotics. The fear is that the NDM-1 enzyme will jump to superbug strains already resistant to many other antibiotics, making infections untreatable.

normally used to fight bacterial infections in the body. In the European Union, untreatable bacterial infections kill some 25,000 people annually.

Such is the magnitude of the problem that some medical experts are now predicting an oncoming crisis whereby there will be no effective drugs available to treat patients with serious infections, setting back medical science by almost a century.

The antibiotics revolution

As recently as the early twentieth century, bacterial infection was a killer. The prognosis wasn't at all good for anyone unlucky enough to sustain an open wound in unhygienic conditions – such as the soldiers who fought in the trenches of World War I. The work of

The French chemist Louis Pasteur, father of the antibiotics revolution, at work in his laboratory.

microbiological pioneers such as French chemist Louis Pasteur, who made the first vaccines against rabies and anthrax, had revealed bacteria to be the cause of these infections (as well as other illnesses such as bronchitis and pneumonia). Yet, at the time, there was no way to treat these conditions. Antiseptics existed, but these were usually harsh chemicals only suitable for external use. There was nothing to treat a major internal infection.

That all changed in 1928, when the Scottish bacteriologist Alexander Fleming discovered penicillin. Fleming found that a chemical produced by the *Penicillium* mould is toxic to bacteria. It was the first antibiotic – a term later coined by American biologist Selman Waksman. Development work by others throughout the 1930s proved penicillin's clinical value – and led to techniques by which it could be mass-produced. The pieces of the puzzle all came together in time for the bloody climax of World War II, where the drug is believed to have saved many thousands of lives – not to mention the millions who have benefited from antibiotics since.

Antibiotics work by blocking the biochemical reactions that bacteria use to survive and multiply. They function by disrupting the cell walls of the bacteria, inhibiting the activity of enzymes and other proteins, or blocking the transcription of DNA in order to prevent bacterial cells dividing. And they worked just fine – at least, for a while.

Remarkably soon, a strain of bacteria called *Staphylococcus aureus* emerged, which the antibiotics were unable to kill. It had become resistant to the drugs. This was in 1947, just a few short years after penicillin was rolled out clinically. In the early 1960s these hardened bacteria received their descriptive name – methicillin-resistant *Staphylococcus aureus*, or MRSA – as they were immune to the effects of methicillin, a common penicillin-type antibiotic in use at the time. MRSA killed 17,000 people in the US during 2005 alone.

The biological arms race

What doctors were witnessing was a practical demonstration of evolution in action. The theory of evolution had been put forward by English naturalist Charles Darwin in 1859 to explain the origin of species: he theorized that new species came about as existing ones evolved and adapted to new environments. For example, a colony of moths with light, dappled wing markings for camouflaging them on trees would soon find themselves being eaten by predators if suddenly relocated to a new setting where the trees were much darker. Some of the moths, however, would by random chance have wings slightly darker than the others. These moths would be slightly better camouflaged and thus slightly less likely to get eaten. They'd also be more likely to survive long enough to reproduce, and pass on the genes for slightly darker-coloured wings to their offspring. In this way, the population of moths with light-coloured wings would gradually evolve into a new darker-coloured variety, better able to survive in the new conditions.

And it's the same story with disease-causing bacteria. An antibiotic drug changes the bacteria's environment in such a way as to kill most of the bacterial cells. However, a few cells will be naturally resistant to the drug, through random happenstance, enabling them to survive and replicate. These surviving cells hand their resilience genes down to their offspring, which in turn multiply, becoming more resistant to the drugs with each new generation.

For researchers, keeping one step ahead of the evolving bugs is rather like an arms race. In 1953, a scientist named Edmund Kornfeld discovered a new antibiotic called vancomycin, from a soil sample collected from the jungles of Borneo. So powerful was this antibiotic that it was able to kill MRSA, and continued to prove effective for several decades. (In actual fact, vancomycin predated methicillin, and it was only the appearance of methicillin-resistant bacteria that brought vancomycin into favour.) But we were eventually – and perhaps inevitably – confronted by a new threat: VRSA (vancomycin-resistant *Staphylococcus aureus*). Bacteria are nothing if not adaptable.

Quest for a cure

We are caught in a kind of Catch-22. We depend upon antibiotics to cure our diseases, but we know that the more we use them, the stronger the bugs get. So we need to be sensible about when to take them. Antibiotics should only be used when prescribed by a doctor, and then the entire course of tablets must be taken: terminating the course early, because you're feeling better, gives strengthened bugs a greater chance of survival. Don't be tempted to take them if you merely have a cold: a cold is a viral infection, whereas antibiotics only kill bacteria. Antibiotics are also abused in veterinary medicine, and agriculture – routinely added to animal feedstock as a growth enhancer. (Antibiotics promote growth by suppressing populations of bacteria in animals' intestines, which helps them digest their food more efficiently, and can result in a lower percentage of fat and a higher protein content in the meat.) Our first strategy must be to stop this abuse so we give bugs minimal opportunity to evolve and

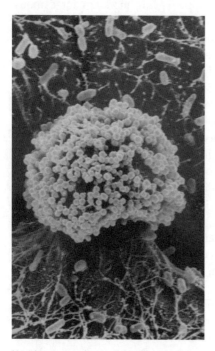

No, it's not some broccoli that's been left in the fridge too long: this is what MRSA looks like, viewed on a water droplet, under an electron microscope.

Nature's antibiotics

Nature had been at work on planet Earth for billions of years before human scientists arrived on the scene. It is not surprising, therefore, that some of the chemicals and microorganisms that exist in the natural world have extraordinary antibacterial properties.

The first antibiotic to be discovered revealed its existence to the world when a blotch of *Penicillium* mould happened to start growing in a Petri dish in which a bacterial sample was being cultivated. A chemical given off by the mould killed the bacteria, and this – in its isolated and refined form – was what became known as penicillin. Yet long before this discovery, an old wives' tale traditionally advised treating infected wounds with mouldy bread – a crude application of a similar process.

Of course, *Penicillium* isn't the only natural antibiotic. A whole host of plant extracts, such as tea-tree oil, thyme and echinacea, are known to fight infection. They are all components of the branch of complementary medicine known as phytotherapy. Use of these alternative antibacterial medicines could greatly reduce our reliance on the conventional antibiotic drugs that biological science has manufactured.

Another natural way to attack superbacteria is by enlisting the help of their disease-causing cousins, viruses. Certain kinds of virus, known as bacteriophages, only attack bacterial cells – leaving the healthy cells of a patient untouched. Studies have reportedly shown that this technique – phage therapy – can achieve an infection-fighting success rate of up to 95 percent. It is especially effective against *E. coli* and *Staphylococcus aureus* infections.

Still more of nature's microbe fighters came to light in new research published during April 2011. Scientists at the University of Wales Institute Cardiff found that manuka honey – made by bees feeding from New Zealand's manuka tree – blocks the pathways by which streptococcus and pseudomonadaceae bacteria attach to healthy tissue during infection. When it comes to fighting off harmful bacteria, nature has much to teach us, it seems.

grow stronger. Indeed, the EU banned the use of antibiotic growth promoters in animal feed back in 2006.

Hygiene is also crucially important. As is making sure we invest sufficient resources in our side of the microbiological arms race – that is, by developing new antibiotics. Many pharmaceutical companies are neglecting this area in their research and development programmes because it's not especially lucrative. It may be the case that governments need to intervene here by subsidizing this important research.

New developments in biology could have much to offer. In research published in March 2011, scientists at the University of Oxford found that resistance to antibiotics is determined in bacterial cells by certain enzymes (proteins that bring about chemical reactions). These enzymes can, in turn, be blocked using special chemical inhibitors. Other studies, meanwhile, are uncovering more and more natural chemicals that appear to have great medicinal value in staving off superbug infections (see box above).

There are plenty of ways to beat superbugs – some microbiological, some logistical. But, as is the case with so many hazards posed to us by the natural world, we need to act now – before it's too late.

The real Andromeda Strain

bugs from space

In the 1971 movie *The Andromeda Strain*, based on the novel by Michael Crichton, a killer alien bug contaminates the Earth and begins wiping out the populace. Could such a scenario ever actually happen?

NASA has certainly taken the notion seriously. On 24 July 1969, the *Apollo 11* astronauts returned to Earth, having just made the historic first manned landing on the moon. But their journey was far from over. Rather than kicking back with a well-earned beer, Neil Armstrong and colleagues were quickly ushered into a small quarantine chamber, where they spent the next three weeks. The fear was that the astronauts might have brought back with them harmful lunar bugs.

And there soon came to light evidence that microbes can survive short journeys through space. In November 1969, the *Apollo 12* mission landed a stone's throw from the touchdown point of *Surveyor 3* – a robotic lander that had flown to the moon two and a half years earlier. When pieces of the probe were brought back to Earth and analysed, scientists found thriving colonies of earthly bacteria.

Are we aliens?

The idea that microorganisms can cross the gulf of space between the planets has a long history. Called panspermia, the idea was first put on a solid scientific footing in 1903 by the Swedish chemist Svante Arrhenius. It later became a candidate explanation for how life arose on Earth. Many scientists found it incredible that life has arisen so quickly on our planet. While it may seem anything but, 3.5 billion years is a very short timescale for primitive chemicals to be converted into intelligent beings like us. Panspermia was a magic bullet of a theory in this respect. It shifted the difficult stage in the process – the formation of the first cells – to another location in the solar system, or possibly beyond. These cells were effectively delivered to Earth in a cosmic parcel – which subsequently evolved into us.

This application of panspermia to explain the origin of life on the planet has become known as exogenesis. Among its proponents were the biologist Francis Crick (co-discoverer of the structure of DNA) and the astrophysicist Fred Hoyle. But there was trouble ahead for the theory. Following the dawn of the space age in the 1950s and 60s, scientists began to better understand the space environment – and with that understanding came a problem for panspermial theories of man's evolution. Space is not a welcoming domain for fragile biological cells. Far from it. It is icy cold, devoid of oxygen and bathed in deadly radiation from the sun.

The radiation was the most severe problem – it was estimated that unshielded microbes subjected to the intense ultraviolet radiation from the sun could last no more than a few days. This is just about enough to get between the moon and the Earth, but nowhere near long enough for an interplanetary journey – which will take months at the very least.

Martian meteorites

There was a simple solution, however. Embed the bugs inside chunks of rock. It's not as daft as it sounds. Analysis of some meteorites found on Earth has revealed pockets of gas within, the composition of which exactly matches the atmosphere of Mars. Scientists believe these rocks were blasted from the surface of the red planet

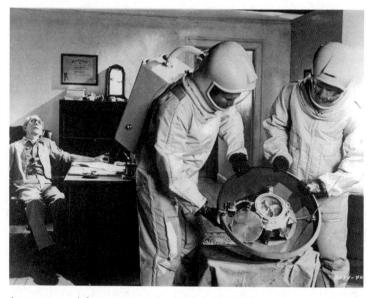

Astronauts search for ways to stop the deadly Andromeda Strain virus (which has just claimed another victim) in the cult 1971 sci-fi disaster movie of the same name.

by the impacts of comets and asteroids, and during violent volcanic eruptions. The implication is that if there was ever life on Mars it could have been transferred to Earth within these meteorites. And, presumably, vice versa: life from Earth could have migrated to the red planet.

In 1996, NASA famously reported that it had found evidence for fossilized microbes inside one of these so-called Martian meteorites. This claim has since been called into question. Nevertheless, studies have confirmed that the protection afforded by encasing a microbe in a lump of rock is more than sufficient to protect it in transit between Mars and the Earth. It'll also guard it against the intense heating up during entry into the Earth's atmosphere. Studies suggest that ablation – wherein bits breaking off the surface of a meteorite entering a planet's atmosphere carry away heat – should keep the inside cool. This was backed up in the aftermath of the *Columbia* space shuttle disaster in 2003, when biological samples from onboard experiments were recovered intact from locked compartments in the wreckage. In 2007, scientists at the European Space Agency attached microbe samples encased within slivers of rock to the outer heat shield of the returning *Foton-M3* spacecraft – and some of these samples did indeed survive.

SARS from the stars

In 2000, British astrophysicist Fred Hoyle – a longtime advocate of panspermia – along with his colleague Chandra Wickramasinghe, published a theory that alien bugs brought to Earth by panspermia could be responsible for some of the deadliest influenza pandemics in history.

Writing in the journal *Current Science*, they argued that flu virus particles may have been deposited in the planet's upper atmosphere inside dust left by passing comets – and that these are then periodically forced down into the lower atmosphere by the energy released during periods of increased solar activity. The sun's output waxes and wanes over an eleven-year cycle and, during peak activity, the Earth is barraged by solar flares and other outbursts from our star. The pair of scientists pointed out that some of the most virulent flu outbreaks have coincided with solar maxima (peak activity), including the 1918 Spanish flu pandemic, which is estimated to have killed more than fifty million people.

In 2003, Wickramasinghe went further, publishing a letter in medical journal *The Lancet*, claiming that severe acute respiratory syndrome (SARS), an outbreak of which, in the Far East, had reached near-pandemic proportions early that year, could also be of extraterrestrial origin. He wrote: "A small amount of the culprit virus introduced into the stratosphere could make a first tentative fall out east of the great mountain range of the Himalayas, where the stratosphere is thinnest, followed by sporadic deposits in neighbouring areas." The US Centers for Disease Control and Prevention were sceptical of the claim, arguing instead that evidence pointed to the disease jumping to humans from civet cats.

Since then, Wickramasinghe has conducted high-altitude balloon experiments, in which he claims to have recovered microorganisms in the air from as high as 41km up. He argues that this is far higher than living cells can be blown from the surface of the Earth. Meanwhile, further evidence in support of panspermia has emerged from analysis of the Murchison meteorite – which landed near the town of Murchison in Victoria, Australia, in 1969. It has been found to contain complex organic chemicals, including amino acids (the building blocks of proteins) and uracil (one of the base chemicals in RNA – a molecule closely related to DNA).

Galactic outbreak

In the 1990s, a variant panspermia theory was developed – called radiopanspermia. According to this theory, organisms were enclosed not in big meteorites, but tiny grains of dust. Studies showed that these dust grains not only offered microorganisms sufficient protection against the harsh radiation fields in space, but also enabled the bugs to remain light enough that they could be blown by radiation out of their home star systems and into the void between the stars. From here, so the theory goes, they could drift into other star systems.

The process would require a very luminous star. A red giant – the kind of star that our sun is due to evolve into in around five billion years' time – would be ideal. Calculations suggest that the bugs could be blown through interstellar space at a rate of around twenty light years per million years. Organisms moving at this speed would take a few billion years to cross our galaxy – much less than the age of the universe (currently around fourteen billion years).

And so the next time you get the flu, bear this in mind: you could be experiencing a cosmic infection that's been spreading across the galaxy since long before life even got going on Earth.

Saving us from ourselves

Our home planet may often make life tough for us humans, with its volcanoes, hurricanes, viruses and miscellaneous natural disasters. But we give as good as we get: it's as if we are increasingly determined to wreck the planet that we evolved on. In doing so, we are shooting our entire species in the foot on an existential level. Are we our own worst enemies? And have we been far too slow to realize it? Is it too late to do anything about it?

Perils of a warming world

feeling hot, hot, hot

Humanity is currently facing what could turn out to be the toughest challenge of its entire two hundred thousand-year history. The Earth is steadily warming up. And if we are to believe the scientific consensus, then this is almost certainly due to carbon dioxide and other greenhouse gases emitted by human industry. In short, it's our fault.

Research published in 2009 warned that if current warming trends continue then the planet could heat up by as much as 5°C during the course of the twenty-first century. That in itself doesn't sound bad. That is, until you begin to consider the full consequences, such as sea level rise and the associated flooding, droughts and extreme weather phenomena – which some climatologists say we're seeing the first signs of already.

The planetary greenhouse

Global warming is caused by a physical phenomenon known as the greenhouse effect – though it doesn't work quite the way a greenhouse does. The glass windows of a greenhouse allow light from the sun to pass through and then heat up the inside. The heat creates rising thermal air currents, which cannot escape because they are trapped by the solid glass.

But with the planet it's a slightly different story. Sunlight passes through the atmosphere and heats up the ground. As with a greenhouse, some of this heat is re-emitted as thermal currents, which circulate through Earth's atmosphere. But a good deal is re-emitted from the ground back upwards as radiation – hot things radiate their heat to the surroundings. We might expect this radiation to escape freely back into space, offering a way to keep the planet cool

But whereas the radiation arrived as predominantly visible light, it leaves as infrared – a form of radiation that has a longer wavelength than visible light. The trouble is that the atmosphere isn't as transparent at infrared wavelengths, and so some of the radiation gets absorbed as it tries to leave. In other words, whereas visible light can pass through the atmosphere unimpeded, much of the infrared light gets absorbed as it tries to leave. It's as if the light coming in is passing through a pane of clear glass but, as it tries to leave, it runs into darkened glass that it can't get through. As time passes, the atmosphere itself re-emits this absorbed radiation evenly in all directions – but that means half of it gets sent back downwards, making the ground warmer than it would otherwise be. Certain atmospheric gases absorb infrared radiation more readily than others – and these are the much-maligned greenhouse gases, which include carbon dioxide, methane and water vapour. Adding more of these gases to the atmosphere, through pollution and industrial activity, makes it trap even more of the infrared radiation trying to leave, warming the planet up even more.

The effect was first hypothesized by the French physicist Joseph Fourier in 1824. He did a simple calculation of the Earth's temperature, given its distance from the sun. Fourier's mathematics predicted that the Earth should be much cooler than it actually is, a discrepancy that led him to speculate that the planet's atmosphere somehow traps solar heat. In 1896, a Swedish chemist called Svante Arrhenius noticed that in laboratory experiments, carbon dioxide proved extremely good at trapping infrared heat radiation. He also knew that the increased burning of fossil fuels throughout the Industrial Revolution must have released massive amounts of CO_2. Arrhenius quickly put two and two together, realizing that not only could this explain Fourier's calculation – but also that it meant the world was going to get considerably hotter over the years and decades to come, as carbon emissions increased.

At first, Arrhenius's breakthrough was seen as good news. For it came hot on the heels of the discovery of another apocalyptic climate scenario – the realization that the Earth had passed through numerous protracted cycles of bitter cold during its prehistory, known as ice ages (see p.57). But now here was a way to counteract the cooling effect of an ice age – and better still, we didn't have to do anything that we weren't already doing.

The first real evidence for Arrhenius's predicted temperature increases was presented in the late 1930s, by the British engineer Guy Stewart Callendar. He collated temperature data spanning the interval 1890 to 1935, finding an average warming of 0.5°C. Meanwhile, levels of carbon dioxide were found to have risen by approximately ten percent in this time. But there was nonetheless little concern. Other research had suggested that the oceans soak up CO_2, putting a brake on climate change and most people, Callendar included, still thought the warming would save us from any future hypothetical ice age.

The penny drops

It wasn't until the late 1950s that this buoyant attitude towards global warming showed any signs of changing. In 1957, Roger Revelle and Hans Seuss (colleagues at Scripps Institute of Oceanography in California) showed that oceans can't soak up anywhere near as much CO_2 as had been thought. Revelle also realized that CO_2 emissions were now increasing at an exponential rate. He concluded that, while the world's population is doubling every few decades, the carbon emissions per person were also doubling in step with improvements in living standards and the rise of consumerism.

In 1958, Charles David Keeler, also of the Scripps Institute, began his own study of atmospheric CO_2 levels. He found that the concentration of the gas had leapt from 280 parts per million (ppm) in pre-industrial times to 315ppm. As Keeling continued his study, the measurements revealed a steady year-on-year rise.

In the 1960s scientists began to realize that warming of the planet wasn't the good thing it had long been thought to be. Slowly but surely, scientific studies began to accrue and their conclusions painted a more sombre picture. Whereas ice ages take place on quite literally glacial timescales – hundreds of thousands and even millions of years – it was now dawning on scientists that global warming could pose a serious threat to the Earth within just a few centuries.

This view wasn't immediately accepted by the whole of the scientific community. Many climate-change sceptics argued that other factors besides human emissions could be to blame for the increased temperatures, such as variations in the brightness of the sun. They also pointed out the many uncertainties in climate models. But in 2007, the Intergovernmental Panel on Climate Change – an international scientific body established by the United Nations to investigate global warming – concluded that the world is getting warmer and posited that it is ninety percent likely that the bulk of warming observed since the mid-twentieth century has been caused by human activity.

Hell and high water

Now the race is on to try to reduce greenhouse-gas emissions before the climate passes a tipping point, beyond which there will be nothing we can do to bring ourselves back from the brink of oblivion. Some scientists, such as British environmentalist James Lovelock, believe this may have already happened. Others are more optimistic, arguing that even if we are unable to rein in our carbon emissions we may still be able to repair the damage done through geoengineering (see overleaf).

If we don't, things could be about to get rather grim. Over the coming decades, melting of the Earth's polar caps could raise sea levels (see p.93) by enough to place some of the world's major cities underwater – including Hong Kong, New York and Mumbai. Dealing with the worst consequences of climate change would have a substantial economic impact that far outweighs the cost of taking action now to nip it in the bud, as was revealed in a 2006 report by British economist Nicholas Stern.

Global dimming

It's not just calamitous events that can plunge the world into a bout of global cooling. Carbon dioxide and other greenhouse gases, which are churned out regularly by industrial pollution, cause the planet to gradually warm up. But some scientists believe that other kinds of pollutants, which exist in the form of solid or liquid particles (like smoke, for example), may be exerting a cooling effect on the planet's climate. These kinds of particulate pollutants are known as aerosols.

One of the landmark studies into the impact of aerosols on the climate was carried out in the wake of the 9/11 terrorist attacks when, for three days, all commercial aircraft in the United States were grounded. Contrails – the trails of water vapour that condense at high altitude in the exhaust from a jet engine – are a major source of aerosol pollution. However, their effect on climate had been difficult to gauge, as there were seldom times when no aircraft were flying which could be used as a control sample in a study.

Researchers, led by David Travis of the University of Wisconsin-Whitewater, took measurements showing that the difference between day and night temperatures was 1°C higher during the grounding of aircraft than otherwise. This suggested that the absence of contrails was either significantly raising temperatures during the day (by permitting more heat to arrive from the Sun), significantly lowering them at night (by allowing more heat to escape into space), or a combination of both. This effect of aerosol pollutants on climate has become known as global dimming.

Some climatologists believe that over the years global dimming may have been masking the true extent of global warming. Others have even suggested we might deliberately pump more aerosol particles into the atmosphere to mitigate global warming (see p.91). However, most environmentalists find this idea of fighting fire with fire unpalatable, believing it will ultimately do more harm than good: altering the climate in this way could affect rainfall and food supplies in unknowable ways.

Indeed, some experts believe global dimming may have been partly responsible for the severe droughts that struck Africa during the 1980s: that air pollution generated in Europe and North America may have made cloud droplets smaller and more reflective over the Atlantic, altering rainfall patterns in Africa so that the monsoon rains never moved north to the Sahel. Furthermore, while this "technofix" might cool the planet, it does not actually reduce the build-up of CO_2 in the atmosphere, which leads to increased ocean acidity (which in itself is a contributor to climate change).

Icebergs calving from the face of the Dawes Glacier in Alaska. Around 98 percent of Alaska's glaciers are shrinking, losing some twenty cubic miles of ice per year. Melting icebergs are extremely bad news for global sea-levels.

Even for those living in regions of the world not directly affected, the sociopolitical consequences of climate change could be dire. Flooded lands would mean mass migrations of refugees and conflicts over resources as starving nations went to war for access to food, farmland and clean water.

Of all the threats facing the Earth and human civilization, climate change is the one most likely to finish us off – and it's one which will require our full attention, and every ounce of our resourcefulness, if we are going to survive it.

Where to go when the planet hots up?

If the worst predictions about climate change were to come true then most of the world would experience catastrophic sea-level rises, leading to devastating coastal flooding, accompanied by massive increases in temperature which threaten to turn most of the planet's now-temperate zones into an unbearable heat trap. If this all makes the central and mid-latitude zones of the Earth's surface uninhabitable, then where might the remnants of the human race hole up?

James Lovelock has suggested that surviving humans might set up home in the Earth's polar regions – the Arctic Circle and Antarctica. In the warming world, conditions in these normally freezing and inhospitable locations would now be quite clement. Lovelock's vision is that we will be living in polar cities – self-sustaining, densely populated settlements where civilization could continue, and where scientists might be able to engage in a last-ditch attempt to find a solution to the cataclysmic mess that we've landed ourselves in.

Lovelock is nothing if not thorough in thinking through what life in such a polar city might be like. Acknowledging that the soil near the planet's poles is deficient in many nutrients, he argues that agriculture might still be possible by introducing certain plant species which naturally channel nitrogen from the atmosphere into the ground.

In 2006, climate campaigner Danny Bloom and artist Deng Cheng-hong produced some of the first visuals showing what polar cities might actually look like. Their designs include areas above and below ground level, urban quarters, as well as farmscrapers – space-saving vertical buildings in which agriculture has been brought indoors using technologies such as hydroponics (growing food crops in nutrient-rich liquid).

Life in such an environment might not be pleasant though. This would be survival as opposed to living. As Dan Bloom himself puts it: "let's hope polar cities are an idea whose time never comes".

Geoengineering
fixing a broken world

If we can't limit our carbon emissions, then can we at least try to fix the damage that these emissions have caused? After all, the fact that human activity is making the Earth warmer proves that we are able to bring about large-scale changes to the planet. So could we therefore contrive ways to alter the planet and put things right? Many scientists think we can. They believe that geoengineering – putting into practice mega-scale engineering projects to cool the planet's fevered brow – may be our best chance to beat climate change.

▶ **Iron fertilization** The best things for soaking up carbon dioxide from the atmosphere are green plants. Via the chemical reaction known as photosynthesis, plants absorb atmospheric CO_2, water and sunlight and produce carbohydrates – upon which the plant feeds. A by-product of photosynthesis is oxygen – essential for all animals to breathe.

Plants don't necessarily need to be taking up space on land. Phytoplankton are a kind of microscopic plant life that live in the oceans. By adding iron fertilizer to the sea, some researchers believe it may be possible to trigger large blooms of these ocean phytoplankton. These soak up carbon during their lifetimes and fall to the deep ocean floor upon their death, where the carbon then remains.

▶ **Artificial trees** Just as fertilizing the oceans is a way to lock away atmospheric carbon using the natural life cycles of plants, so is planting trees. The trouble is that trees take time to reach maturity – and time is increasingly something we don't have much of in tackling climate change. One solution, say scientists, could be the construction of hundreds of thousands of artificial trees.

These devices resemble very large fly-swatters. Air passes through them, where a sodium hydroxide solution then soaks up CO_2. The solution is pumped to a special processing plant, where it is heated, causing the CO_2 to be released. The gas is then trapped and compressed into liquid form, which some scientists believe could then be pumped underground – for example, into disused oil wells.

▶ **Space sunshades** If the sun gets in your eyes, you might put on a pair of shades, or open a parasol. Climate engineers have used a similar principle in coming up with the idea of positioning a large reflecting mirror in space between the Earth and the sun – at the L1 Lagrange point, where the gravity of the two bodies roughly cancel each other out.

However, in order to provide the necessary reduction in sunlight the sunshade will require a surface area of around 3.8 square kilometres. That will be rather tricky to launch into space in one go, and so it seems more likely that a flotilla of smaller sunshades would be used. The cost would be liable to be in the region of $5 trillion – just

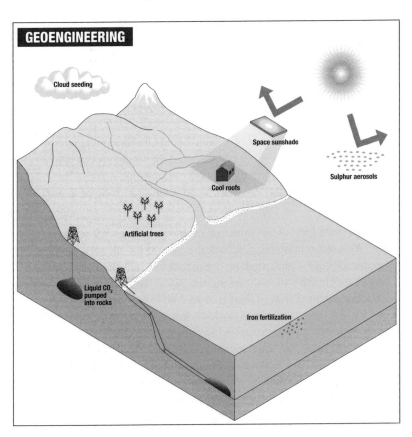

over a third of the United States GDP.

▶ **Sulphur aerosols** Climatologists have long known that the massive amounts of sulphur particles lifted into the atmosphere during major volcanic eruptions can have a cooling effect on the planet's environment. Accordingly, could pumping such sulphur aerosols into the atmosphere artificially provide a stopgap against global warming?

Scientists have suggested that gases such as sulphur dioxide – which react in the atmosphere to form reflective droplets of sulphuric acid – could be dispersed from aircraft, balloons or using artillery shells. There are fears, however, that this technique could lead to harmful acid rain.

▶ **Cloud seeding** If pumping sulphur particles into the atmosphere is too much of an environmental hazard, a safer option might be to use sea water. The idea is to use the equivalent of giant water-sprinklers to pump ocean water up into the sky. The water would soon evaporate, leaving behind crystals of salt. These would drift into the upper atmosphere and encourage droplets of water to condense, in turn forming clouds.

The bright white blanket of all these extra clouds would then serve to reflect solar radiation back into space. The trouble is that the role of clouds in global warming is poorly understood – while they do indeed reflect sunlight, the water vapour they are made of is itself a greenhouse gas that traps heat, like CO_2.

▶ **Cool roofs** One of the principal problems with global warming is that it's a self-reinforcing feedback process. As the planet gets hotter, so the ice caps shrink, making the planet less reflective, thus allowing more sunlight in and making the place hotter still. And so one tack geoengineers have taken is to try and boost the planet's reflectivity artificially. One way to do this is through the use of "cool roofs" – reflective coatings are applied to the roofs of urban buildings.

A joint study by the Lawrence Berkeley National Laboratory, California, and the California Energy Commission concluded that increasing the reflectivity of roofs, and indeed paving surfaces, around the world could offset approximately 44 billion tons of CO_2. That's eleven years' worth at the present rate of emission.

▶ **Biochar** The problem with fossil fuels is that by using them we are dredging up carbon that was previously locked safely away underground. One way to put carbon back underground is by burying dead biological material in a form of synthetic charcoal known as "biochar". Ordinarily, dead biomass returns its carbon to the environment as it rots, but by subjecting it to a thermochemical process called pyrolysis the material can be converted into biochar, a much more stable form of carbon that does not rot.

Water-world Earth

could the planet ever submerge?

The main worry about climate change is the potential flooding that will be caused by rising sea levels, as global warming melts the Earth's polar caps. What should we expect? Just how bad can the flooding get? Could rising temperatures ever melt the icecaps in their entirety, and plunge the whole of the Earth's surface beneath the waves – turning our planet into a featureless sphere of water? And could we survive such a terrifying scenario?

This island Everest

The good news, if there is any, is that it's unlikely the entire planet could ever wholly disappear beneath the waves. There simply isn't enough water locked away in the polar icecaps for this to happen. If all the water at the north and south poles melted tomorrow, then the sea would rise by about 80m. But there are mountains

The third and largest wave of the tsunami of December 26, 2004 invades the promenade on Ao Nang Beach, Thailand. As global temperatures rise, flooding caused by "freak weather" is likely to become much more commonplace.

very much taller than this and so the odds of the Earth becoming a "water world" (as imagined in the 1995 Kevin Costner movie of the same name) do seem fairly remote. Mount Everest, for example, reaches 8848m above sea level. Raise the sea by 80m, and Everest will hardly blink – still standing an impressive 8768m tall. That said, some geologists believe there may be extra water in the form of vast subterranean reservoirs beneath our feet.

Nevertheless a sea-level rise of 80m would still be catastrophic for human civilization on Earth. It would be sufficient to reduce the mainland of the British Isles to a smattering of islands poking above the surface of the sea. Major cities including London, Bristol, Manchester and Newcastle would all be submerged. On the European continent, we would say goodbye to much of Germany, Belgium and France – and all of Denmark and the Netherlands. The United States would be due for similar levels of water damage – with low-lying southeastern states such as Florida, Louisiana and Alabama being the worst hit.

Taking the rise

Sea-level rise isn't all down to melting icecaps. In fact, there are three contributory factors. The thawing of polar ice is the most important one; followed by the melting of glaciers on other land-masses. The third effect is known as thermal expansion: the ocean water literally increases in volume as its temperature rises. This happens because, as materials are heated, so their atoms and molecules vibrate more vigorously. Collisions between the vibrating molecules then force them apart ever so slightly, and the cumulative effect of this happening between every molecule in the material causes it to expand. (It's worth keeping in mind, however, that, compared to melting ice, thermal expansion has a relatively small impact on sea levels.)

Bizarrely, water also exhibits the opposite effect. Most materials shrink as they get cooler, but water expands when it is cooled below freezing temperature. This is caused by the unusual shape of water molecules – each being made from one oxygen atom and two atoms of hydrogen – which causes them to lock together upon freezing into a solid lattice that actually creates more space between the molecules than when they are liquid. We should be grateful for this fact though.

Higher ground: property in the age of floods

When sea levels begin to rise, what can we do to try to hold back the tide? In the Netherlands, urban planners have been wrestling with this problem for many years. Indeed, if it wasn't for sea defences such as dams and flood barriers, a sizeable portion of the country would now be underwater. The Netherlands is an example of how human ingenuity can hold back moderate ocean flooding. However, experts are sceptical that even these measures would cope with holding back sea-level rises of 2m or higher. Indeed, even the Netherlands is beginning to plan a strategy of "managed retreat" – where an area is allowed to become flooded, steadily conceding ground to the sea.

Other options may also be considered, such as building houses on stilts – as is already done in many flood-prone territories in the Far East, for example in Myanmar (the former state of Burma). Other nations are also taking drastic action. The Maldives, off the southern tip of India, are especially at risk. These islands erupted through the surface of the ocean due to volcanic activity thousands of years ago. But now their low-lying landforms are in danger of dropping back beneath the waves, due to climate change. One solution the government is looking at is the construction of artificial islands. The island of Hulhumalé was built in 1997 from sand, hauled from the ocean floor in a massive dredging operation and piled up in a shallow lagoon.

Even the notion that the entire planet may, after all, be engulfed by water may be a contingency that we have to plan for. In 2007, scientists from the University of Washington in St Louis found evidence for a hidden ocean lurking beneath China. The ocean holds a volume of water equivalent to the entire Arctic Ocean. If this, and other similar subterranean bodies of water, somehow spilt their contents to the planet's surface – for example, through earthquakes or volcanic activity – then there is no telling by how much sea levels could ultimately rise.

The expansion of water upon freezing lowers the density of the resulting ice, and this is why it floats. If ice was denser than water, and thus sank upon freezing, then the oceans would freeze from the bottom up rather than the top down. In this case, our oceans would have frozen solid long ago, and life on Earth would probably never have evolved.

The facts

Scientists charted sea levels over the course of the twentieth century, and they found an annual average rise of 1.8mm per year. In 2007, the UN-appointed Intergovernmental Panel on Climate Change (IPCC) predicted that, during the twenty-first century, world sea levels will rise by a total of between 190 and 590mm. In 2009, a group of climate scientists collaborated internationally and published a report known as the "Copenhagen Diagnosis". In it, they used updated research to predict that, by 2100, sea levels would be at least twice as high as the predictions made two years earlier by the IPCC – with the upper boundary being a rise of around 2m.

Just a 1m rise would flood land occupied by an estimated 145 million people. That alone would create a terrible refugee crisis, but it would also indirectly affect over a billion more people, dependent on agricultural land and fresh drinking-water supplies that would now be contaminated by the sea. The most vulnerable areas lie in the Indian Ocean. In the Bay of Bengal, for example, an average rise of just 400mm would mean disaster for Bangladesh, submerging eleven percent of its coastline and creating as many as ten million refugees. A rise of a metre here would place sixteen percent of the country underwater, displacing many more people than that already huge figure. It seems likely that we will all have to live on a much smaller area of the Earth's surface: an overcrowded planet is just another consequence of global warming and sea-level rise that we may just have to get used to.

Of course, ending the twenty-first century with sea levels at 2m higher than they were could just be the beginning. Unless steps are taken, the sea may continue to swell during the twenty-second century as well. And when that happens it won't be long before the rest of the world starts suffering the first-hand consequences of higher tides. A 4m rise, for instance, would be enough to open the floodgates on many low-lying cities such as London, New York and Shanghai – requiring either evacuation of these population centres or a vast outlay of money on preventative flood defences. The same rise would place the city of Miami 60km offshore.

Freak weather

Bodies of water creeping quietly higher and higher won't be all we need to worry about. Earth's weather systems are governed by heat from the sun. Warm oceans evaporate, causing water vapour to rise up, which then condenses at high altitude to fall back down as rain. Such rising thermals create regions of low atmospheric pressure that surrounding air then flows towards, creating wind.

With more heat lingering in the Earth's weather systems, as the world warms, so the weather is going to become more energetic – increasing the frequency and magnitude of extreme weather phenomena such as heat waves, storm surges and hurricanes. High sea levels are bad enough, but when whipped up by a storm surge (a "mound" of seawater, sucked up by the low pressure that generally accompanies a storm), many more areas will be placed at risk. Rising sea levels are the teeth of climate change. Most climatologists agree it's going to take us a good deal of effort not to get bitten.

Pollution: deadly waste?

side-products could be the death of us

Chemicals in the air, water and soil that have a detrimental effect on Earth's environment and the life forms that it's home to are known as pollutants – and the act of releasing them is known as pollution. Recently the use of the term has spread to include the effects of unwanted noise, and light during the hours of darkness (something astronomers are especially concerned about, as it compromises our view of the night sky). However, as we'll see, the type of pollution that's of principal interest when it comes to end-of-the-world scenarios is chemical.

Much pollution is released during single, high-profile events – such as the running aground of the *Amoco Cadiz* oil tanker off the coast of Brittany in 1978, or the Bhopal disaster of 1984 in which a leak of methyl isocyanate gas from a pesticide plant in Bhopal, India, owned by American firm Union Carbide, killed over 3700 people.

Sunrise over the city of Linfen, Shanxi Province, in China. Due to nearby coal mines and related industries, Linfen suffers from terrible air quality, and was the world's most polluted city from 2004 to 2007.

The six big chemical pollutants

The Blacksmith Institute is an organization based in New York that works to combat the effects of toxic pollution, particularly in the developing world. In 2010 it published a study naming the six leading chemical pollutants that threaten the environment today, namely: lead, mercury, chromium, arsenic, pesticides and radionuclides (see table overleaf).

The toxicity of lead has been well known for many years – it can cause brain damage and impair heart function, to name just two of its poisonous effects. It is often released by the mining and smelting of metal ores and from the improper disposal of car batteries, and can pollute the air, water and soil. Mercury is another dangerous metal – best known for its application in thermometers. However, it's also used in large quantities in chemical engineering plants for the manufacture of compounds such as chlorine gas and caustic soda and in batteries. Like lead, you can be exposed to mercury through polluted water, soil or air. It harms internal organs and can lead to brain damage. Chromium, yet another dangerous heavy metal, is a by-product of large metal-working operations, such as steel works.

Poisoning from exposure to chromium can lead to a wide range of problems, including damage to human respiratory, immune and reproductive systems. It also causes cancer.

Arsenic, the next one up, is a known deadly poison. It is used in the electronics industry in the manufacture of semiconductors, and is often given off by smelting plants in the process of extracting other metals from ore. The fifth big toxic pollutant listed by the Blacksmith Institute is the general category of pesticides. The dangers of pesticide poisoning were highlighted in 1962 by *Silent Spring*, written by the American conservationist Rachel Carson. It was particularly critical of the insecticide DDT, which Carson claimed is toxic to many wildlife species, and the book led to the banning of this chemical in the US. Today, pesticides cover anything used to kill unwanted species such as insects, weeds and parasitic types of worms. These chemicals seep into groundwater, and anything drinking this water then runs the risk of damage to the nervous and reproductive systems.

Chemical	Population at risk at pollution sites (million people)	Estimated population affected globally (million people)
Lead	10	18–22
Mercury	8.6	15–19
Chromium	7.3	13–17
Arsenic	3.7	5–9
Pesticides	3.4	5–8
Radionuclides	3.3	5–8

The Blacksmith Institute's top six causes of pollution.

Radionuclides make up Blacksmith's final category. These are chemicals that are radioactive, and as such give out high-energy particles and electromagnetic radiation over time. Radioactive elements occur naturally. However, the development of nuclear technology has led to them being mined and concentrated. Since the mid-1940s, nuclear weapons detonations (both controlled tests and wartime deployment) as well as leaks of radioactive material from nuclear power stations, and their associated waste repositories and reprocessing plants, have caused considerable radionuclide pollution.

The 1986 Chernobyl accident alone released a hundred times more radioactive material than the Nagasaki and Hiroshima bombs combined. The radiation from these chemicals can damage living cells – and in high doses can lead to cancer-causing DNA mutations.

Acid rain

Of course, there are many other pollutants in addition to the "big six". One of these is sulphur dioxide, a chemical given off by various industrial processes – as well as the burning of coal and oil as fuel. Sulphur dioxide has the effect of blocking some of the light from the sun, causing a slight reduction in global temperatures – a phenomenon leading to the artificial winters that follow major volcanic eruptions, which give off massive amounts of the gas.

But sulphur dioxide has another detrimental effect on the environment. It combines chemically with water and oxygen in the atmosphere to form sulphuric acid, leading to the phenomenon of acid rain. This erodes natural features, destroys plant life (especially high-altitude forests), and pollutes rivers, lakes and groundwater – from where its toxic effects can then work their way up the food chain. Happily, curbs on industry and the addition of catalytic converters to cars seem to be reducing our annual sulphur dioxide emissions.

Since the Industrial Revolution in the eighteenth and nineteenth centuries, the biggest pollutant on a global scale has been carbon dioxide, released by the burning of fossil fuels. Time is running out to avoid the effects of the catastrophic climate change that this may bring (see p.84). To this end, nations are working to introduce regulations to limit the emissions not just of carbon dioxide, but many other polluting gases given off by human industrial activity.

Pollution and extinction

Unlike human beings, who seem to be able to survive in almost every corner of the Earth, most species of animal and plant life have grown up in very particular niches. When a particular niche is destroyed by the toxic effects of polluting chemicals, there is a clear and present danger that any species inhabiting that niche may become extinct. Recently it has been suggested by some scientists that the Earth could be in the grip of the sixth major mass extinction of life on Earth – a sweeping extermination of many species from the planet's surface (see p.62).

A study carried out in 2004, and reported in the journal *Science*,

The world's most polluted places

In 2007, the Blacksmith Institute released its list of the ten most polluted places on Earth.

Place	People potentially affected	Type of pollutant	Source
Sumgayit, Azerbaijan	275,000	Organic chemicals, oil, metals including mercury	Petrochemical and other industries
Linfen, China	3,000,000	Ash, carbon monoxide, sulphur dioxide, arsenic, lead	Automobile and industrial emissions
Tianying, China	140,000	Lead and other metals	Mining and metal recycling industries
Sukinda, India	2,600,000	Hexavalent chromium and other metals	Chromite mining
Vapi, India	71,000	Assorted chemicals and heavy metals	Industrial activity
La Oroya, Peru	35,000	Lead, copper, zinc and sulphur dioxide	Mining and associated smelting of heavy metals
Dzerzhinsk, Russia	300,000	Substances involved in chemical weapons manufacture, plus lead and phenols	Poorly regulated chemical weapons manufacture during Cold War
Norilsk, Russia	134,000	Airborne particulates, sulphur dioxide, heavy metals, phenols, hydrogen sulphide	Major metal mining and associated smelting
Chernobyl, Ukraine	unknown	Contamination from radionuclides such as uranium, plutonium, caesium-137 and strontium	Reactor core meltdown at the Chernobyl nuclear power plant in 1986
Kabwe, Zambia	255,000	Lead and cadmium	Lead mining and processing

suggested that pollution may be at least part of the cause. Researchers from the Open University, in Milton Keynes, found a strong correlation between areas in the UK where the diversity of plant species is on the wane and areas where there are high levels of nitrogen pollution. They found that as much as one species is being lost for every 2.5kg of nitrogen per hectare above the ambient background level (and in some areas, levels are 30kg per hectare over the norm). Follow-up research by the team now suggests that the effect extends across much of Europe, while a related study by the University of Minnesota has uncovered evidence for similar effects in the continental US, and there is now further evidence in India and China. Whereas pure nitrogen is harmless, the trouble stems from its compounds, such as nitrates and ammonia, which are released by agricultural fertilizers and industrial activity. The scale of the problem posed by nitrogen pollution is only just starting to be understood.

So it seems pollution may already be causing extinction on a global level. Dealing with this presents a big dilemma for us humans. Science, technology and industry have done much to improve our quality of life – and they continue to do so. And yet, if we are not careful, the pollution that results from these endeavours may undermine all their many benefits – to our extreme cost.

When population outstrips resources
too many people, not enough planet

There's a worrying possibility that there may soon be too many human beings on Earth for the planet to support. As the human race becomes more numerous, so the per capita resources at our disposal are becoming scarcer and scarcer. Now we're starting to feel the pinch – hundreds of millions of people in the world are undernourished and over a billion don't have easy access to clean water. If the human race continues to expand at the same rate, while the natural resources we need to survive grow ever less plentiful, we may witness mass extinctions of species, and experience wars over access to land and water and increases in the severity of pandemics of the sort described in Part 2 of this book.

Improvements in medicine, and other life-prolonging technologies, have helped increase life expectancy over the twentieth century. Technological improvements in agriculture have given us the ability to mass-produce our own food. Steve Jones, head of the biology department at University College London, puts it this way: "humans are ten thousand times more common than we should be." He points out that without intensive farming there would be perhaps just half a million human beings on the Earth today.

As it stands, there are nearly fourteen times that many – 6.8 billion of us at the last count, all clamouring for space. And that's up from just 1.6 billion at the start of the twentieth century. The figure is expected to reach 9.5 billion by the year 2050.

Malthusian catastrophe

Up until recently, world population was doubling roughly every forty to fifty years. This kind of behaviour, whereby a quantity increases by a multiplicative factor in a fixed time, is known as exponential growth. It was the British social scientist Thomas Malthus who first concluded that the world's population was increasing at this rate, back in 1798. His reasoning was simple: the more people there are, then the higher the birth rate will be. A population of one thousand people would have more children in a year than a smaller population of one hundred people. And mathematicians have long known that when a quantity is proportional to its own rate of change, an exponential law of increase is sure to follow. But Malthus noticed something else. Food production only increases in linear fashion – meaning it rises by a fixed increment in a fixed time, rather than by a multiplicative factor. And this could only mean one thing: there will, inevitably, come a point at which there are more people on the Earth than it's possible to feed.

When are we likely to reach this Malthusian catastrophic point? If you believe the United Nations Environment Programme (UNEP), then we already have. UNEP's Global Environmental Outlook study, published in 2000, was compiled by 1400 scientists over a period of five years. It found that humans are already using over thirty percent more land than the planet can sustainably provide. Other estimates of the total number of people the Earth can support vary, with most ending up between four and sixteen billion.

The dystopian sci-fi movie *Logan's Run* (1976) depicts a future society ruled by a central computer in which everyone over the age of thirty is forcibly "renewed" (executed). The eponymous Logan (played by Michael York) is a state executioner who is forced to go on the run when his time prematurely comes up.

The perils of overcrowding

If nothing is done about overcrowding on our planet, food shortages are just one of the major consequences that we will have to deal with. Already a trend seems to be emerging in the data, with 832 million people starving in the world in 1995 – a figure that had risen to 923 million by 2007. The UN's Food and Agriculture Organization predicts that in order to feed the billions of extra human mouths on the planet in 2050, we will require present-day food production rates to have risen by seventy percent. Which will be no mean feat, given that we're already farming a total land area equal to that of South America.

But it's not just the demand for farmland that will impact upon food production. Agriculture uses up water – eighty percent, in fact, of our planet's present fresh water supplies. There is already concern that the amount of fresh water available for drinking may be in danger of running out: we currently use some fifty percent of the world's

Case study: Easter Island

During its heyday in the seventeenth century, Easter Island, one of the Polynesian islands in the Pacific Ocean, is believed to have been home to a civilization consisting of some fifteen thousand people. This was no ragtag bunch. They were a cultured society, as evidenced by the hundreds of ornately carved stone statues, known as *moai*, that they left dotted around the island – not to mention cave paintings and detailed wood carvings. And yet, when European explorers discovered the island in the early eighteenth century they found it inhabited by just a handful of tribes, living in squalid conditions, and engaged in continual warfare and cannibalism.

What happened? Anthropologists believe that the ancient people there mined their small island of every last scrap of its resources. With nothing left to support them, and no way of escape – Easter Island is over 2000km (1200 miles) from the nearest land – their entire civilization collapsed. The story remains today a cautionary tale of what happens to societies who dare to overexploit their natural environment.

fresh water supply, which is in itself only some 2.53 percent of the world's total water (the rest being saline). Then there's oil to consider. Producing food and hauling it to our doorsteps all takes energy, which has to come from somewhere. At the moment, the bulk of that power is generated by the burning of oil. But this is in jeopardy too – with geologists warning that oil reserves could start to go into decline as early as 2015 (see p.125).

The environment will also suffer as the population rises. Everybody does their own little bit to pollute the planet, through simply being alive – and the more of us there are, the worse the situation. Climate change in turn leads to sea-level rise, and a decrease in food production as agricultural lands are inundated by the ocean.

As demand for food rises with the population, so deforestation increases as we clear jungles and forests to make more farmland available. As habitats are wiped out, so extinctions of species become more frequent: ecosystems will fall in on themselves. Expansion of both cities and agriculture bring man further into the habitats of other animals, making it easier for disease agents to jump between the two species – increasing the likelihood of pandemics.

Of course, food availability – and all the problems that come with it – will ultimately cause the size of the world's human population to adjust itself until a stable equilibrium is reached. But that's merely a way of avoiding stating that a lot of people will starve to death.

State control

One state solution to an ever-increasing population would be that of enforced family planning. If a state decreed that a couple were allowed to bear a maximum of two children then, in theory at least, the population should stabilize (or even start to drop slightly, given that not everyone chooses to reproduce). Putting that theory into practice, however, is less straightforward. This was the case with China's one-child policy, which has enjoyed, at best, mixed success.

It officially restricts married, urban couples to having only one child, while allowing exemptions for several cases, such as rural couples, ethnic minorities and parents without any siblings themselves: it applies to approximately 35.9 percent of China's adult population. According to official figures, China had three to four hundred million fewer people in 2008 than it would have had otherwise. It claimed the fertility rate in China had dropped from over three births per woman in 1980 (already a sharp reduction from more than five births per woman in the early 1970s) to approximately 1.54 in 2011.

Quite apart from the human rights issues, there's the unfairness of the penalty: couples that had more than one child were fined, which meant those wealthy enough to pay for it could still have more children. But the biggest problem caused by reducing the population too abruptly became apparent – a large elderly population must be cared for by a disproportionate number of the young. As the first generation of law-enforced only children became parents themselves, one adult was left having to support his or her two parents and four grandparents: the "4-2-1 Problem". The older generation is thus more likely to have to depend on retirement funds, state support and charity.

Are there really too many of us?

Whereas the global number of people on the planet jumped from 2.55 billion in 1950 to six billion in 2000, more than doubling, the projected figure for 2050 is only just over half as much again – 9.5 billion. This is still a huge number, but it is a substantial slowdown.

Childhood's end

might we one day stop making babies?

The 2006 movie *Children of Men* presented a bleak vision of the Earth's future. It is the year 2027 and, all over the world, government and society has collapsed. Terrorism is rife, and disease pandemics grip what looks set to be humanity's final generation. The cause of the apocalypse? Not an asteroid, not climate change – humans have simply lost their ability to have children. The youngest person in this world is nineteen, and the human species as a whole is estimated to have fewer than one hundred years left.

Could this stark vision of humanity's exit from the Earth ever come to pass? Well, medical studies suggest that infertility could well be on the rise. In 2000, a study by a collaboration of scientists in Denmark found that thirty percent of men aged between nineteen and twenty in the country had sperm counts low enough to impair their fertility. What's more, the team collated historical data showing a gradual decline in the quality of male sperm during recent decades. Other research has confirmed this on a worldwide scale, showing a steady decline in sperm counts amounting to around one to two percent per year.

The causes

Research in the last decade has fingered several culprits. Causes of male infertility include physical damage and diseases, such as mumps. Diabetes is another potential cause, meaning that the rise in obesity across the world could be harming male fertility levels. But foremost among them are agricultural pesticides. A 2003 study by the US Centers for Disease Control and Prevention found a correlation between low sperm count (defined as fewer than fifteen million sperm per millilitre of semen) and the presence of the pesticide chemicals alachlor, atrazine and diazinon in a man's bloodstream.

Only 2 of the 86 men who participated in the study were farmers – in other words, almost all of the subjects had no ostensible contact with agricultural pesticides – leading the scientists to conclude that the chemicals were most likely being ingested through drinking water. Meanwhile, another study, conducted by a collaborative group of Japanese scientists and published in 2007, found that

When the whole human race becomes infertile in *Children of Men* (2006), the world descends into chaos, martial law is imposed and liberal democracies become military dictatorships. Refugees flock to the UK, where the army deal with them ruthlessly.

the insecticide permethrin halved sperm counts in mice that were exposed to it for six weeks.

Infertility arises in women too, of course. Specific causes include damage to the fallopian tubes, by which eggs are transported from the ovaries to the womb – this can result from infections, such as chlamydia – as well as age, with the conception rate for a 38-year-old woman being twenty percent less than it is in a woman of 35. Smoking is also a factor – in both men and women. Despite the best medical science, however, doctors are still unable to explain the cause in 20–25 percent of infertile couples.

The solutions

Although there are no known treatments for low sperm count in men, there are medications that stimulate the ovaries in women, thus increasing the chances of conception. And there are physical methods to assist sperm entering the uterus.

In extreme cases, where none of these measures have helped, a doctor may prescribe a course of in vitro fertilization (IVF), where an egg is surgically extracted from the mother, fertilized artificially with sperm from the father, re-implanted into the mother and then

How to live forever

Physicist Max Tegmark, of the Princeton Institute for Advanced Study, believes that a kind of immortality could arise naturally through the laws of quantum mechanics – the mind-bending, counterintuitive branch of physics governing tiny subatomic particles. One interpretation of quantum theory says that there exists a multitude of parallel universes, and that some of the weirder quantum effects are due to interference between these universes.

Each parallel universe contains copies of everything that we see in our universe – including copies of you and me. In each of the different universes history plays out slightly differently, so that every possible course of events takes place in a universe somewhere. This means that whatever fate befalls you in this universe, there is always a universe somewhere in which you would survive.

Tegmark believes that under certain circumstances it's possible for a person's consciousness to always end up in the universe in which they live, granting them a special kind of "quantum immortality" – albeit one that isn't of a great deal of practical use.

brought to term.

In *Children of Men*, however, it seems nothing has worked. Putting aside the likelihood of such widespread infertility at a global level, it's worth asking what other techniques we might have at our disposal. Perhaps the science of cloning could help us out in such a scenario. Cloning is a technique for producing offspring that are an exact genetic match to one parent. The first mammal to be cloned from an adult cell was Dolly the sheep, born in 1996 at the Roslin Institute of the University of Edinburgh. The nucleus of a sheep egg cell was removed from the mother and replaced with the nucleus from another animal. The nucleus contains all the genetic material of the cell, so that when it was re-implanted into the mother animal's womb and brought to term the result was a sheep that was a carbon copy of the nucleus donor.

This technique might help to avert a hypothetical fertility crisis, if the crisis is predominantly due to a problem on the male side. However, if the problem were to lie with the ability of females to grow babies in the womb and deliver them, then cloning of this kind would be of no use at all.

But help could still be at hand: the use of artificial wombs, sometimes known as ectogenesis. In 2002, researchers at Cornell University's Center for Reproductive Medicine and Infertility announced successful experiments they had conducted using an artificial womb. In their studies, embryos proved able to attach themselves to the walls of the artificial womb – just as they would inside that of a real mother.

The laboratory womb was made from cells taken from a real endometrium – the womb lining – and then grown onto a biodegradable scaffold that was shaped like a uterus. This research could be invaluable in helping women who have suffered several miscarriages, or given birth prematurely – as well as potentially assisting in the process of conception. However, this experiment was terminated after fourteen days, in line with US regulations governing experiments with human embryos.

A childless world

If even these measures failed, and humanity did find itself doomed to shuffle off with no heir apparent, how might the final decades and years of our species unfold? While its premise might be far-fetched, the depiction of the end results in *Children of Men* is entirely feasible. Humanity would fizzle out a lot sooner than you might expect. There would be economic strife, as the workforce became progressively older and smaller. Riots, social discontent and ultimately complete societal breakdown would set in; all concern for the future of the planet would become an irrelevant impedance to enjoying the few short years we would have left. The last people on the planet would be senior citizens. With no one around capable of caring for them in their twilight years, they would die quickly, and probably painfully. And then humanity would be over.

Generation d'uh

dumb and dumber and dumber

Dr Richard Lynn, a psychologist, won a professional notoriety of sorts when he published his book *Dysgenics: Genetic Deterioration in Modern Populations* (1996). The book suggested we ought to be concerned about the fact that, in the Western world at least, intelligent people (meaning those with a high IQ rating) are having fewer babies than people with lower IQ.

This, the book concluded, is creating a kind of dysgenic pressure that threatens to multiply the number of low-IQ people in the world. Lynn ascribed this discrepancy in the fecundity of low- and high-IQ people to intelligent women pursuing careers and delaying having children until much later in life – when they have fewer fertile years remaining, leading to fewer offspring.

The Flynn effect

Lynn's theories are controversial for several reasons. For one thing, the inheritability of IQ is highly debatable: how much of one's intelligence is nature and how much is nurture is an argument that will no doubt continue to seesaw until the end of the world. There is also the question of how much IQ itself can really tell us about the capabilities, decision-making skills, potential and overall capabilities of any given human being.

However, even leaving all that aside, there is plenty of evidence that IQ actually appears to be creeping up with time, not down. Despite fewer children being born to brainy couples, on average people seem to be getting smarter. Known as the Flynn effect – after its discoverer, the US-born psychologist James Flynn – the phenomenon suggests that IQs have risen by approximately three points per decade since the beginning of IQ testing in the years following 1900.

IQs are calculated so that the average score in any era is one hundred. What Flynn had found was that this average score of one hundred was in effect steadily being recalibrated, so it corresponded to an increasingly higher level of intelligence. If a group of people from 1930 – all with IQs of one hundred, as measured by tests from that era – could travel forward in time and take an intelligence test today, their average score would be more like 75 on the modern scale. This would tip them towards the bottom of today's scale.

So what's going on? Flynn puts it down to wholesale changes in the way people think. Back at the start of the twentieth century there was no TV and no Internet for us to easily inform ourselves with. People's judgements were shaped largely by their own limited experiences and intuitions. Nowadays, on the other hand, we are generally better informed, and more accustomed to thinking about things logically: Flynn proposes that the increase in our IQ denotes positive changes in abstract problem-solving ability. Other experts have pointed to factors such as better nutrition allowing better brain performance and improvements in education in the general public.

Survival of the wittiest

There is at present a heated debate amongst biologists about whether or not the human species is still evolving. Some say that our ability to make deliberate alterations to our bodies though cybernetics, genetics and plain old ingenuity – advanced tool-making such as the manufacturing and wearing of spectacles – has eclipsed any changes that occur naturally via evolution.

Others, however, think evolution is taking place at a faster rate than ever before. Not only that, but it's our brains that are doing the lion's share of the evolving. These biologists say that as our environment becomes increasingly filled with technology, so our brains are having to improve and adapt, just as Darwin hypothesized was the case with the physical form of living creatures.

Crucially, they say, evolution is also encouraging diversification in brain function. Whereas in the past some of us were brainy (good at mental work) while others were brawny (better at physical tasks), in the future we may all become brainy – but we'll each excel at disciplines involving different brain areas. Some of us will be good at maths and sciences, others the arts, while for some of us our strengths will lie in other areas altogether. If these biologists are right then evolution will save us from dumbing ourselves down into oblivion, and keep human IQs rising. And that would certainly seem like the cleverest outcome of them all.

Will the obese inherit the Earth?

could we be eating ourselves out of existence?

Obesity is a growing problem around the world: many doctors believe it to be the most serious health issue currently facing humanity. The World Health Organization (WHO) now estimates that one in ten of the entire human race is obese, and that as such the condition has reached epidemic proportions. According to data gathered by the US Centers for Disease Control and Prevention (CDC), obesity in the US rose from around thirteen percent of the adult population to almost 27 percent between 1960 and 2007– more than doubling. It's worth bearing in mind that these global figures are skewed by the rich world: 95 percent of the world's hungriest and malnourished people live in developing countries while, in 2009, 63.1 percent of American adults were either overweight or obese. Incidents of obesity are increasing in the developing world (in the Middle East and North Africa in particular) but the link between obesity and income seems to be undeniable.

How heavy do you need to be in order to be classified as obese? The present definition uses the body mass index (BMI), which is arrived at by dividing a person's mass in kilograms by the square of their height in metres. A normal BMI is somewhere in between 18.5 and 25. Once you know this number, you can then look up your weight classification on the table below to see how you measure up.

BMI has drawn some criticism as a measure because it takes no account of the fact that muscle is denser than fat – meaning that it's

What does your BMI say about you?

The table below allows you to look up your body weight classification according to your body mass index (BMI), calculated by dividing your weight in kilograms by your height in metres squared.

BMI range	Category
less than 16.0	Underweight
18.5 to 25	Normal
25 to 30	Overweight
30 to 35	Obese
35 to 40	Severely obese
40 to 45	Morbidly obese
greater than 45	Super obese

quite possible for a superfit body builder to have a BMI of more than thirty, classifying them as obese. Given the rarity of superfit body builders among the general population, however, BMI remains the most practical and easy-to-apply measure of unhealthy body mass that we have.

Obesity can lead to heart disease, diabetes and a host of other medical complications – even increasing a person's susceptibility to cancer. But can it really threaten the future of our civilization? Some commentators have suggested that it can, because the carbon footprint of an obese person (the amount of planet-warming carbon dioxide that their lifestyle contributes to the environment each year) is that much more than the footprint produced by someone of normal weight. A report from the London School of Hygiene and Tropical Medicine had this to say: "Because food production is a major contributor to global warming, a lean population, such as that seen in Vietnam, will consume almost twenty percent less food and produce fewer greenhouse gases than a population in which forty percent of people are obese." Furthermore, "transport-related emissions will also be lower because it takes less energy to transport slim people". It concluded that "a lean population of one billion people would emit 1.0 GT (one thousand million tons) less carbon dioxide equivalents per year compared with a fat one".

Food production and transport is already a major source of carbon emissions. The average Western citizen generates two tons of carbon dioxide per year purely as a result of the food they eat. That's the same amount of CO_2 per head as is generated by three transatlantic flights. On a related note, United Airlines announced in 2009 that it would charge passengers extra if they were unable to lower both armrests; some other US airlines have similar policies.

Weight watching

The obesity epidemic is an interesting symptom of the environment that we humans have created for ourselves. It is now changing at a pace faster than natural evolution can keep up with. Many millennia ago, before the dawn of agriculture – and long before supermarkets and convenience food outlets – much of an adult human's life was taken up in the search for food. Discovering a source of energy-rich fat or sugar was a find you had to make the most of – by devouring as much of it as you could. Now such sugary and fatty foods are plentiful – yet evolution has been slow to respond and we still have our primal cravings for these foods. Hence our swelling waistlines.

It's even possible obesity could be contagious. Research in the late 1990s at the Pennington Biomedical Research Center in Louisiana found a connection between incidences of obesity and infection with a virus called AD-36. A gene in the AD-36 virus was observed to be causing fat accumulation in infected animals. The gene responsible is called E4Orfl, and researchers are hoping to be able to use it in vaccines and anti-viral medicines. However, it is unlikely that AD-36 is responsible for any more than a minority of cases of obesity: people are overweight for a number of reasons.

If obesity is wrecking our health and our planet, then what can we do to stop it? Governments run health awareness campaigns, while on an individual level, measures such as counselling, medication and even surgery that limits the capacity of the stomach are all commonplace. Some healthcare professionals have long been calling for taxation to be added to fattening foods – similar to that which already exists on alcohol and tobacco. In the UK, the government tries to encourage people to cycle to work, with special discounts (in the form of tax-free loans) for bicycles.

It's rather sad if this game of carrots-and-sticks is the only form of healthy eating advice we are capable of responding to. But with the number of overweight adults in the world predicted to reach 2.3 billion by 2015, they may well be our best bet.

Survival of the... whatever
making ourselves worse by making ourselves better

There is a school of thought that says the measures we take to help out the weak and needy in our civilized society are actually enfeebling our species, diluting the gene pool and making us less able to cope in times of crisis. Proponents of this idea argue that we have been rendered more likely to get snuffed out by the next large asteroid strike, disease pandemic or other global calamity that might happen to come along. They argue that, many millennia ago, life for human beings was very difficult indeed.

In order to survive, a human being had to be fit, strong or intelligent – and preferably all three. Not only was such an individual more likely to survive, but so were his or her children – because the individual passes the genes for these beneficial qualities on to them. In this way, for generation after generation, the harshness of life acted as a filter to ensure that the human race was built upon the healthiest gene pool possible – by, quite literally, removing any weak elements.

Nowadays, however, life is somewhat less taxing. True, most of us have to work when we'd rather not, and money is sometimes tight. But we don't have to chase our dinner across the savannah each day, in the knowledge that the slow ultimately go hungry. And we don't run the risk of getting eaten by sabre-toothed tigers, and other ferocious beasts.

We also now have healthcare, of course. Many of those who would have perished from illness, injury or other physical shortcomings in past eras can now survive and thrive. Someone whose poor eyesight would, centuries ago, have led them to an early grave, can now see the world thanks to spectacles, contact lenses and corrective eye surgery. This means we live in a less savage, less hardscrabble society, but also that the genes for defective vision are now passed on to their children – genes which, in the past, would have been filtered from the population.

Charles Darwin: father of evolutionary theory. The extent to which he was sympathetic to eugenic theories remains an oft-debated topic.

The spectre of eugenics

This weakening of the gene pool has been termed dysgenics. Arguing that we should try to oppose it deliberately sounds horribly reminiscent of the eugenics programmes of the early twentieth century. Eugenics is the opposite of dysgenics, though based on the same principles, and is concerned with the deliberate removal of what are perceived as weaknesses from the gene pool. At its worst, it led to the extermination of millions of Jews in Nazi gas chambers. The First International Congress of Eugenics in 1912 was supported by many luminaries of science and politics, such as its president, Leonard Darwin (son of Charles), its honorary vice-president Winston Churchill (rather ironically, given his opposition to Nazi Germany) and Alexander Graham Bell, the inventor of the telephone.

The US and Canada have operated eugenics programmes of some kind. They weren't genocidal, like Nazi Germany's, but they did include horrendous measures such as compulsory sterilization, wherein citizens whose genetic make-up was deemed to be inferior were forced to undergo surgery or courses of drugs that rendered them incapable of having children. In the US, state laws were written in the late nineteenth and early twentieth centuries, prohibiting marriage and enforcing sterilization of the mentally ill in order to prevent the "passing on" of mental illness to the next generation. These laws were upheld by the US Supreme Court in 1927 and were not abolished until the mid-twentieth century: all in all, some sixty thousand Americans were sterilized on grounds of mental illness.

In fact, not only is eugenics an abhorrent philosophy, but it does not even bring about the goals of its advocates: the notion that it makes for a more productive society is wholly flawed. Here's why.

The "comparative advantage" argument

Bryan Caplan, an economist at George Mason University, in Virginia, has attacked the founding logic of eugenics using a principle from economics called the law of comparative advantage. This law, in essence, states that two groups of people can mutually benefit by working together, even if one group is "superior" to the other in every way so long as their relative levels of ability are different.

Here's an example. Let's imagine a society in which there are just two tasks that need to be performed: building walls and growing potatoes. There are two groups of people – the High Flyers and the Drop Outs. Every day, a single High Flyer can build two walls or produce ten potatoes (averaged over the year). Meanwhile, a Drop Out can build just one wall or grow three potatoes. The High Flyers are demonstrably better at both tasks.

But consider this. If one High Flyer is transferred from building walls to growing potatoes, then we are two walls down but ten potatoes better off. Meanwhile, if three Drop Outs are switched from growing potatoes to building walls, then we gain three walls but lose nine potatoes. Do both and, on net, the society is one wall (three minus two) and one potato (ten minus nine) better off. Having two populations of different relative abilities – even though one of them is worse at everything – thus facilitates a boost to the society's overall productivity.

What doesn't kill us...

The same argument applies to the idea that dysgenics is weakening human society on Earth. In general, the existence of subsets in the population – each with a different spectrum of abilities – encourages people to specialize in what they are good at, and then to trade those abilities with each other to the mutual benefit of everyone. Dysgenics doesn't necessarily weaken society.

But what about susceptibility to disease – which surely is of no benefit to anybody? The argument goes that improvements in healthcare paradoxically increase the prevalence of disease in the world: fewer people die from conditions that were previously fatal, thus allowing the genes for those conditions to spread. The problem with this argument, however, is that "bad genes" – such as those which today cause disease – might not always be so bad.

Take type-2 diabetes, for example. Those who suffer from this condition are essentially very good at turning the food they eat into fat. So good, in fact, that they suffer ill effects from it if they eat too much. But what if our circumstances on Earth suddenly changed? If climate change and/or population growth made it difficult to grow sufficient crops, leading to a food shortage, then a global famine would result. Those with type-2 diabetes would be genetically well-equipped to survive it – capable of extracting the most reserve fat from their limited food. Whether a gene is bad or good depends on the environment in which a human society is living – and that's continually changing.

Even genes that are debiliting in the short term might be "correctable" using gene therapies and other new areas of science such as nanoengineering and synthetic life (see Part 4: Rage of the machines). A key point about these important developments and others – they ultimately make us stronger, not weaker. For we are no longer just human beings. We are humanity plus the technology we create around ourselves, and that is a powerful combination.

The big burn-out
us humans don't know what's good for us

People seem to have an unerring habit of willingly engaging in behaviour which they know is no good for them. They drink to excess, they smoke and they overeat; or, at the opposite extreme, push themselves to punishing lengths in the name of achievement. Sportspersons force themselves to injury-inducing extremes of endurance, while the career-minded deny themselves leisure time, spending their evenings and weekends toiling in pursuit of the next promotion.

Such self-destructive drives occur in society as a whole. We know climate change, ultimately, will be potentially catastrophic and yet we fail to curb our carbon emissions, preferring to enjoy the short-term benefits and luxuries that fossil fuels facilitate instead. We continue to wage wars that cost billions, while millions of people go without food. Multinational corporations are seemingly obliged to wring every last drop of profitability from their staff and customers, over and above the ultimate well-being of either. Rather like an overworked employee, is human civilization staggering towards one big nervous breakdown?

Economic collapse
One prime example of irresponsible corporate actions throwing the world into turmoil was the economic backlash from the US subprime mortgage crisis. You may well wonder what this has to do with

end-of-the-world scenarios. Well, it is crucial to understand just how enmeshed our existence has become with the systems we have built to look after our money and possessions. So interconnected – and international – are all the links in the chain, that it's clear we are scarily only ever one big crisis away from collapse.

American lenders gave mortgages to homebuyers who did not really have enough money to meet the repayments. They then sold these loans as securities to other finance companies, both in the US and overseas. In 2006, interest rates began to rise substantially and many sub-prime homeowners found themselves unable to make their repayments. The housing market was also slipping into decline, meaning that properties were losing value, ending up being worth less than they were at purchase (known as negative equity). And this in turn made it difficult for owners to remortgage their properties at a more affordable rate. As a result, many ended up defaulting on their payments.

The banks and finance companies repossessed the properties, but themselves lost billions because of negative equity. And because these loans had been sold on around the world, the crisis quickly spread to become a global problem. Banks in many countries were pushed to the brink of collapse. And knowledge that the banks were in trouble led many thousands of account holders to withdraw their money, creating a run on the banks, as financial speculators smelled blood and swooped, which made the situation even worse. (This is, in fact, a great example of an "information hazard" – see p.184.) Indeed, some of these banks would have gone under, had it not been for massive government bail-outs. The US government alone stumped up $700bn to shore up its ailing finance sector.

Just how bad can an economic crisis get? It will never be quite in the same league as an asteroid impact or a supervolcano, but things can still get considerably worse than they did between 2007 and 2010. The Great Depression, suffered by the US in the 1930s, went some way in that direction, with many banks actually failing – and account holders losing all their money. Unemployment reached 25 percent. A considerable proportion of today's most affluent nation were living out of tents. This was one of the worst economic crises that the developing world has seen.

But it could have been yet worse. Today's world is far more driven by consumption, spending and credit than that of the 1930s. Thus the lack of money being circulated as a result of unemployment (fewer people having less money to spend) becomes more of a problem more quickly. Companies go bust, as they no longer receive income from their products, fewer people earn, and so on. If no one is earning then no one pays taxes to the state. The state can shore its accounts up by borrowing from the banks, but when the banks have all gone under, then the state itself may come in danger of collapse. If this happens all around the world – as it started to in 2006 and 2007, then the total breakdown of civilization is a distinct possibility.

Social justice

The last financial crisis could be said to have stemmed from an inability to regulate our own behaviour – less as individuals, more at the societal and organizational level. The profit motive is written into the behaviour of corporations – they are beholden to their share-holders to maximize profits – which places a dangerous premium on returns. In the 1970s, the American political philosopher John Rawls arrived at a theory of social justice by using a thought experiment known as the "veil of ignorance". In essence, Rawls contended that the fairest system of society could only be put in place by politicians who were ignorant of their own place within it. A policy-maker acting as if they had no knowledge of their own circumstances cannot engineer policies for personal gain: they run the risk of penalizing themselves. A politician would be unlikely to condone slavery if they didn't know what criteria would dictate who was to be enslaved and who would be free.

Rawls's theory is something of an idealism of course. It is similar to the idea that the person best suited to wielding power is the person who least desires it. And yet it holds valuable lessons for governments about the importance of fairness in society – and how policy might bring it about. The future of our world is too important to be entrusted to the selfish and ill-conceived actions of a society which, at times, simply cannot help itself.

Misery loves company: depression's evolutionary roots

Recent research has challenged the traditional view of depression as a malfunction of the brain, and suggested instead that this source of misery and anxiety for millions could actually have arisen as a result of evolution – as a benefit.

In 2009, Paul W. Andrews, of Virginia Commonwealth University, and J. Anderson Thomson, of the University of Virginia Student Health Center, published research in the journal *Psychological Review*, suggesting that depression emerged as a way for us to focus on solving problems in our lives. They argue that the way in which depressed people ruminate deeply about nothing other than their problems is an extremely efficient way to get those problems solved.

They have even found that people in a depressed state demonstrate an enhanced capability for analytical thought, enabling them to achieve higher scores in intelligence tests. In particular, the scientists have found that those suffering from depression are better able to break complex problems down into a number of smaller, more tractable ones.

They also point out that several of depression's so-called symptoms are especially conducive to long periods of sustained concentration – for example, losing interest in pleasurable activities that might be considered a distraction, such as eating or sex, and instead preferring to sit in isolation. If these researchers are right then depression is simply an exaggerated, extreme form of a natural biological strategy: telling you that you have important problems that need solving, then putting you in the optimum state of mind to find solutions to them.

In 2011, new research emerged to support this view. Researchers from Clarkson University, New York, writing in the *Journal of Abnormal Psychology* noted that depressed individuals perform better than their peers in sequential decision tasks: open-ended tasks in which part of the problem is deciding when to actually stop and make a decision, such as selecting from job applicants, dating or simply shopping.

Woe is us
everybody gets the blues

An estimated fifteen percent of the adult population of most developed countries suffer from severe depression. And in all too many cases the condition leads sufferers to take their own lives. In 2006, the World Health Organization (WHO) estimated that suicide is the cause of around a million deaths per year – more than war or homicide – which means that somebody commits suicide somewhere in the world every 32 seconds.

There are as many as twenty million attempted suicides annually. In the Western world, females make more attempts, though males are generally more successful, making men four times more likely to die by suicide than women. In China and India, however, the situation is reversed and female deaths by suicide are higher. The highest overall suicide rates seem to occur in Eastern Europe and Russia – with Lithuania topping the table at 38.6 deaths per hundred thousand people. In Western nations, the rate is closer to ten per hundred thousand.

As might be expected, rates are generally higher amongst those who spend much of their time alone – divorcees, empty-nesters and the retired – although, surprisingly, seasonal variations tend to peak in spring and summer rather than autumn and winter. There is a higher incidence of suicide amongst homosexual people than in heterosexuals.

However you look at it, suicide has reached epidemic proportions. In 1998, the WHO cited suicide as the world's twelfth biggest killer. Experts predict that by 2020 it will have risen in the rankings to second place – with only heart disease claiming more lives.

Tired and unhappy

The leading cause of suicide is depression, a complex condition that generally first presents itself in individuals during late adolescence and early adulthood (although studies suggest that four percent of children aged five to sixteen may be affected). Often a traumatic event will trigger the beginning of depression in someone's life – such as the death of a close family member, or the break-up of a relationship. Depression is also hereditary – if your parents or grandparents are known to suffer, then there is a greater likelihood that you will too.

Treatments for depression take two forms – medication and psychotherapy. The leading medication nowadays comes in the form of antidepressant drugs known as selective serotonin reuptake inhibitors (SSRIs). Serotonin is a neurotransmitter – a chemical that helps to carry signals across the brain and through the nervous system. Low levels of serotonin have been implicated in depression – and are believed to be caused by brain cells re-absorbing the chemical. SSRIs simply block this re-absorption. There are other forms of anti-depressant drug too. Medication is generally effective in between thirty to forty five percent of depressed people.

Meanwhile, the most effective form of psychotherapy for depression and anxiety disorders is known as cognitive behavioural therapy (usually abbreviated to CBT). Here, a patient works with a therapist to identify the negative thought patterns (cognition) that lead to depressive behaviour, and then learns how to control and override these thoughts.

The fast lane

But why is depression becoming so prevalent? Well, perhaps it isn't after all – it could be simply that we are less reluctant to report it. Until recently there was considerable stigma attached to mental illness – and many people would suffer in silence rather than risk the ridicule they imagined would result by coming forward for treatment. However, the rise in suicides would tend to suggest that what we are seeing is a genuine rise in cases – rather than just a rise in the number of cases diagnosed.

In 2009, 1500 farmers in the Indian agricultural state of Chattisgarh committed mass suicide after crop failures drove them into unmanageable debt. It's perhaps easier to understand why people at the extreme end of poverty might be driven to take such desperate decisions. But even those in the rich West who are supposedly doing well don't seem to be especially pleased about it. It seems that as we gain material wealth and possessions, so we covet even more. And when we don't get what we want, we become miserable.

You can't take it with you

A group of psychologists at the University of Liege, in Belgium, has come up with a fascinating theory that could hold the answer to why our society seems to be increasingly unhappy. It's based on an idea called the "experience-stretching" hypothesis, which essentially says that too much of a good thing lowers your enjoyment of it. They've used this to argue that as the rich enjoy the spoils of their labours, so they become used to the finer things – to the point that they subsequently find it difficult to obtain any pleasure from the more mundane side of life (which is, after all, what most of us must experience day to day). Rather like an addict waiting for their next fix, day-to-day life then becomes unbearable. And the result is depression.

It's not just a theory. The scientists conducted psychological tests in which hundreds of participants were asked to imagine various pleasurable scenarios – such as the satisfaction of completing an important task or the sense of well-being following a romantic break. Then they were asked to answer questions from which the team could attempt to quantify just how much enjoyment they were experiencing.

A subset of the participants was primed before the test by the simple expedient of being shown a large pile of money. The results revealed lower "enjoyment readings" for the answers these people gave. This applied even to such participants whose real-life income was high. It supports the notion that wealth – or rather, all the factors associated with the acquisition of money – really does inhibit our ability to savour the small pleasures in life.

Peak oil: the looming energy crisis
could the black stuff be about to run dry?

The world uses an astonishing amount of energy. In 2008, human civilization on Earth got through a total of 143,851 terawatt-hours. A terawatt-hour is the amount of electricity needed to maintain an electrical power of a million watts for the space of an hour. Put another way, 143,851 terawatt-hours is about the same as it would take to run a small kettle continuously for fifteen billion years, about the age of the known universe.

Despite the rise of nuclear power and renewable sources, about 33.5 percent is still generated by burning petroleum oil – more than any other. The trouble is, many geologists now believe the oil is run-

An estimated thirty percent of the world's undiscovered gas and thirteen percent of its undiscovered oil may lie in the Arctic. If predictions about declining oil prove correct, nations will scramble to exploit Arctic reserves, despite the ecological harm it will do – to both the climate and to Arctic residents such as these polar bears.

ning out. Some say dwindling reserves could force production into decline by as early as 2015: a scenario that has become known as peak oil, meaning that production has reached its maximum and that future production will henceforth be on a downward curve.

Needless to say, if the oil runs out before we've had time to develop alternatives it will be extremely bad news for industry, the world economy and, ultimately, everyone who relies on energy to light and heat their homes, get to work every day, and put food on the table.

Black gold

Oil is fuel that's retrieved from the decayed bodies of ancient plants and animals, buried by silt and soil, then compressed and heated over millions of years. By the time it's discovered by man, the silt and soil has long turned into rock – and that's why the only way oil can be extracted is by drilling down into the Earth's crust.

The peak oil theory was first proposed in the mid-1950s by American geophysicist M. King Hubbert. He worked out the mathematics describing the rate at which a finite resource can be harvested. Then he fitted this theoretical model to observed data on oil production in the continental United States. The model predicted that US oil production would reach a peak between 1965 and 1970. It duly did, reaching a maximum of 9.6 million barrels per day in 1970 – and has been in decline ever since.

In 1974, Hubbert applied the same mathematical model on a global scale. It predicted that world oil production would peak in 1995. This didn't happen – but for good reason. In the late 1970s, demand for oil dropped slightly due to the emergence of energy-efficient cars and a decline in the use of oil for heating. By the mid-1980s, however, the rapidly swelling world population had picked up the slack once more – and oil production was on the rise yet again.

New predictions

In 2005, a report was produced by the French government that applied Hubbert's analysis to the latest data on the global oil industry. The French team developed a number of models in which the annual increase in demand was varied between zero and three percent, while extra oil provided by new discoveries varied between zero and fifty billion barrels per year.

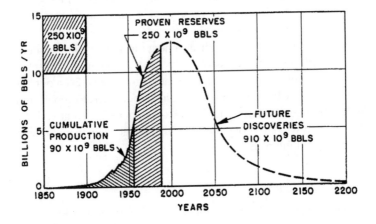

Geophysicist M. King Hubbert's orginal graph, drawn by hand in 1956.

The most optimistic scenario, with the growth in demand at zero and new discoveries at fifty billion barrels, predicted peak oil in 2125. However, this choice of parameter was highly unrealistic. Using the more plausible figures of three percent annual increase in demand and ten billion barrels a year in new finds led to the alarming forecast that oil production would reach its peak in 2013.

The 2007 world financial crisis damped down oil demand once more. But even taking this into account, the worst-case-scenario geologists still believe we could reach peak oil by 2015, with production most likely reaching a maximum of 95 million barrels per day. By 2010, it had already passed 87 million barrels per day, so if they're correct, then we are not far off.

This prompted businesses to begin lobbying world governments. Companies including the Virgin Group, Foster and Partners architects as well as banks and travel firms launched campaigns to raise awareness of the looming "oil crunch", and urged authorities to take action. And with good reason too. Oil is the lynchpin of the economy. Take it away and, with no replacement, cars, buses and trains all grind to a halt. With so many people commuting to work from suburban homes, day-to-day business as we know it would cease. Foreign travel would also become a thing of the past. But it gets much worse than that. All the trappings of the modern world require energy to produce. The electricity to heat and light our homes must be generated. Food must be transported. Offices and factories all require power in order to function.

Most concerning of all, with no energy to power our technology we will be sitting ducks when it comes to defending ourselves against the multitude of other threats facing the planet. Even our battered climate, which you might imagine would start to repair itself in the absence of oil burning, is unlikely to benefit – so great is the damage that we have done that averting climate change will require technological interventions.

Rising fuel bills

Merely waiting until the oil runs out is clearly the stupidest thing to do. It would be far better if we could invest the time and money now to come up with a replacement energy source – or, more likely,

Five oil alternatives

When oil reserves finally dry up, humanity could find itself in a tight spot if it hasn't invested in alternative energy sources. Here are some possibilities:

Thermal depolymerization

Making oil usually means subjecting organic material to terrific temperatures and pressures for millions of years. But what if you could compress the procedure into a few hours? The process called "thermal depolymerization" has the capability to turn organic waste material from the food industry (for example, turkey offal) into oil at the rate of over two barrels per ton.

Nuclear electricity

Nuclear power has controversial, and sometimes catastrophic, safety history. New reactor designs theoretically promise a much more reliable future for this industry – using alternatives to water as a coolant, for example, which cannot turn into high-pressure steam and explode. New solutions are also being investigated to the nuclear waste problem, such as cooking the waste in secondary reactors which turn it into harmless, non-radioactive chemicals.

The hydrogen economy

How do you run a car on nuclear power? The answer is to use electric cars, powered by nuclear-generated electricity. But charging ordinary batteries takes hours. The alternative is to store electricity using hydrogen. Electricity is used to extract hydrogen from water. The hydrogen can be used to fill up your car in a matter of seconds, and a fuel cell in the car then gradually converts it back into electricity as needed. The only waste product: water.

Biofuel crops

What if petroleum grew on trees? Various schemes exist to extract viable fuel from plant matter – such as biodiesel, made from rapeseed, and bioethanol, made by fermenting plant sugars. There are legitimate concerns, however, that growing enough of these crops to meet demand is already taking up too much of the planet's surface, posing a threat to the environment and taking away land that could be feeding the world's poor.

Deep hot biosphere

If the late British physicist Thomas Gold is correct, then all the hysteria over peak oil may be misplaced. He believed that oil deposits are created not by dead prehistoric organisms but by living ones, thriving deep underground. As these subterranean bugs digest natural methane deposits they secrete oil. It's a radical theory but if this continually replenishing source actually exists, then oil reserves may never dry up.

The Savannah River Site (SRS) is a nuclear power station in South Carolina. There, the first mixed oxide fuel (MOX) plant is being constructed. MOX fuel allows weapons-grade plutonium to be converted into fuel suitable for commercial power reactors. One attraction of MOX is that it's an alternative to storing surplus plutonium – it cuts down on the security risk of theft for use in nuclear weapons. MOX is just one of several new technologies that are making nuclear power more feasible as a large-scale fossil-fuel alternative.

a portfolio of different energy sources running in tandem – which could then be phased in gradually as natural oil ran out. Experts say such replacement technologies should be implemented between ten and twenty years ahead of the peak. Still, better late than never.

In an ideal world, replacement power would come from renewable energy sources – such as solar panels, wind power and tidal energy systems. These are sources that do not pollute or otherwise compromise the environment. The ability of renewables to meet world energy demand was – and still often is – regarded with scorn from many quarters. However, a report published in May 2011 by the Intergovernmental Panel on Climate Change (IPCC) suggested that within forty years renewable sources could be providing up to eighty percent of the world's energy needs – if governments act now. We now have the technological capabilities to transport power across vast distances: the idea of renewables providing an entire country's power becomes a lot more feasible when you can use, say, solar energy from a vast desert region in a different continent to power cities hundreds of miles away.

The annual investment required would amount to around one percent of global GDP – or around $600bn. Other short-to-long-term options are to push ahead with existing alternatives such as nuclear power and biofuel, both of which come with a cost to the environment. One way or another, surviving peak oil is going to cost us dearly. So let's not waste time quibbling. This is simply the price we must pay if we want to keep the lights on.

How to mend monoculture
agriculture as it should be

Monoculture is the name given to agricultural land on which a single plant or animal species is being cultivated. The more monoculture we have on the planet, the worse it is for the environment. That's because monoculture eats away at biodiversity – the range and richness of biological species found in any particular ecological niche. High biodiversity in an environment is rather like having a rich gene pool in a population – it makes the environment healthier and better able to cope with the knocks that are inevitably thrown at it from

The Algaeus Sapphire Prius is one of a new breed of cars that is happy to run on green phytoplankton-derived fuel cultivated in algae farms.

time to time by natural phenomena.

The trouble is that human activity is leading to more and more of the planet's natural habitat being converted to monoculture and this, the ecologists warn – could push our already strained environment to the point of collapse.

A lonely number

It's a simple mathematical equation – as the Earth's population increases, so we need to devote more of the planet's surface to growing food. Nourishing the seven billion people on Earth today already requires a vast amount of space: the amount of land us humans live on is tiny when compared to the amount committed to agriculture.

This land use is not geared solely towards food production. Biofuels, which their advocates claim are one of the potential solutions to climate change, are fuels based on fresh plant matter (as opposed to fossil fuels, based on mineral oils pumped up from underground). Examples of biofuels might include biodiesel, the vegetable-oil-based fuel that could fill your car's tank, and ethanol, which is a kind of flammable alcohol made by fermenting plant sugars.

Trying to replace harmful fossil fuels is laudable, but biofuels are controversial, as the space required for their cultivation may wreak counter-productive environmental damage. The most land-efficient kind of biofuel is produced from algae grown in large tanks, which can produce an annual yield of fifteen thousand gallons of fuel per hectare of land. However, the US Department of Energy has estimated that to replace all the petroleum fuel used in the US with algae-derived biofuel would require a land area of nearly forty thousand square kilometres (fifteen thousand sqaure miles) – about the size of Switzerland. And as the increasing population requires an increasing amount of fuel to sustain it, so that already-huge space will grow even bigger.

Why do we need biodiversity?

According to experts, there could be as many as one hundred million species living in the world today. And each and every one of these is important. It's the interactions between species that are

Bruce Dern starred in the 1972 movie *Silent Running*, playing a deep-space gardener. After all plant life on Earth becomes extinct, a few specimens are preserved in enormous, greenhouse-like geodesic domes, just outside the orbit of Saturn.

responsible for maintaining a balance in the chemistry and biology of the natural world. This balance has arisen over the course of many millions of years of natural evolution. And now human activity threatens to disrupt it over a timescale that is just the blink of an eye by comparison.

A high level of biodiversity means that if a particular species goes extinct, then it is more likely that another similar species might evolve into the ecological niche left behind – which will then perform all the services to the environment that the old species carried out. Biodiversity tends to make the environment more stable and more resilient to the effects of climate change, which we know are already beginning to make their presence felt.

Forests and jungles are the parts of the Earth's surface that boast the greatest biodiversity. Worryingly, these are the terrain types most at risk of being cleared to make new agricultural land. The Amazon rainforest, for example, is being cleared at a rate of hundreds of square kilometres every month.

There's an economic dimension to all this as well. Certain plants, for instance, have a financial – and, of course, social – value as medicines. If an ecosystem collapses through lack of biodiversity then we risk losing these treatments. An EU-funded study in 2008 estimated that the annual cash value of the damage that human beings cause to the world's biodiversity totals almost £40bn. Some of the poorest people on the planet – those who depend directly on natural resources for their livelihoods – stand to be the hardest hit.

An unlikely solution?

According to Professor Dickson Despommier, an ecologist at Columbia University, New York, the monoculture problem could be solved at a stroke – all we have to do is build more skyscrapers. He thinks the future of food production lies in land-efficient high-rise greenhouses, powered by solar energy and urban sewage. These vertical farms, or farmscrapers, are a way to meet the increasing demand for farmland without threatening biodiversity.

Despommier's calculations suggest that a thirty-storey building, one New York City block in size, could feed fifty thousand people – providing fruit, vegetables, meat, fish, poultry and fresh water to drink. Each offers a sealed, controlled environment eliminating the possibility of disease or insect attack – thus removing the need for many harmful pesticides. Specially engineered lighting mimics the properties of sunlight so plants can continue to photosynthesize and grow at night. Crops can then be cultivated 365 days a year, oblivious to outside weather conditions. This continuous production means that every acre farmed indoors is equivalent to between four and six acres of traditional outdoor farmland.

Flower power

Electricity for light and heat in a farmscraper would be generated by renewable means, such as solar panels and wind turbines – and by burning waste stalks and roots from the farm in high-temperature incinerators. Crops would be grown hydroponically – in nutrient-rich water rather than soil. Building vertical farms in, or close to,

A prototype of a vertical farm, designed by the company Pantagon; one of these giant greenhouses is currently being built in the city of Linköping, Sweden.

cities means that urban "grey water" – treated liquid waste – can be used for irrigation. A typical city produces billions of gallons of grey water every day. What's more, plants act as natural filters, giving off pure water vapour from their leaves, which can be captured and condensed. So the vertical farms double as massive water purification facilities.

Virtually all crop types can be grown indoors – from basic vegetables and grains to fruits such as avocados and date palms. Even biofuel crops, such as rapeseed, can be grown successfully under glass. Livestock, meanwhile, would be housed in the lower floors, with tanks for farming fish, and open areas for rearing chickens – both for eggs and poultry – and red meat species, such as sheep.

With eighty percent of Earth's population set to live in cities by 2050, city-based farmscrapers could drastically reduce food miles. And there's no reason why these novel buildings should be used exclusively for creating new agricultural land. Once enough of them are built, existing natural farmland can be returned to nature – restoring biodiversity to formerly monocultured areas. In this way, farmscrapers could enable us to repair at least some of the damage we've wrought upon our weary planet.

Fighting the bad fight
why can't we all just get along?

The Industrial Revolution changed the way we work, the food we ate and the buildings we lived in. It also radically altered the way we fought each other. New communications technology enabled arguments in real-time to take place between governments on opposite sides of the world. Transportation capabilities advanced too: the early nineteenth century saw the development of the first steam ships that could cross the Atlantic Ocean in a matter of days. And this allowed us to take our troops and weaponry across the world – not just our belligerent words. It's worth reminding ourselves just how global the reach of our weaponry has become; how scarily easy it would be for a nation to bring about a world armageddon.

The war to end all wars?

The expansion of our sphere of conflict came to a head in 1914, with the eruption of World War I – which involved virtually all of the world's major powers. The human cost was colossal, with a total of 10 million dead, and each side losing over a half of its military personnel as either killed, wounded or missing. At the time, some regarded World War I as the final war, the scale of which could never again be matched – let alone exceeded. However, David Lloyd George, who was Britain's prime minister through much of it, knew differently, stating: "This war, like the next war, is a war to end war."

And how right he was. Lloyd George lived to see most of World War II, an even more devastating world conflict in which over seventy million perished. Many of these were civilians, as the rise of strategic bombing as a military tactic brought the destruction wrought by warfare to the world's cities. London, Hamburg and Tokyo have since become famed for the punishment they sustained. Though the worst was yet to come. The atomic bombings of Hiroshima and Nagasaki between them killed almost a quarter of a million. Suddenly, it became terrifyingly clear that warfare – aided by technology – could wipe out vast numbers of civilian lives in an instant. With weapons of mass destruction becoming ever more powerful, how soon would it be before war threatened the future of humanity itself? It wasn't long before world events provided the answer to that question.

An uneasy détente

After World War II, a period of intense rivalry followed between the Communist nations, led by the Soviet Union, and the free western world, led by the United States – the Cold War. There was no direct military action between the US and Russia, just a frosty exchange of threats, posturing and espionage. And probably just as well. With the further development of nuclear weapons and the rapid accumulation of massive nuclear arsenals by both sides, the potential now existed for a war that could destroy the world.

The fierce rivalry and political tension came to a head during the Cuban missile crisis of 1962. In response to the US stationing of medium-range nuclear missiles in the UK, Italy and Turkey, the Soviet Union established missile bases on the Communist island state of Cuba – from where they could strike the continental United States within minutes. The US was not pleased, to say the least, and put a blockade around Cuba, turning back a number of ships suspected to be carrying weapons. Soviet leader Nikita Khrushchev warned President Kennedy that his actions were liable to lead to nuclear war between the two nations.

Khrushchev and Kennedy were ultimately able to strike a deal whereby the Soviet Union would vacate its position on Cuba if the US removed its missiles from Europe. Both sides upheld their ends of the bargain, and the world breathed a deep sigh of relief. It was the closest human civilization had come to an all-out nuclear exchange – and remains the closest we've ever been since.

The Cold War raged on until the early 1990s. Today, both the Russian Federation (the former Soviet Union) and the US have dismantled much their nuclear stockpiles, although both still operate stripped-down arsenals. Other nations now possess nuclear weapons: the UK, France, China, Israel, India, Pakistan and North Korea.

Nuclear winter

The smoke and soot generated by the fires ignited in a major nuclear exchange could well plunge the Earth into an artificial winter. Fears over the nuclear winter scenario first arose in 1973, during the height of the Cold War. Nuclear stockpiles then were massive. Yet a study published in 2007, in the *Journal of Geophysical Research*, found that – even with today's reduced global nuclear arsenal being about a third of the size it was during the Cold War – a full-scale nuclear war would still cause global cooling of up to 8°C.

Just to add cheer to an already bleak scenario, some have even suggested that a nuclear winter could be followed by a nuclear summer. Several years after the nuclear exchange, when the particulate pollutants blocking the sun have cleared, the atmosphere will still be choked with carbon dioxide from all the fires. This is a potent greenhouse gas. Global cooling could therefore suddenly switch to fierce global warming – and our frozen planet would be rapidly thawed and then roasted.

As if that wasn't bad enough, the nuclear detonations may also have stripped away much of the ozone layer, which shields us from the sun's harmful ultraviolet rays. Anyone tough enough to have survived a nuclear holocaust, followed by the mother of all winters and then the summer from hell, would next have to brave a great outdoors that carried a massive risk of skin cancer.

Most of these operate their nuclear capability under the guidance of the Nuclear Non-Proliferation Treaty (NPT), instigated in 1970 to limit the spread of nuclear arms. The exceptions however, are India, Pakistan and North Korea. Most worrying of these is North Korea – a nation ruled by a brutal regime, known for its human rights abuses, secrecy and unwillingness to participate in the international community.

The war on terror

One legacy of the Cold War lives on. Both the US and Russia are suspected to have developed "suitcase bombs": nuclear weapons small enough to fit inside a suitcase that could be carried onto enemy soil by an agent and then detonated. By today's standards, the explosive yield of these nuclear weapons was small, equivalent to around six kilotons of TNT (the blast at Hiroshima was thirteen)

– but that's nevertheless enough to cause a huge loss of life within an urban centre.

In 1997, a former Russian security official went on the record admitting that the Soviet Union produced some 250 suitcase bombs, and that the whereabouts of around a hundred of these devices was now unknown. This raised concerns that some may have fallen into the hands of terrorists.

In much the same way that the first computers were operated solely by government institutions yet now every household has one, so weapons technology has gradually become more obtainable. In recent decades we've seen terrorists carrying out attacks using both chemical weapons (the Tokyo subway nerve gas attack of 1995) and biological agents (the US anthrax attacks of 2001). The fear is that terrorists – or other independent organizations, not bound or monitored by international treaties – could conduct further attacks with weapons of mass destruction, including nuclear devices.

When the only nuclear threat came from other sovereign states, the best deterrent was to have nuclear weapons of your own. But when dealing with terrorists this deterrent evaporates. And so the value of intelligence gathering and espionage has gradually taken precedence over sheer military muscle.

Even so, the spectre of all-out world war may yet return to haunt us. As climate change starts to place the world's landmasses beneath the waves so – as some security experts have pointed out – the lack of land could well drive desperate nations to war over food, living space and resources. And that may well be the beginning of the war to end all others.

The shape of WMDs to come
the ever-nastier ways we find to kill each other

Despite arms-limitation treaties and the best efforts to prevent the unruly nations of the world from acquiring them, weapons of mass destruction, or WMDs, may yet be humanity's undoing. The term is first thought to have been used in 1937 by Cosmo Gordon Lang, the archbishop of Canterbury (head of the Church of England), in a comment deploring the heavy bombardment of the town of Guernica during the Spanish Civil War. Although only conventional weapons had been used, the Archbishop speculated how such atrocities could only worsen as the destructive power of weaponry increased.

WMDs today break down into three principal categories: nuclear, chemical and biological. Chemical and biological weapons have been with us a long time. As far back as 10,000 BC, warriors would use poison-tipped arrows to vanquish their foes. However, the mass application of chemical weapons didn't come until World War I, when poisonous agents – such as mustard gas, chlorine and other toxic chemicals – were employed by all sides. Around four percent of combat casualties during the war were due to gas.

In the 1930s, however, deadly nerve gas agents were developed. These cause loss of life by disrupting the chemical pathways between the brain and the body's internal organs. The first class of nerve agents, the G-Series, was accidentally discovered in Germany by a researcher neamed Dr. Gerhard Schrader, working to discover new types of insecticides: the Nazis realized the agents could be used as deadly weapons on humans.

Herbicides or plant pathogens deployed over agricultural land can rob a nation of valuable food crops – as proven by US forces in Vietnam by the use of the notorious defoliant Agent Orange. This herbicide gained its name from the orange-striped vats it was shipped in. Sprayed in vast quantities in the jungles of Vietnam, its purpose was to erase the ground cover of Vietnamese guerrillas, and to drive rural rebels towards the US-controlled cities. Vietnam estimates 400,000 people to have been killed or maimed, and 500,000 children born with birth defects, due to exposure to a toxic chemical compound that Agent Orange was contaminated with.Biological weapons, on the other hand, involve the use of dangerous microorganisms to cause harm to enemy personnel or property. Anthrax bacteria or Ebola virus particles, sprayed over an advancing column of troops, lead to considerable loss of life and incapacitation.

Again, biological (or germ warfare, as it's also known) is not a brand new invention. There is evidence that, during medieval sieges, catapults were sometimes used to launch plague-bearing corpses over the battlements of a beseiged castle in the hope of triggering an epidemic in the opposing army.

What Einstein would have done: world government

When asked for his predictions about the future of warfare, Albert Einstein famously replied: "I know not with what weapons World War III will be fought, but World War IV will be fought with sticks and stones."

The great physicist was a committed pacifist until the rise of Adolf Hitler. He felt partially responsible for the invention of nuclear weapons – his theory of relativity had provided scientists with the crucial relationship between mass and energy (the equation $E=mc^2$) that underpins how these weapons work. A letter from Einstein to President Roosevelt, alerting him to the military applications of nuclear physics, and stressing that Germany might well be close to making an atomic bomb, eventually led to the Manhattan Project – the US effort to build a working nuclear weapon. After the atomic bombings of Japan at the end of World War II, Einstein dedicated much of his remaining life to campaigning for peace and trying to limit the spread of nuclear arms. "I have always condemned the use of the atomic bomb against Japan," he once wrote. Shortly before he died, he confessed: "I made one great mistake in my life ... when I signed the letter to President Roosevelt recommending that atom bombs be made."

Einstein came to the conclusion that the only sure path to avoiding future world wars was to abolish national barriers and unify all the nations on Earth under one banner – through the establishment of a single world government. He wasn't an idealist though. He realized that world government wasn't going to happen overnight, and so for the interim recommended the establishment of what he called a "supranational organization" – essentially a world police force. It would have its own independent military and the authority to intervene and break up scuffles between nations before they erupted into full-scale conflict.

Einstein's suggestion came just a few years before the establishment of the United Nations. However, he would later remark that the UN did not possess sufficient power over nation states, nor the ability to act independently, for the organization to be fully effective.

The nuclear genie

The weapon of mass destruction that strikes fear into the heart like no other is the nuclear bomb. Since the bombings of Hiroshima and Nagasaki, nuclear weapons have become drastically more powerful. The bomb dropped on the Japanese city of Hiroshima exploded with a thirteen-kiloton blast (the force equivalent to detonating thirteen

Smoke billowed 20,000 feet above Hiroshima after the US Air Force dropped "Little Boy", an atomic bomb, on the city on 6 August 1945.

thousand tons of TNT). Nine years later, the US detonated its Castle Bravo dry fuel thermonuclear hydrogen bomb. Its blast was the equivalent of fifteen million tons of TNT, or fifteen megatons – over one thousand times the strength of Hiroshima.

Today, most of the world's developed nations have seen the error of their ways and treaties are in place to limit the number and the type of nuclear weapons in use. Accordingly, nuclear stockpiles are now just a fraction of what they were during the uncertainty and paranoia of the Cold War. And emphasis has shifted away from city-busting multi-megaton devices to smaller weapons designed to crack open especially tough military targets – such as underground bunkers (see p.15).

The primary concern now is that, as the relative degree of technological expertise required to build nuclear devices becomes smaller, it is becoming ever easier for rogue states and even independent terrorist organizations to construct them. The good news is that, while even a localized nuclear blast will cause loss of life, it's unlikely the global threat posed by these renegade nuclear factors could ever equal that of a global-scale nuclear exchange.

The bad news, however, is that just as the nuclear genie has been stuffed back into the bottle, so science is now uncovering the potential for new and even more devastating weapons of mass destruction.

Anti-weapons

One of these is antimatter. This was discovered when physicists applied Albert Einstein's theory of relativity to quantum mechanics – the physics of tiny subatomic particles. The resulting mathematics revealed that every particle of matter has an opposite number with key properties – such as electric charge – reversed. Moreover, if a particle of matter ever comes together with its antiparticle, the result is the complete conversion of the particle masses into energy.

It's an often-quoted statistic that the Nagasaki A-bomb was powered by a lump of plutonium about the size of an orange. But if the bomb's designers had chosen to use antimatter instead, they could have gotten the same oomph from just half a gram of the stuff.

Of course, it's not quite that simple. Antimatter is costly and time-consuming to produce: using current technology, the making of a gram would take a hundred million years and cost $60tr.

But there is another source of antimatter to hand. If you can get a flight to Jupiter, that is. Tons of antimatter are believed to drift into the solar system every year and become trapped in orbit around Jupiter, caught by the planet's sizeable magnetic field. A suitably equipped space mining mission could be sent to retrieve a tank-load of this super-explosive which could, in the future, lead to weapons with the potency of an atom bomb, yet no bigger in size than a hand grenade.

God-rods, nano-bombs and synthetic viruses

One territory which could become more and more of a battleground is space. In 2007–08 both the US and China demonstrated the capability to shoot down Earth-orbiting satellites using surface-launched missiles. Space-based observation systems have already played a key role in intelligence-gathering during warfare; in the future, they could take a worryingly active role.

Weapons deployed from space to the ground look set to be incredibly destructive. One species of space-based ordnance is known by the cheerful moniker of "rods from god". A solid metal pole dropped from Earth orbit would hit the ground at hypersonic speed, exploding with the equivalent yield of a small nuclear weapon. The idea has been considered by the US military since the 1950s. Each rod would be made of tungsten (due to its high melting point), measure around thirty centimetres in diameter and be up to nine metres in length – about the size of a telegraph pole.

There's good reason to believe that other cutting-edge scientific developments, such as nanotechnology – engineering on scales of nanometres (billionths of a metre) – might bring about terrifying new forms of weaponry too. Many commentators have mused over the "grey goo" scenario – in which self-replicating nanoscale robots might devour the world (see p.156). Could we also one day see nano-devices that are engineered to interact with and disrupt the biochemical processes needed for life? Perhaps they would inject hostile genetic material into the victim's cells. Or simply tear their molecules apart atom by atom. Synthetic biology (p.151) is yet another new area that offers the terrifying potential to interfere with life's essential processes using microscopic agents, all purposefully designed from the ground up in a laboratory.

As history has taught us, new technologies often come with a considerable burden of responsibility – lest we use them to wipe ourselves out. But unless we call a halt to all avenues of scientific research, discoveries are always going to be made that place ourselves and our civilization in potential jeopardy. Ultimately, perhaps we should stop worrying about what we know and concentrate instead on endowing our civilisation and society with the maturity to apply powerful new knowledge with the sense and responsibility that it deserves.

Rage of the machines

4

Human beings are unique in their ability to understand the world in which they live, by gathering knowledge through science, and then applying that knowledge creatively – the pursuit that we call technology. While most technology is undoubtedly beneficial, now and again we become victims of our own success as a new device or breakthrough backfires in our faces spectacularly. Could the occasional tendency of science and technology to turn round and bite us ever pose a threat on a global scale? Could a scientific or technological advance ever prove to be the Pandora's box that we wish we'd never opened – spelling disaster for our species and our planet?

Some might say we have already sown the seeds of our species' destruction, citing the spectre of nuclear weapons that has hung over world affairs ever since 1945. Perhaps even more of a threatening situation is that of global warming: human consumption of fossil fuels is almost certainly behind the worrying trend that now threatens the stability of the Earth's long-term climate. In this section, we'll take a closer look at the potential blowback of other fields of science and technology which are either just reaching maturity or which look set to do so over the course of decades to come.

Problems with particle accelerators

could they eat the Earth?

When told that scientists are about to switch on a giant machine 8.5km wide that will accelerate subatomic particles to within 3m per second of light speed – so fast that as little as a billionth of a gram of matter would pack as much punch as detonating 170kg of TNT – most people would probably want to know what happens if the thing goes wrong. It's a reasonable question.

And so it was hardly surprising that, in 2008, as physicists at the CERN particle physics laboratory on the Swiss-French border prepared to activate their Large Hadron Collider (LHC) accelerator machine, they were greeted by a chorus of concerned voices from around the world. And not just members of the public – even some scientists came forward too, brandishing calculations which they cited as proof that the LHC is a doomsday scenario waiting to happen.

The super collider

The Large Hadron Collider is the world's largest and most powerful particle accelerator. It occupies a circular tunnel 175m beneath the CERN complex that measures a huge 27km in circumference. Dotted around the tunnel are over 1500 powerful electromagnets which accelerate electrically charged subatomic particles – such as protons and atomic nuclei – and then curve their path so that they travel around the loop continuously, gathering speed on each circuit. At full power, the particles circle the LHC ring eleven thousand times every second. Running the LHC's electromagnets requires 96 tonnes of liquid helium coolant and an awful lot of electricity – so much that the facility is switched off over the winter period, when fuel prices are deemed too high.

The LHC was built to carry out experiments that will further our scientific knowledge of the subatomic particle world. It does this by crashing the high-speed particles together, re-creating the conditions that existed just a billionth of a second after the Big Bang in which the universe was born. This produces a shower of

The law of unintended consequences

"The best laid schemes of mice and men, go oft awry." So said Robert Burns, in his poem "To a Mouse". It's not just in science where, no matter how well you plan for the future, happenstance can often wrong-foot you. And this fact has become known as the law of unintended consequences. It can be thought of as a sort of cross between Murphy's law (what can go wrong, will go wrong) and the butterfly effect (the way small changes can lead to momentous consequences).

Over the years there have been some dramatic demonstrations of the law at work. For example, when Australian sugar cane crops became blighted with cane beetle, the government thought it might be a good idea to introduce the predatory cane toad to the country. Previous introductions of the creature to control crop pests in New Guinea and the Caribbean had proven highly successful.

But in Australia it turned out to be a catastrophe. The toads had little or no interest in the beetles, but instead decided to tuck into the food chain that was supporting Australia's native population of reptiles – snakes, lizards and crocodiles – with a massive negative impact on the country's biodiversity. The cane toad is now itself a major pest in Australia and anyone finding one on their land is encouraged to kill it – the recommended humane method being freezing.

Nowadays, policymakers try to mitigate unintended consequences by adopting the precautionary principle. This says that when deciding whether or not to adopt some new untested measure about which there is no consensus view regarding the consequences, then the onus lies with the parties proposing the action to prove that it is safe. It is a principle that has now been incorporated into the law of the European Union. We can only hope that those making the big decisions in science – the ones that could quite literally cost the Earth – exercise the same caution.

debris fragments which scientists can then study to figure out how exactly subatomic particles work.

Black heart

The LHC's very purpose, therefore, is to kick-start processes in physics about which we know very little. And that's the root of the concern. One worry is that the high density of matter generated in some particle collisions could trigger the formation of microscopic

The Large Hadron Collider: highly unlikely to be generating a plethora of microscopic black holes in the near future.

black holes. A black hole is an object so dense that not even light can escape from its intense gravitational field. The fear is that these tiny black holes would then grow by pulling in the matter around them until they eventually devoured the entire planet.

According to the standard model of particle physics the LHC will not crank out enough energy to produce black holes – even at full power. But there are speculative theories that extend the standard model – by supposing that space could have more than the three dimensions of our everyday experience. In these theories, the extra dimensions are tightly rolled up, as it were, and are impossible to see. They are like the surface of a hose pipe in this regard, which looks one-dimensional from a distance even though it is in fact two-dimensional. The LHC could be quite capable of making black holes in these models.

Scientists at CERN insist that even if black holes are cooked up in collisions in the LHC, they pose no danger to the Earth. In the early 1970s, the physicist Stephen Hawking, then a professor at Cambridge University, used quantum theory (the branch of physics that governs the subatomic world) to show that black holes aren't one-way funnels that simply devour matter. They actually give off a steady stream of particles and radiation too. More importantly, the rate of this outflux increases as the black hole gets smaller – so that any microscopic black holes appearing in the LHC should evaporate away to nothing almost as soon as they form.

Indeed, this view seems to be the consensus of most particle physicists. Meanwhile, initial experiments in the LHC have failed to produce any evidence for extra dimensions. So it seems, for now at least, that the Earth is safe from this particular doomsday scenario.

Strange brew

That hasn't silenced the scaremongers though. Another way the LHC might do for us, they warn, is by creating so-called "killer strangelets". These are clumps of quarks (the tiny building-block particles from which larger, more familiar particles such as protons and neutrons are made). Quarks come in three principal types: "up", "down" and "strange". Protons and neutrons contain just up and down quarks but, as the name suggests, strangelets have strange quarks mixed in too.

Where does the doomsday scenario come in? Well, some physicists have made calculations that suggest that if a stable, negatively charged strangelet ever comes into contact with ordinary matter it will convert the ordinary matter into more strangelets. And so any strangelets churned out by the LHC could potentially assimilate the whole Earth into strange matter – with disastrous consequences for all concerned.

It's not the first time we've heard this song. Similar charges (no pun intended) were levelled at the Relativistic Heavy Ion Collider (RHIC), a particle accelerator at Brookhaven National Laboratory, in New York State, before the device was switched on in 2000. The RHIC operates with just one twenty-eighth of the energy of the LHC at full power, but – perhaps counter-intuitively – the chance of strangelets forming diminishes as the energy increases. And so the fact that the RHIC has now been operating safely for more than ten years makes it very unlikely that killer strangelets are a danger worth worrying about at CERN.

Worse things happen in space

If that doesn't convince you, another argument for the safety of the LHC, and all particle accelerators to be constructed in the foreseeable future, is that far more violent and energetic particle collisions take place regularly in outer space.

For example, ultra-high-energy cosmic rays from space routinely smash into particles in the Earth's upper atmosphere in collisions packing hundreds of millions of times the energy mustered by the LHC's particle beams. And yet we don't suffer any ill effects.

Quantum leaps: how clever physics could save the day

The scientific knowledge that will be gathered in the course of research at the Large Hadron Collider (LHC), and other particle accelerators like it, is a million times more likely to help us avert future disasters than be the cause of them. Blue-sky fundamental physics research has played its part in improving scientific understanding to benefit human life. For example, next time your sat nav gets you safely from A to B (without any irritating excursions via X, Y and Z) say thank you to Albert Einstein. His general theory of relativity is used inside sat nav units to correct time signals from the satellites high above for distortions introduced by the Earth's gravitational field. Without general relativity – perhaps one of the more esoteric theories in science – satellite navigation would be impossible.

Even in quantum physics, the area where the LHC's research is most relevant, developments made during the early twentieth century have led to modern technologies such as computers and the lasers upon which Blu-ray players and high-speed fibre optic communications links rely. Averting disaster, in whatever form it might take, will almost certainly involve some of these technologies. And of course, quantum theory and relativity ($E=mc^2$) gave us nuclear power, which may turn out to be the only non-fossil-fuel energy economically viable enough to take us forward into the twenty-second century. The LHC will probe particle physics at unprecedented scales. It may well reveal new sources of energy that could underpin the spacecraft propulsion systems of the future – upon which we may rely should our planet ever become uninhabitable. And it's hoped it will provide insights into how gravity meshes with the other forces of nature – an area of research that could prove invaluable in defending our world against gravitational hazards, such as comet and asteroid impacts.

When it comes to guarding the Earth against threats to its very existence, knowledge will be our most powerful weapon. And scientific research in obscure areas can often lead to the most profound breakthroughs.

Meanwhile, in exotic cosmic objects such as neutron stars and white dwarfs (the super-dense remnants left behind after the deaths of some stars) the effects of cosmic ray collisions are thought to be even more extreme. And yet these objects are observed by astronomers night after night and are never seen mysteriously winking out of existence.

In the light of this evidence, the idea of the LHC destroying the Earth seems fanciful to say the least. And those who continue to believe such notions – when the LHC has been safely operating since 2009 – are sadly misguided. As CERN physicist and science popularizer Professor Brian Cox bluntly put it in *The Daily Telegraph* newspaper: "Anyone who thinks the LHC will destroy the world is a twat." There are many things that threaten the future of civilization on Earth. But renegade particle accelerators are not one of them.

Synthetic life
real-world Frankensteins

In May 2010, scientists at the J. Craig Venter Institute in the United States announced that they had created life from scratch. They had painstakingly designed the DNA molecule for a new species of bacteria, and then manufactured it from basic chemicals in their laboratory. When they implanted the new DNA into the heart of an existing bacterial cell, subsequent divisions of the cell produced copies of their new custom-built bacterium. The Venter team had manufactured the world's first ever synthetic life form.

What was their motivation for doing this? What new technologies might the discovery bring? And, moreover, what threats might it unleash to the future of life on Earth?

DNA is a long, chain-like molecule that every living thing has at the heart of each of its cells. It is actually made up of a broad family of molecules, from which the component chemicals – called the bases – can be arranged in different sequences. The precise order of the bases in your DNA is used to store information – such as what colour your eyes are, how big your nose is, your susceptibility to particular illnesses and the consistency of your earwax. This information is known collectively as your genetic code. All life forms – at least, those on Earth – have one.

Gene machines

In the 1970s, biologists realized that tinkering with the genetic code of life forms offers a way to alter their physical traits. They found that they could isolate the stretches of DNA containing the genetic code for certain desirable traits and then cut and paste those into the DNA of other organisms. For example, taking the genes that stop an Antarctic fish from freezing to death in icy water and then splicing them into the DNA of a potato could potentially yield frost-resistant spuds.

This practice became known as genetic engineering. Synthetic life, synthetic biology or synbio, as it's sometimes known, has been described as "genetic engineering on steroids". Because rather than chopping and changing DNA between existing organisms, synthetic biologists aim to create new life from the ground up. In fact, synbio is probably more deserving of the genetic engineering tag than its predecessor field, which might better be described as mere genetic editing.

So why do it? Organisms are effectively biological machines, meaning that a synthetic biologist is an engineer building devices to serve useful purposes – not from plastic and metal, but from biological cells. Indeed, many researchers working in this field are from backgrounds in engineering and design, who have simply picked up the biological knowledge they need along the way. Craig Venter, leader of the team who created the first synthetic life form, believes a major application of synbio will be in using synthetic bugs to manufacture biofuels – enabling humans to stop burning CO_2-producing fossil fuels, and do so without the deforestation needed to grow biofuel crops conventionally (see p.129). Other research is employing synbio techniques to combat cancer and even to detect hidden landmines.

Dolly the sheep: the first clone to be created via "somatic cell nuclear transfer". She was born to a surrogate mother, via a cell taken from an adult mammal.

DNA pollution

So it seems there are plenty of useful potential applications for synthetic biology. But what about the dreaded law of unintended consequences? Environmental campaign groups are urging scientists to consider the dangers of introducing synthetic DNA into the wild – either deliberately or by accident – lest we suffer potentially disastrous consequences. They could have a point. The planet's delicately balanced ecosystem has evolved gradually, with the genetic make-up of new and emerging species continually held in check by interactions with other species at every stage in their development. The danger is that releasing a synthetic organism which hasn't been tempered by these interactions during the course of its evolution could bring about sudden, drastic changes to the ecosystem. What if, for example, the new organism was to out-compete or prove toxic to other species in the food chain, causing ecological collapse? This is known as genetic pollution; in the worst-case scenario its consequences could be catastrophic to the interconnected biodiversity of our planet, and would most probably be irreversible.

Another danger is long-term toxicity to humans. What if we accidentally engineer a microorganism that causes a terrible disease, but one which only strikes months or perhaps even years after the new organism is released? We could end up becoming the victims of a pandemic, inadvertently unleashed by our own bumbling hands. It wouldn't be the first time life on Earth has suffered in this way. In the 1970s, the synthetic pesticide DDT was banned after evidence revealed its toxicity to wildlife – it had pushed the US bald eagle almost to the brink of extinction.

Of course, not all harmful substances are manufactured by accident. Synbio will almost certainly be sequestered to build biological weapons – either by nation states or, as the technology becomes more accessible, by terrorist organizations. Anyone wanting to do this wouldn't even need to design their own disease – the genetic code of virulent pathogens, such as the 1918 Spanish flu, is easy enough to find all over the Internet. At the present time, turning such a sequence of genetic information into an actual virus is a task beyond most amateurs, requiring PhD-level science knowledge and costly equipment. But that might not be the case forever...

The age of the amateur geneticist

Physicist and futurologist Freeman Dyson, of the Institute for Advanced Study at Princeton, has noticed a parallel between the development of synthetic biology and the electronics industry. Sixty years ago, electronics was in its infancy and the only people carrying out research were in universities and other big-budget research institutes. But slowly the scale and the cost of the equipment needed to build electronic devices came down. Today, anyone with a little know-how, a small amount of money and an electrical store nearby (or an Internet connection to order components online) can be an amateur electronics engineer.

Dyson thinks the same thing is about to happen in synbio. He imagines gardeners being able to buy kits that enable them to create hybrids by far more precise and efficient genetic means than by taking cuttings and cross-pollinating flowers (as they have done for centuries). At the same time, he's suggested that animal breeders will be able to go nuts with DIY genetic modification tools, allowing them to rustle up new breeds of dog, pigeon – and pretty much any other species that takes their fancy.

Crazy as this might sound, it has actually already begun. Genetic components called BioBricks are now freely available for researchers to order online and use in their own genetic creations. The process already smacks of amateur electronics. For instance, connecting up acid-sensitive bacteria with a BioBrick for fluorescent protein gives

Trust me, I'm a bioengineer

The good news is that official synthetic biology research – as carried out in universities and research institutes – is governed by a number of well-established safeguards drawn up more than three decades ago in response to initial breakthroughs in the field of genetic engineering.

These guidelines specify the minimum level of biosafety containment required when dealing with a particular kind of organism, and insist on other precautions, such as requiring researchers to always experiment on neutered animals so that there's no chance of them breeding. These regulations were put together at the 1975 Asilomar scientific conference, held in Pacific Grove, California.

Most experimental life forms used in synbio research are, at present, microbes. They are usually extremely weak, and – so scientists working in the field contend – would be extremely lucky to survive outside the laboratory environment. For example, they have little to no immunity to the diseases that natural organisms are exposed to during the course of their development. Opponents of synthetic biology argue that evolution can rapidly acclimatize an organism to the harshest environment. This is especially true if the creature is a single-celled life form, for whom the time between successive generations is just the timescale of cell division, which can be as little as a few minutes, making the pace of evolution extremely rapid.

In the light of this, some laboratories have gone further, deliberately tweaking the organisms they work with to inhibit them if they ever escaped. One way to achieve this is through the introduction of a "terminator gene" – a section of genetic code that causes cells to self-destruct after a set number of divisions. The good news is that corporations have an additional motivation to invoke this particular safety step – namely, that the terminator gene also serves as patent protection, preventing clients or competitors from growing copies of the synthetic cells. Biosafety guidelines are regularly reviewed and updated, and bioethics has itself now become an active field of research.

you a biological detecting device that glows in the presence of acid. Simple as that. Anyone can order BioBricks. And while the user agreement does contain a clause prohibiting intentionally harmful use of the technology, it's hard to see how that could be enforced. Before it's too late.

Biologists working in an official capacity at universities and research organizations are taking laudable steps to conduct their work ethically and with care. But it seems the real threat from synbio could come from the kitchen tables and garden sheds of the hobbyists and enthusiasts of the decades to come. Perhaps this is an area where governments should legislate now – before we discover that the damage is already done.

Grey goo

A swarm of tiny robots that devours the Earth, leaving behind nothing but a quivering grey mass: that, in essence, is the "grey goo scenario" for the demise of our planet. The concept was put forward by American engineer Eric Drexler, as a possible consequence of the vision of nanotechnology that he had first suggested in his 1986 book *Engines of Creation*. Nanotechnology is engineering on the scale of nanometres (billionths of a metre or, equivalently, millionths of a millimetre). It is quite often also known as "molecular engineering" because it involves manipulating and fixing together pieces of material so small that they consist of individual molecules. Indeed, some proposed nanomachines are only slightly bigger than the largest chemical molecules, and many are much smaller than biological cells.

Why would anyone want to build such things? The simple answer is that tiny machines are able to do things that large-scale machines cannot. In fact, the traditional view of machines doesn't always apply to these entities: they are able to move molecules around and manipulate matter at the cellular level – processes that are more akin to the action of drugs and chemicals than normal engineering. So nanomachines can in some regards be thought of as programmable chemicals.

The nano revolution

Nanotechnology is still in its infancy but it has many proposed applications. For example, Robert Freitas, of California's Institute of Molecular Manufacturing, has put forward a nanotech design for an artificial red blood cell called a respirocyte, which can carry hundreds of times more oxygen than its biological counterpart. Other researchers have suggested that we might not be too far away from realizing such science-fictionesque inventions as healing robots that swim through your bloodstream, repairing cell damage and alerting you (and your doctor) if they detect the onset of any serious illness.

The engineer Dr J. Storrs Hall, of the Foresight Nanotech Institute, in Palo Alto, California, has drawn up futuristic plans for a "utility fog": a cloud of tiny nanorobots (which he dubs "foglets") that could replace seatbelts in cars and perform a range of other life-saving roles. In normal use, the cloud surrounds the user invisibly – allowing them total freedom of movement. But in the event of a collision,

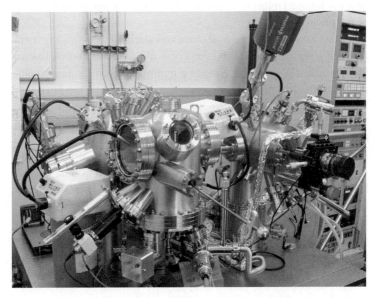

A Scanning Tunnelling Microscope: nanotechnology's equivalent of the surgeon's scalpel, it is capable of imaging and manipulating surfaces at the atomic level.

arms extending from each tiny robot would allow them all to lock together, forming a mesh that holds the user in their seat while spreading the force of the impact evenly across the body.

This might sound fanciful today, but manipulation of matter on the tiniest scales promises the development of engineering materials with truly astonishing electrical, thermal and mechanical properties. There can be no doubt that nanotechnology is already beginning to offer many benefits. But what are the drawbacks?

Fade to grey

The problems kick in when scientists start talking about nanobots that can self-replicate. These bots function autonomously – following a preset internal program, with no external control – and can build copies of themselves using the materials they find in their immediate locale. The grey goo scenario is one particular vision of what might happen if these self-replicating nanomachines ever got out of control and converted the Earth's entire biomass into nanomass – a process Robert Freitas has named "ecophagy", a literal eating-away of the environment.

Ecophagy would happen at an exponentially accelerating rate, and might be over before we even know it's started. It's rather like an old Chinese allegory: if you place a grain of rice on the first square of a chessboard, then two grains on the next, four on the next, and keep doubling every time, by the final square you have over one hundred thousand billion tons of rice. Imagine that it takes a nanobot an hour to make a copy of itself. After one hour you have two nanobots. In the next hour, these both make copies of themselves, so you have four, then eight, sixteen and so on. In around seventy hours there would be more nanobots on Earth than there are grains of sand (about ten to the power twenty, multiplied by seven; or seven followed by twenty zeroes).

Goo fighters

If this is a possibility, why would anyone want to build self-replicating nanobots? As Drexler himself has pointed out, it would be far safer to run them off in a conventional, stationary and nonautonomous factory. However, he points out two contexts in which we might make exceptions.

The first is space exploration. In the 1940s, Hungarian-American mathematician John von Neumann suggested that the most efficient way to explore our galaxy, the Milky Way, would be to release a swarm of self-replicating robots that could travel from star to star, building copies of themselves from the materials they encountered. As they multiplied they would explore the galaxy at an exponentially faster rate – far more quickly than any single probe could – radioing home their findings as they went.

The other exception might be weaponization. It is not hard to imagine a government or terrorist cell releasing self-replicating nanobots deliberately as an act of war or aggression. Geek culture has even thrown up names for such speculative scenarios: "khaki goo" refers to a military nanobot attack, while the name "black goo" is reserved for acts of terror.

But there's another possibility too. Human beings are all too good at making mistakes. And so perhaps nothing more than a human programming error could cause a swarm of nanobots to run amok. Here's a scenario. An explosion at a chemical processing plant has vented a cloud of toxic vapour into the atmosphere, which is now drifting towards a densely populated area. A bright young nanotechnologist figures out that a swarm of specially adapted nanorobots, dropped from an aircraft flying above the cloud, could digest the deadly chemicals, turning them into harmless gases. With no time to lose the plan is put into action, and within minutes of the drop the toxic cloud has gone. But celebrations are short-lived, as grim-faced scientists realize that the nanobots are still eating – and not just toxic gases.

Stop the bots

As Eric Drexler points out, we have enough of a job controlling fruit flies and viruses – nanorobots may simply be too small and too robust for us to deal with. We could perhaps hope that the natural world will be too harsh an environment for the bots, and that they will be outcompeted in their bid for the Earth's resources by the biological organisms that have spent millions of years adapting to it.

Know your goo

Grey goo A mass of self-replicating nanobots that has gotten out of control, exceeding its useful remit of destroying toxins, which will, if left unchecked, eat the entire world.

Blue goo Goo police: a second wave of nanobots released deliberately to destroy the grey goo.

Black goo Grey goo that has been released deliberately by terrorists.

Khaki goo Weaponized grey goo used by the military of a nation state.

Green goo A plague of biological organisms engineered by nanorobots.

Fingers crossed on that one.

Is there a more reliable counter-strategy? Cautious bot-builders might consider incorporating a few trapdoors into their designs that would allow us to rein in a renegade nano-swarm. For example, the bots might be programmed to stop reproducing after a fixed number of generations. Or perhaps they could be designed to always maintain an overriding control link to a central bot – which could, at any time, issue a command causing all the bots to self-destruct.

If, however, we haven't acted with such foresight then we could have a near-impossible fight on our hands. In this instance it might even be that the only plausible method to actively stop the rogue nanotechnology would be... more nanotechnology. Scientists have conjectured we would need "blue goo" – which can loosely be thought of as police nanobots that would be programmed to hunt down and destroy their malicious grey goo counterparts. Let's hope we've got the programming right this time, so our blue saviours don't turn against us too. Even if the probability of a grey goo assault is low – and even if it sounds more sci-fi than science fact – it remains a scenario of immense consequence. It would only have to happen a single time for the Earth and everything on it to be eaten alive by the machines.

Changing the course of history

destroying the future by destroying the past

Armageddon angst, for most people, is all about fretting over events that may or may not happen at some point in the future. Will a killer asteroid career into the Earth? Will global warming turn the planet into a drowned world? Or will a rogue state like North Korea kick off World War III?

But what if global calamities could also be unleashed by fiddling with events in the past, radically altering the course of history – perhaps for the worse? Just such a scenario could be possible if backwards time-travel ever became a technological reality. It might only take a subtle tweak to events long ago to set off a domino effect that brings about cataclysmic changes to the present day – or even which erases the present day entirely.

Science-fiction authors have enthusiastically explored the idea. In the Ray Bradbury story "A Sound of Thunder" (1952), a big-game hunter signs up with a company offering safaris in the past, and takes a trip back to the Cretaceous period, 66 million years ago, to bag himself a *Tyrannosaurus rex*. To minimize the dangers of rewriting history, he's only allowed to shoot dinosaurs that are soon to die naturally, and he must stay with his guides at all times. However, when the hunter sees the *T. rex* he panics and flees, inadvertently crushing a butterfly underfoot as he goes. This tiny premature death turns out to have grand consequences. The United States was a democracy when the hunting party set out, in the year 2055. But on their return they are horrified to find that a dead butterfly – followed by 66 million years of toppling causative dominoes – have placed the country in the grip of a hard-line fascist dictatorship.

Time-travel can really screw things up. In the *Terminator* movie series, a robot army threatens to exterminate humankind and take over the world. The secret to the robots' success is clever artificial intelligence technology. But, as we learn in the second film, *Judgment Day* (1991), this technology was initially developed from a microchip recovered from the remains of one of the very same robots, which had time-travelled back from the future. Where then, did the creative spark for the microchip first come from? It seems to have appeared out of thin air.

This is an example of a time-travel paradox, wherein meddling with the order of cause and effect throws up impossible incon-sistencies. The *Terminator* plot is what physicists call a "Bootstrap Paradox", because it's rather like pulling yourself up by your own bootstraps.

But it's not the only kind. What if you went back in time and killed your maternal grandmother before your mother was born, thus undermining your own existence? If you don't exist then you can't have killed her. But if you didn't kill her then you do exist. And so on. It's one big logical inconsistency. Scientists call this one the "Grandmother Paradox". And it's not hard to see how it could be scaled up – what if you went back to the dawn of life on Earth four

How to build a time machine

Could it ever be possible to build a real time machine? It might surprise you to learn that scientists already have. In 1905, Albert Einstein put forward his special theory of relativity. This is a theory describing the motion of objects moving at very close to the speed of light. Its radical predictions replaced the centuries-old laws of Newton and Galileo for describing the physics of fast-moving objects.

Special relativity brought with it some rather odd effects. For example, it showed that anything travelling close to light speed actually gets shorter in its direction of motion – an effect known as length contraction. But Einstein's mathematics also revealed something weird about time: in the reference frame of a fast-moving object, time slows down. This effect, known as time dilation, means that on board a spacecraft travelling at 99 percent light speed, every year that passes corresponds to seven years back on Earth. This dilation factor increases as the spacecraft goes faster – at 99.9999 percent light speed, every year on the ship corresponds to 707 years back on Earth. When this spacecraft returns to Earth after a year measured in its own frame of reference, the astronauts on board will find that they have travelled 706 years (707-1) into the Earth's future.

The theory was subsequently proven in experiments involving high-speed aircraft, demonstrating that time-travel into the future really is possible. The trouble, however, is getting back again. In 1986, a group of physicists at the California Institute of Technology (CalTech) figured out one way by which it might be done. The theory underpinning the idea billion years ago and prevented the first self-replicating chains of amino acids from forming?

Could time-travel even ever be possible? Many professional scientists consider time-travel paradoxes and the potential havoc they could wreak to be one very good reason why time-travel must logically be an impossibility according to the laws of physics.

Foremost among these temporal-displacement party poopers is Professor Stephen Hawking. Such is his loathing of scientific discussions of time machines that he has invented a new law of physics to forbid them. It's called the "chronology protection conjecture" – it's a conjecture because, even though the arguments for it are, he believes, compelling, there is as yet no evidence that it actually exists. However, Hawking speculates that natural quantum fluctuations – tiny packets of energy that continually pop in and out of exist-

is again down to Einstein, though this time it's not his special theory of relativity, but his general theory. Einstein arrived at the general theory of relativity in 1915, as a way to incorporate gravity into his theory, and he achieved this by bending the flat space and time of special relativity. One consequence of this is the possible existence of objects called wormholes – tunnels through space that offer a shortcut between otherwise remotely separated regions of the universe.

The CalTech team realized that if one mouth of a wormhole were to be placed on a spacecraft and then flown off at near light speed then – because of time dilation – a time difference could be introduced between the two mouths. But because a wormhole is a two-way street, this time difference could be used to travel both forwards and backwards through time. Of course, given the fact that we're not all gadding back and forth through time on a regular basis, you've probably guessed that it's not all that simple. The problem is that even after you've found yourself a suitable wormhole, holding it open is no mean feat, as its intense gravitational forces will tend to pull it shut.

The good news for wannabe Dr Whos is that there is a theoretical kind of matter – which physicists call exotic matter – that has negative mass and thus exerts negative gravity, which can prop a wormhole tunnel open. The bad news is that calculations indicate that supporting a man-size wormhole will take a quantity of exotic matter equal to the mass of Jupiter – while, as the name suggests, exotic matter is extremely rare.

In Terry Gilliam's movie *12 Monkeys* (1995), Bruce Willis (who features rather a lot in this book) plays a reluctant time-traveler, sent into the past to discover how and where a deadly toxin, which has left the outside world uninhabitable, was first released. Can he change the past to alter the future?

ence throughout the whole of space – would be magnified by any time machine that was ever built, and destroy it.

The principle is rather like that of going back in time to meet your younger self, and then doing that over and over again until there are several copies of you all at the same point in time. Likewise, quantum fluctuations from the future go back through the machine, and keep on doing so over and over until there are so many of them, all at the same instant in time, that their combined energy becomes huge and cooks the time machine.

Hawking's chronology protection conjecture would, as he himself puts it, "keep the world safe for historians" – and, indeed, for the rest of us, if there's a grain of truth behind the dystopian science-fiction stories. Yet many other physicists think time-travel is a very real possibility – one that is consistent with the laws of physics and only kept from humanity's grasp by our technological limitations. Limitations that, they say, we will one day overcome.

Paradox lost

Does that mean the human race is destined to one day wink out in a puff of chronological confusion? Not necessarily. A number of ideas in modern physics now make it possible to neatly dodge some of the most destructive consequences of time-travel.

One of these ideas is known as self-consistency. It was first put forward as far back as 1975, by the Russian physicist Igor Novikov. In a nutshell, it says that nature always finds a way to ensure a self-consistent course of events. Stated simply, the Novikov principle asserts that if an event exists that would give rise to a paradox, or to any change to the past whatsoever, then the probability of that event is zero. In short, it says that it's impossible to create time paradoxes.

A physicist named Joseph Polchinski put forward, in response, a restatement of the Grandmother Paradox, only using a billiard ball as an example. He suggested that, were time-travel to be possible, one could launch a ball into a time machine in just such a way that it emerged in the past to collide with its earlier self, preventing it from entering the time machine in the first place. The principle of self-consistency dictates, however, that – no matter how you aim your throw of that ball – there must be a path in which it would strike its earlier self a glancing blow that knocks it into the time machine on just the right course so that it emerges to deliver that glancing blow.

That might sound like a fudge of logic. But research suggests that self-consistency arises as a natural consequence of the principle of least action – one of the fundamental postulates of physics. This principle states that a quantity called the action, which can broadly be thought of as a measure of the energy locked away in a physical system, is always minimized. It's a powerful principle that enables physicists to derive Newton's laws of motion, Maxwell's equations of electromagnetism and Einstein's theory of relativity, all from first principles. Now it seems to be telling us that time-travel is self-consistent.

Of course, self-consistency wouldn't be much use when it comes to preventing our fictional big-game hunter and his squashed butterfly from ushering in the next Hitler. But there is another idea that might do the trick. It revolves around parallel universes.

Into the multiverse

In 1957, an American physicist called Hugh Everett put forward a rather radical interpretation of quantum theory – the set of physical laws that govern the microscopic world of atoms and particles. Quantum physics is a very counter-intuitive area, home to some hard phenomena to swallow – such as a particle being in different places at the same time until it is measured, when it then "collapses" into

Could we send a warning message into the past?

Perhaps we're being too ambitious in expecting to send human travellers to explore history first hand. What if we could just send a message back through time? This in itself could be extremely useful. As soon as future humans realize they've screwed up, a quick message to the world leaders of the past could swiftly set things straight. Note to self: stop burning coal, shake up sub-prime mortgage industry and send maintenance men to Chernobyl.

But how might you do this? There is a kind of subatomic particle – hypothesized to exist by physicists – that has just this backward time-travel property, and on which a message to the past could conceivably be written (in much the same way that radio messages today are encoded using particles of electromagnetic radiation called photons).

These odd particles are called tachyons (from the Greek *takhus*, meaning swift), because physicists believe that, if they exist, then in addition to travelling back in time they must also move faster than the speed of light. For this reason, you could never see a tachyon approaching – all you'd see would be two images after it had passed, one approaching and one receding.

Tachyons were predicted from the theory of special relativity, which permits a whole class of subatomic particles travelling faster than light speed. Aficionados of Einstein's theories might argue that special relativity prevents anything from moving faster than light. But in fact, all special relativity says is that it's impossible to cross the light barrier, from either below – or above. That means it's impossible for you or me to ever travel faster than light in special relativity. But also that particles which are created travelling faster than light can never go slower – in other words, tachyons are destined to roam the cosmos at superluminal speeds forever.

Experimental studies have been conducted to try to detect the presence of tachyons in our universe, but to date there is no evidence for their existence and they remain purely a theoretical curiosity.

a single definite location. Everett explained these weirdnesses as being down to interference between parallel universes. If he's right then our universe is just one of very many that exist side by side, like pages in a book. This universe of universes is sometimes known as the multiverse.

In his opinion, a particle in one universe is accompanied by copies in all the others. And whenever a quantum event takes place that has a number of possible different outcomes – say, colliding with another particle – then every possible outcome actually happens somewhere, in one (or more) of these myriad parallel worlds. This picture, which has become known as the "many worlds interpretation" of quantum theory, also means that somewhere out across the multiverse, there exist other copies of you and me, all living out subtly – and necessarily wildly different – lives. It's a controversial theory, but one which is gaining currency amongst physicists today.

Some of them – such as Professor David Deutsch, at the University of Oxford – think it may even have a bearing on time-travel. They say that hopping back in time is a quantum event that takes you into the past not of your own universe, but one of its parallel companions. And that means that whatever acts of temporal vandalism a time traveller may commit, they will have no effect on the universe that he or she has come from, thus circumventing any paradoxes. Go back and stop life emerging on Earth and it's a different Earth that you've sterilzsed – not this one. And so your own existence is never called into question. Send a high-tech robot to its struggling inventor fifty years ago and it falls into the hands of a copy of him in another universe; he still needs to design it from scratch in this one.

The many worlds theory gets rid of troublesome temporal paradoxes and makes it impossible to alter history in your own universe. But before you crack open the Champagne, just remember that it brings with it a new danger – meddling time tourists from the universe next door.

The techno singularity
hyper-intelligent bytes and chips

What if a computer could acquire the ability to think? Not just to make decisions – computers do this already – but to be aware, and to have conscious thoughts and desires? More to the point if such a thing were to exist, then could this artificial intelligence ever exceed the brainpower of the smartest human beings? And what might happen if it did?

This is a scenario that futurologists call the technological singularity. The name was first coined in 1983, by the science-fiction writer Vernor Vinge. It came from an analogy he drew with gravitational physics, in which the term singularity refers to a point of infinite density at which the predictive power of physical laws breaks down. Vinge reasoned that a technology-based singularity will be much the same, in that the unknowable nature of a machine superintelligence makes it impossible for a futurologist to predict what life will be like afterwards, or whether life will even be possible at all.

We are the weakest link

A superintelligence would have to be created by humanity's own hand. But once in existence it could soon come to dominate over us. That's because, once we've figured out how to build a machine that's even slightly more intelligent than we are, then the machine will be better than us at building an improved version of itself. That improved version will be smarter still, and better at improving itself once again. The process continues and the rate at which the machine's intelligence is increasing soon becomes exponential, leaving our primitive biological brains way behind.

American inventor and futurologist Ray Kurzweil estimates that computers could become powerful enough to sustain such a superintelligence by as early as 2013. A human brain cell's neurons can fire at around two hundred times per second, but modern computer processors already operate at speeds of around 2Ghz – two billion times per second. This means that every thought a human brain could have during an average lifetime of seventy years can already be processed by a modern computer in about three and a half minutes.

But of course hardware is only part of the problem. If I could give you a computer billions of times more powerful than anything in existence today, then without any programming it would still be no more intelligent than my shoe. The key to building a superintelligence is software.

Not everyone takes the view that the singularity is really going to happen. Many renowned artificial intelligence researchers and neuroscientists – including Daniel Dennett and Steven Pinker – argue that the notion of humans creating a machine superintelligence, when we don't even understand fully how intelligence arises in our own brains, is at best far-fetched.

Thinking machines

Creating machines that think has certainly proven harder than initially anticipated. Research in this area began soon after the birth of the digital computer, during the early 1950s. The first scientific conference on the subject was held at Dartmouth College, New Hampshire, in 1956. And it was here that a young American computer scientist called John McCarthy coined the term artificial intelligence, now commonly abbreviated to AI.

This was soon followed by the emergence of two different approaches to AI research, dubbed "neat" and "scruffy". The neats applied logic and careful computer programming to try to re-create intelligence. While the scruffies spliced together odd pieces of software code on a largely trial and error basis to see if they could get anything resembling intelligent behaviour to emerge.

Both camps have enjoyed some success. The scruffy approach led to the development of neural nets – software that tries to mimic the mess of connections between neurons in the human brain. Neural nets are used today for spotting patterns in large datasets and have also demonstrated a capacity for learning. Meanwhile, the neat approach led to the development of effective chess computers – culminating in a historic match in 1997, in which IBM's Deep Blue computer defeated grandmaster Garry Kasparov.

But spotting a pattern or making lightning-fast searches through a database of chess moves doesn't constitute what most of us would consider true intelligence – self-awareness, and the ability to comprehend the world and our place within it. A genuinely intelligent computer would be able to hold a conversation with you, have opinions and get your jokes. This will require a breakthrough in our present understanding which may happen tomorrow, or may not take place for many decades.

Is superintelligence dangerous?

A superintelligence that decided we are a threat, an obstruction or simply a commodity to be exploited would be a danger because so many aspects of our society are controlled by networked computers. The emergence of a hostile and superior machine intellect also forms the basis for most "robot uprising" scenarios (see p.174).

In some ways, if we were to encounter a hostile superintelligence we might be better off meeting a highly developed one rather than a merely mediocre one. We can expect most intelligent machines to have goals – objectives that benefit them or increase their chances of survival. The question is, would the machine be ruthless in the pursuit of those goals or would its actions be tempered by some kind of emotional intelligence? As American AI researcher Eliezer Yudkowsky, of the Singularity Institute for Artificial Intelligence (SIAI), once said: "The AI does not hate you, nor does it love you ... you are made out of atoms which it can use for something else".

Could a computer really become hostile? It would be wrong to write off the possibility. After all, throughout history, humans themselves have been hostile and exploitative towards many other species – and to other human races which they have considered inferior. Why should a computer intelligence be any different? The singularity is defined by uncertainty so, first and foremost, AI researchers should proceed with caution.

Robots for peace

One safe environment for AI development that has been proposed by researchers is an AI Box. This effectively isolates the AI in a simulated world, and the only information that's permitted in or out is plain text – allowing simple two-way communication, and enabling programmers to modify their code.

Another option, which is advocated by the SIAI, is to try to ensure that all AIs will be friendly by encouraging programmers to imbue their creations with a moral, ahem, code so that any emerging intelligence will feel sympathy towards humanity and act in our interests. That might sound lame, but the idea has attracted support from Kurzweil and other prominent scientists and futurologists. Sustaining such friendship would also likely require the same respect from us towards the machines. So turning them into a race of robot slaves is probably out of the question.

We should hope that computer scientists working in AI move forward with due care and foresight. Ray Kurzweil believes we will run into the singularity before this century is out. And if life afterwards turns out badly, there will probably be very little that we can do to change our fate at the mercy of a machine intelligence immeasurably superior to our own.

Putting the brake on Moore's law

At the heart of all the speculation about whether or not the Earth is due to plunge headlong into the uncertainty of a technological singularity lies a mathematical relationship known as Moore's law.

It's named after Gordon Moore, the co-founder of American microchip manufacturer Intel. In 1965, he noticed that the number of components that could be squeezed onto a silicon microchip wafer was doubling roughly every two years. Taking into account the increase in the quality of the chips, it meant that computer processor speed was doubling every eighteen months. This regular doubling of computer power is in part what's led computer scientists such as Ray Kurzweil to predict that we're heading for exponential growth of technology – and that's what many believe could bring us to a singularity.

However, it seems several effects may undermine Moore's law. One is heat. Put your hand on top of a running computer and it's hot. Computer chips generate a great deal of waste heat, which must be dissipated if they are to operate efficiently. It now seems that some new chips are operating so fast and throwing out so much heat that they threaten to melt the very silicon into which the structure of the circuit is etched.

That's not the only problem. Components on chips are now getting so small that they are approaching the limit, imposed by quantum mechanics (the physics of subatomic particles), beyond which it's impossible to stop electric charge from leaking between different parts of the chip. Ray Kurzweil believes we'll reach the quantum limit by 2019. But he doesn't think this will be the end of Moore's law, instead speculating that new technologies will be discovered to keep the pace of computer hardware moving.

One such technology could be quantum computing – an idea that turns the quantum limit on its head, using quantum physics to produce a new breed of superfast computer processor. It works by exploiting the fact that quantum particles can be in several places at once. And so an electron that normally encodes just a single piece of information can now encode many, and then process all those pieces of information at a stroke. When it comes to computing, it may be that quantum theory has the last laugh.

Rise (and fall?) of the machines
bots get too big for their bytes

In the *Terminator* movies, Skynet – a computer system designed to control the whole of the US's defence infrastructure – becomes self-aware and decides to do away with people. It initiates full-scale nuclear war, killing billions of humans, and then creates an army of robot warriors – the Terminators – to finish the job.

As we've seen, the emergence of a superintelligence such as Skynet is taken seriously by many futurologists. With computers governing everything from defence systems to air traffic control to electricity grids, it's not hard to imagine how this metallic mind could make life very difficult for the human species. But could it ever hope to send legions of armoured Terminators beating a path to your door? And, if so, just what can you do about it?

Silicon soldiers

The military already has some eight thousand robots operating in the field, performing tasks that include retrieving wounded soldiers, bomb disposal and bomb delivery, in the form of the aerial combat drones that have seen action in Afghanistan. You could argue that none of these machines make their own decisions to shoot – they're all controlled remotely by humans. But there are already other robotic entities which do pull the trigger of their own accord.

One example is the guidance computer in a cruise missile, which is trusted to fly a high-explosive warhead to a target and then detonate it. And there are systems in use in Afghanistan, to shoot down incoming artillery shells, that have to be automated because human reaction times simply aren't quick enough.

But even these devices simply link the decision to fire to the input from a simple sensor. A true autonomous battle robot has complex software between the sensor and the firing. And all our concerns about robots taking over the world hinge on whether this software could ever inculcate a consciousness. As we've seen, this seems eminently possible.

Walk this way

What form might our robotic assailants take? We all have robots, in elementary form, in the house, such as washing machines to clean our clothes and automatic thermostats to keep us warm, and there are even robotic vacuum cleaners and lawn mowers in existence that scurry about under their own steam. But are bipedal walking robots really a possibility over the course of the coming decades?

In 1986, Honda developed its first robot capable of walking on two legs. Called E0, it was still primitive, only able to walk in a straight line on a flat surface – and each step took between five and twenty seconds. Fourteen years later, Honda's research came to fruition when it unveiled the now-famous Asimo. This robot stunned the world with its powers of balance and agility. Its latest incarnation can not only walk, but does so up and down stairs, round corners and can even run at 6kph.

The secret of their success was to copy human-style walking empirically, rather than trying to arrive at the answer by hardcore mathematical analysis (a "scruffy" rather than a "neat" approach – see p.169). Even so, they still have some way to go in order to truly mimic the complexity of human locomotion. Asimo has 34 so-called degrees of freedom – the ability to move one body joint left and right or up and down. By comparison, a human being has over two hundred.

There are now many bipedal robots able to walk with ease, including Reem-B, built by the United Arab Emirates' Pal Technology Robotics, which has 41 degrees of freedom, and Hubo, a humanoid robot developed at the Korean Advanced Institute of Science and Technology.

The friendly and helpful-looking Honda Asimo: every home should have one.

Stopping a Terminator in its tracks

So what sort of firepower would you need to stop a perambulating Terminator? Standard 9mm bullets are likely to bounce harmlessly off its armour. However, there are plenty of options for hand-held weapons that pack a little more punch. For example, you might like to try armour-piercing bullets, 40mm anti-tank grenades or a saucy number called Frag-12. That's a 12mm high-explosive cartridge that fits in a standard shotgun, and which can poke one-inch-diameter holes in quarter-inch-thick steel. Of course, the average homeowner – especially if you're in Europe – is unlikely to get hold of such goodies. But if you do, beware of using the exploding ones in confined spaces: the back-blast may well finish you off.

The bad news is that even these top-shelf fireworks may be insufficient to stop the most determined and well armoured of robotic assailants. Is there anything else that the soldiers who turn up to save us could use? One relatively new addition to military arsenals that might help are electromagnetic pulse (EMP) weapons. These release an intense electromagnetic wave that induces a high voltage in any conducting material it encounters, which is often enough to cook the sensitive circuitry – microchips and other delicate components – in modern electrical systems.

The first EMP weapons were nuclear bombs – though that's a rather counterproductive solution for dealing with a few Terminators that are menacing your street. Instead, the US military is now working on EMP grenades, hand-held electromagnetic weapons that can be deployed by troops in combat to knock out anything with wires. Let's hope the squaddies that turn up to liberate us are packing a few of those.

Last resorts

But let's say you're on your own and backed into a corner with robots advancing on all sides and no one in khaki to help out: what options do you have? You might hope to be able to stop a hostile robot by pulling out the plug – or removing the battery. However, a rather ghoulish project under development by the US Defense Advanced Research Projects Agency (DARPA) could well have put the kibosh on that particular line of defence. Their Energetic Autonomous Tactical Robot (EATR) is able to fuel itself by ingesting organic material, leading to the grim possibility of a combat robot that can tuck into the corpses of its fallen adversaries – and thus which needs no external power source.

We might reasonably hope that the human designers of any robots that have the potential to turn on us might have built in some failsafe measures into the robots' programming – "kill switches", or emergency shut-downs that only humans can activate.

Does Hollywood offer any inspiration in terms of easy ways of destroying a robot? Well, if all else fails, try bamboozling their logic circuits with the old conundrum of a question "Everything I say is

The Terminator, played by Arnold Schwarzenegger, in the 1984 movie of the same name. Even killer robots sometimes have to use good old-fashioned technology, like the humble pair of pliers. Don't try this at home – unless you happen to be an android assassin sent from the future to alter the course of history and ensure droid domination.

a lie. Am I lying?" That, apparently, can make them explode. And ensuring you're not listed in the phone book under the surname Connor can't do any harm either.

Y10K and other bugs
updated your virus software recently?

If computers don't try to destroy us deliberately, there's every chance they could get us by mistake – that is, by a mistake of our own doing. If the hype was to be believed, they almost did. When the clocks rolled over from 1999 to 2000, a lack of foresight on the part of software designers nearly threw the world's computer systems and electronic networks into turmoil.

It was called the Millennium Bug, or Y2K bug, and it arose from abbreviating the four-digit numbers used in computers to record the year down to two digits, so for example writing 1999 simply as 99. Because 2000 is greater than 1999 but 00 is less than 99, this could then throw up all kind of errors and inconsistencies as computers tried to make logical comparisons between dates – arriving at the impossible conclusion that tomorrow happened yesterday.

Spanner + works = problem
The feeling that there might be trouble ahead started to gain traction among computer scientists in the mid-1980s. The name Y2K was put forward in 1995 by an American computer programmer called David Eddy, and it was at around this time that public awareness of the problem began to gather pace. The realization that the bug could affect some essential computers – such as those managing nuclear power stations or air traffic control systems – brought genuine concern, and serious efforts then began that it was hoped would mitigate the threat.

It's been estimated that, globally, a total in excess of $300bn was spent preparing for the impact of the Y2K bug and fixing the instances where it did actually occur. However, these were few and far between. Perhaps the worst case was the failure of a number of swipe card machines used in stores to take payments by credit and debit card. But this was hardly a disaster – little more than an inconvenience.

Some commentators took Y2K's failure to bite as a sign that the threat had been exaggerated by scaremongering in the media, citing the fact that most small businesses – many of which had done little or nothing to protect themselves – suffered no ill effects. Others pointed out that many of these companies would have been using proprietary software packages for which updates fixing any Y2K-related issues would have been circulated in advance.

It's possible that we could be due for more bugs like this in the future. And, as computer systems play an increasingly important role in civilization – and our very survival – we had better be ready for them.

What causes date bugs?

The Millennium Bug was caused largely by the limitations of early generations of computers. These had very little memory in which to store information, and so programs had to be written as efficiently as possible. That meant that using four digits to record a piece of information was frowned upon when it could be done in two. To be fair to the programmers, this was back in the late 1960s and early 70s – and they had no idea then that their software creations and precedents in programming technique would still be in use at the end of the century.

We no longer have to worry about such hardware limitations, but that doesn't put us in the clear. As 2009 turned into 2010, a few computer systems were caught out by a kind of Millennium Bug aftershock. Dubbed Y2K+10, it happened because of confusion between different kinds of number systems used by some computers. In particular the system known as binary-coded decimal encodes the number ten as 0x10. However, in the alternative hexadecimal system, 0x10 is the code for the number sixteen. This meant that some mobile phones and PS3 consoles displayed the date on 1 January 2010 as 1 January 2016 – while millions of German bank debit cards were rendered inoperable. The situation was rather like trying to compare values in metric and imperial units without first converting them.

The shape of bugs to come

Scientists have already figured out some of the future Millennium Bugs that lie in wait for us. The first is due to hit in 2038. Known as the Y2.038K bug, this one will affect Unix computers – typically used in academic institutes and scientific research, as well as for military and medical applications. Unix systems record the date and time in seconds as a binary number made up of 32 binary digits, or bits, measured from 1 January 1970. But at exactly eight seconds after 3.14pm on 19 January 2038, those 32 bits will become inadequate to record the number of seconds that have elapsed. Solving this problem is no simple matter. The most obvious solution is to add some bits to the date, say making it a 64-bit number, but then ensuring compatibility with existing software and other protocols is not straightforward.

There's more. Some of the fixes to the Y2K bug that were implemented only made the shift to three-digit years, rather than four, meaning that we're just going to have a repeat performance in the year 2900 – which, to any affected computers, will now be indistinguishable from the year 1900. This trend of running out of digits can only continue. Even those perspicacious computer scientists who made the shift to four digits right away would, if they were still around, see problems arise in the year 10,000 – the rather far-sighted Y10K bug.

The spreadsheet program Microsoft Excel suffers from this now. It measures dates as the number of days from 30 December 1899. Enter the number 2,958,466 as a date – which corresponds to 1 January 10,000 – and you'll get an error message. Even if you take the number of digits used to represent the year to five, you're still going to face a Y100K problem. In fact, pretty much the only safe option is to use enough digits to get you to the conjectured end of the universe. But as no one knows for sure when that will be, it's little help.

The Y10K and Y100K bugs are especially frightening because, as more and more of our infrastructure becomes computerized in the future, the potential damage caused by such rollover glitches only increases. And the inevitable complexity of the advanced systems that will be in place by this time will, of course, make them all the more difficult to fix.

On the plus side, we can realistically expect that the present calendar system – the Gregorian calendar – will no longer be in use by the year 10,000. So maybe all computer systems will be given a future-proof upgrade as well. And even if we do get caught out by a future date-related bug, perhaps its computer-paralysing effects might be just what it takes to save us from the aftermath of a technological singularity. Though don't hold your breath.

Human 2.0

are you ready for your upgrade?

Charles Darwin's theory of natural selection determines how species in the wild – human beings included – evolve and adapt to the environment in which they're living. So animals in water evolve streamlined bodies with fins and tails, while those up trees develop strong arms and legs for climbing. But imagine if human beings could steer the course of their own evolution. What adaptations might we give ourselves?

Some would say humans already are plotting their own evolutionary path – and that the first glimmers of this revolution can be seen in the form of anyone who has ever had plastic surgery, wears a pacemaker, has had an organ transplant or who simply wears spectacles.

But these examples of human beings deliberately altering their bodies are small fry compared to what some scientists and philosophers now have on their drawing boards. They call themselves "transhumanists" and they are working to alter the human form so radically that the result will be an entirely new, posthuman species – which they call H+. They believe that, just as medical researchers today pursue technologies and techniques to improve our minds and bodies, so new emerging areas of science such as nanotechnology, genetic enhancement and cybernetics, now offer enhancements to the human condition that we have only just begun to appreciate.

They are adamant that forthcoming discoveries in these fields will enable us to shore up our frail bodies against the ravages of disease and ageing. And that they could give us virtually superhuman powers in terms of improvements to both our mental and physical performance.

A Detroit policeman is given a new lease of cybernetic life in the 1987 movie *Robocop*, with high-tech weaponry built into his metal body. While the film is a violent shoot-'em-up, it does delve into questions of how human it's possible to be once you're more machine than man.

Holding back the years

Prominent among this new generation of transhumanists is American innovator Ray Kurzweil. In 2005, he made the startling statement in *New Scientist* magazine that he had absolutely no intention of dying – ever. He pins his hopes on the fact that progress in all fields of science and technology is now growing at an exponential rate.

The first step is to use all the technology that's available right now to slow down his ageing process as far as possible. So he lives a superhealthy lifestyle, consuming umpteen cups of green tea and alkaline water, and over one hundred supplement tablets every day. He never eats sugar or foods rich in carbohydrate. And he regularly takes intravenous chemicals that he believes will keep his cells functioning in tip-top condition.

This is what he calls "bridge one", and he believes it will be enough to sustain him for long enough to get to the next step – yes, bridge two. Here he's referring to a portfolio of more advanced technologies, such as gene scans for serious illnesses as well as other technologies to prevent serious diseases that he might be prone to – as well as gene therapies that go some way towards curing and preventing disease by modifying the patient's DNA.

His bridge three is an impending revolution in nanotechnology. Kurzweil says that in the coming decades he will be able to inject a swarm of tiny nanorobots into his body that will be able to swim through his bloodstream patching up the effects of ageing. The robots will repair the gradual erosion to his molecules – the damage from which is what causes the visible signs of ageing. They'll also keep an eye open for the early symptoms of serious illness, such as cancer, and take corrective steps – for example, repairing a cancerous mutation in a cell, or simply destroying the cell to prevent the disease spreading.

Chop and change

The range of technologies in the transhumanist's (anticipated) toolbox is impressive. As well as nanotechnology robots, researchers plan to use gene selection methods to screen human beings for defects before they are even born. Any serious defects found in an embryo that might lead to disease or weakness can be "corrected" through the use of gene therapy techniques.

Gene therapy works using viruses. Ordinarily, a virus operates by injecting its own DNA into a host cell, which then reprogrammes the cell to make more copies of the virus. But in gene therapy, the virus has been altered to do the dirty work of injecting new human DNA, which in turn has been deliberately modified by scientists. As well as curing diseases, gene therapy has the potential to increase muscle strength, improve lung capacity and boost human brainpower.

Another emerging technology is cybernetics – the melding of electronic and mechanical components with the human body. Cybernetics has already yielded primitive electronic eyes, ears and even limbs to replace those lost by amputees. As with gene therapy, cybernetic modifications to the human body have the potential to make it stronger, faster and smarter, as engineers develop the science-fiction dream of interfacing computer components with the brain.

Imagine the possibilities if the agility of human thought were coupled to the vast memory and search capabilities of a computer. What if it could then be connected to the Internet? Some have even speculated that, if your thoughts could be gathered by a brain implant, they could in theory be transmitted by radio to another implant wearer – yielding the possibility of a synthetic telepathy of sorts. Dr Robert Freitas, Senior Research Fellow at the Institute of Molecular Manufacturing in California, estimates this could be reality within forty years.

Too much of a good thing?

At what price does this bold new vision of humanity come? Some futurists and thinkers have warned that it could be far more costly than the benefits would merit. Of course, all the individual technologies – nanotech, genetics and robotics – carry with them risks that have been explored elsewhere in this section. But some more subtle concerns have arisen too.

American philosopher Francis Fukuyama argues that to have someone else's specification for what it means to be human imposed upon you is a compromise of democracy. Others have issued more sinister-sounding prognostications, noticing familiar overtones of eugenics in the speeches and rhetoric of the transhumanists. To their credit, most transhumanists actively reject eugenics and insist that their intentions are for the good of all. Nevertheless, making such modifications to yourself is unlikely to come cheap. And this will naturally widen the class divide, as the rich use their wealth to buy better bodies – quite literally, turning themselves into a physically superior race.

Many view transhumanism as just an extension of the age-old quest for the fountain of youth – a desperate bid for survival by those unable to come to terms with their own mortality. On the other hand, perhaps the ultimate solution to nightmare scenarios of "technology taking over" – whether it's robots or genetically engineered organisms – might be to simply apply those same technologies to ourselves, to give us the same advantages. After all, if you can't beat them, join them.

The planet that knew too much

information hazards

Otto von Bismarck, the nineteenth-century German statesman, once remarked that laws and sausages have something in common: it's usually best to see neither being made. Even so, most of us would like to believe that, in general, the more we know and the more information we are able to gather about the world, the better off we are. Knowledge, after all, is power. Isn't it?

Not necessarily, according to a growing number of scientists and philosophers. They seem to have taken von Bismarck's comment to the extreme, warning that the discovery and dissemination of all kinds of knowledge can bring with it hidden dangers; they say we are sometimes better off simply not knowing the truth. In the worst cases, knowing too much can lead to mass panics, the collapse of markets and even threats to the very future of our species.

These dangers posed by knowledge are known as information hazards. The most obvious kind is that arising from the development of powerful new technologies. There is mounting concern that we don't let the same thing happen with today's budding new areas of biotech, artificial intelligence and nanotechnology – fields for which Bill Joy, the former CTO of Sun Microsystems, has coined the term KMD (knowledge-enabled mass destruction).

Ignorance is bliss?

But information hazards don't just apply to the dissemination of scientific knowledge. The amount of info made available to the public by authorities during times of crisis can also constitute a potential danger. A case in point is containing the outbreak of infectious diseases, such as swine flu. This is a need-to-know minefield – governments and bodies such as the World Health Organization must try to steer a course whereby they release enough information to make the public aware of the risks, but not so much as to trigger panic. Release too little information and the public may suspect that the government is downplaying the risk, and therefore overreact. The government then has to downplay the risk even further. Taken to its logical conclusion, this leads to a total breakdown in the flow of credible information. On the other hand, if the government sounds the alarm and nothing happens, no one will listen the next time there's a real danger.

Incompetent marshalling of information in this way may already have left the public sufficiently distrusting of government advice to make it easy for cranks and conspiracy theorists to gain a foothold. This happened in the UK with the controversy over the measles,

Spanish flu: publish or perish?

A classic example of an information hazard from biotechnology arose in October 2005, when the research journal *Science* chose to publish the genetic code of the Spanish influenza virus. A team of American researchers had reconstructed the virus, which killed more than fifty million people worldwide in 1918. *Science* had elected to stand by its policy on gene sequencing research, by which it will only publish the research if the accompanying genome is made publicly available in the GenBank online database.

Shortly after, futurologist Ray Kurzweil and computer scientist Bill Joy, the former CTO of Sun Microsystems, published an editorial in *The New York Times* decrying the decision. They pointed out that re-creating a real virus from this data would be easier for a small group to achieve than building an atomic bomb. And, more importantly, the virus could cause far greater devastation – killing over ten times more people than the detonation of an atom bomb over a major city.

In February 2009, London's Royal Society held a workshop to explore how the risks posed by bioscience research should be addressed. It concluded that it's important not to exaggerate the threats posed by emerging technologies, but also that *natural* biological pathogens – such as the 1918 flu virus – were much more likely to be misused by rogue groups than any created in the lab.

The workshop's chairman, Professor Geoffrey Smith, a virologist at Imperial College London, defended *Science*'s publication of the virus genome. He argued that placing the data in the public domain was essential to silence conspiracy theorists, and added that there are already numerous stages – from funding to publication – at which the security threat posed by such biotechnology research is reviewed.

Kurzweil has since been working with the US Army to develop a rapid-response system to deal with the sudden emergence of new biological viruses – whether natural or engineered.

mumps and rubella (MMR) vaccine. A single scientist was able to cause a panic that led many parents to forego getting their children vaccinated. Some of these children died as a result.

A flow of reliable information from authorities is imperative to prevent the order of civilization collapsing into anarchy. And yet that may require a certain degree of economy with the truth.

Crying all the way to the bank

While we're on the subject of being economical, the state of the world's economy is, of course, essential for the stability of civilization. Stocks and share prices are one example of how information can affect financial markets. These are driven not necessarily by the actual performance of companies, but by how investors perceive them to be performing, and how they anticipate they will be performing in the future. In other words, what information about the company investors have at their disposal. The power of information in share dealing is well recognized and the exploitation of information that isn't freely available is illegal (insider trading).

The recent failures of some financial institutions could be seen, in some cases, as instances of too much information being released. In 2007, when members of the public learned that the UK's Northern Rock bank was in trouble, account holders promptly acted on that knowledge – by withdrawing their money. The resulting run on the bank pushed it to the brink of collapse. It could be argued that had the bank's troubles not become public knowledge, it might have pulled through on its own. As it happened, the UK government was forced to step in and guarantee deposits. However, this strategy isn't always a good idea as it too can be interpreted as a sign of weakness, causing further loss of public confidence: the public might conclude that the government is simply throwing good money after bad and still move their accounts elsewhere. Notably, the British government adopted a very different strategy when it came to Lloyds TSB, keeping its balance-sheet woes, and the government bail-out it had received, firmly under wraps for months.

Similar info hazards may come to afflict the insurance industry. Recently, companies have emerged that offer private genetic health scans, allowing individuals to assess their likelihood of succumbing to various ailments over the course of their lifetime. Anyone whose gene scan shows them to be at low risk of getting sick will naturally be inclined to purchase less cover, while those at high risk are going to buy more. No one who's paid for a gene scan and knows they're at risk will share that knowledge with their insurer, because this will push up their premium – and, indeed, medical privacy legislation may forbid it anyway. With no way to tell the healthy from those destined for illness, insurance companies would be forced to raise premiums for everyone. This would deter even more of those at low risk, driving the premiums beyond affordability, which could possibly undermine the entire insurance market.

Are we living inside a computer program?

Matrix scenarios

Most of us have experienced virtual reality (VR) in one form or another – whether it's trying out a sophisticated headset at a science museum that immerses us in a simulated world, or playing escapist online games such as *Second Life* or *World of Warcraft*. Some respected philosophers have posed an interesting existential question: how would we know if everything we see around us – in what we regard as the real world – is in fact nothing more than an elaborate computer simulation, constructed by an advanced intelligence many millennia ahead of our own?

Long before this scenario was explored in the *Matrix* movies, it was investigated by philosophers such as René Descartes in the seventeenth century. His notion of a split between the mind and the body was an early suggestion that there exists a divide between physical reality and what our senses actually perceive. In the early 1990s, artificial intelligence researcher Hans Moravec was among the first to seriously entertain the idea that reality could be an artificial construction put together inside a computer.

The simulation argument

Our perception of the world boils down to a flow of information relayed to the brain by our senses. Computers process information, so it seems reasonable to imagine that a sufficiently advanced computer could furnish our brains with enough information to provide a convincing picture of reality. And if computers were ever able to attain artificial intelligence, then it's also reasonable to assume that simulations of human brains could be placed within this reality.

Nick Bostrom was the first to make the case for this scientifically, in terms of logical hypotheses. In what he called the simulation argument, he put forward three statements and showed that at least one of them must be true. The statements are:

1. The chance that a species at our current level of development can avoid going extinct before becoming technologically mature is extremely small.

2. Almost no technologically mature civilizations are interested in running computer simulations of minds like ours.

3. You are almost certainly living in a simulation.

Possibility 1 says that civilizations generally become extinct before they discover the technology needed to create their own artificial reality. We should hope – from the point of view of the survival of the human race – that this proposition is false. Possibility 2 seems unlikely, given our experiences of ourselves. With the ever-increasing power of computers and the interest in artificial brains, if anything this would be a top priority – it clearly already is for the transhumanists.

If neither possibility 1 nor 2 is true, argues Bostrom, then the rapidly advancing pace of computer technology would enable an advanced civilization to run simulations of a vast number of artificial brains – so many that the number of simulated brains would vastly outweigh the number of real biological ones. And so, the probability of any randomly selected brain being simulated would be very much greater than the probability of it being biological: meaning that you and I are most likely living inside a computer.

An increasingly virtual reality

In February 2007, a 26-year-old Chinese man keeled over and died after spending a marathon seven days playing online computer games such as "World of Warcraft" – only leaving his keyboard for toilet breaks and brief naps. A survey in early 2010 revealed that UK employees using social networking sites during work time are costing the country's economy an estimated £1.38bn every year. We have a serious Internet addiction, it seems.

Sights and sounds from our environment stimulate the brain as much as fatty and sugary foods do our stomachs and taste buds. And many computer games and online experiences provide amplified stimuli that are more intense and attention-grabbing than reality itself, making them highly addictive. Some online games have incorporated "anti-obsession" features, which reduce a player's score if they play for longer than a few hours at a time. However, enterprising gamers found ways to crack these safeguards more or less immediately.

Is this the real life?

If the world really is a computer simulation, is there any way we could ever know? It seems not. If the program's creators are immeasurably more intelligent and technologically superior than ourselves, they will have expertly concealed all the seams in their fabric of reality. Even any bugs in the software that might have occurred are likely to be erased from our experience (remember: in this view we are just aspects of the program ourselves). Although perhaps reports of paranormal activity – odd deviations from normality, superstitions, bizarre coincidences – could be signs of just such bugs occurring.

It may be that the creators wish, at some point, to reveal themselves to us. Or perhaps they have left clues locked away in the structure of the artificial world we inhabit. This was the case in Carl Sagan's novel *Contact* (1985), in which scientists discover a message encoded in the digits of the fundamental mathematical constant Pi.

It's an interesting train of thought, given current debates over religion, and the fact that many atheist scientists such as Professor Richard Dawkins are speaking out aggressively against the notion that our universe might have had a creator. Arthur C. Clarke once said that any sufficiently advanced technology is indistinguishable from magic. So perhaps running simulated realities is a technology that's indistinguishable from divine creation.

Proof of life

The strongest evidence that we are living in a simulation would be the activation of simulations of our own. This would of course prove beyond doubt that such technology is possible and – say proponents of the theory – make it unlikely that we're the first to develop it.

On the other hand, if we aren't living in a simulation, one way it could be proven is by demonstrating that some aspect of our world is uncomputable (a phenomenon that it would be impossible for a computer to calculate). As far as we know, the laws of physics that we experience are computable. However, Oxford University physicist David Deutsch has argued that an idea in mathematics called Gödel's incompleteness theorem may prevent us from generating perfect simulated realities.

Gödel's incompleteness theorem is rather like a mathematical version of the paradoxical sentence "This statement is false". Which, if true must be false, and if it's false must be true. Gödel used this to argue that there are certain truths in mathematics that cannot be proven using mathematics. Similarly, says Deutsch, there may be certain aspects of reality that a computer – which is built from that reality – cannot simulate.

We should probably hope that this is the case. The passage of time that we would experience within a simulation is just "computer time", and so can be stopped and started; paused on the whim of the creators at any point without us even noticing. But if they ever decided to switch us off permanently, it would be an end to humanity that we would be utterly powerless to prevent. That's if we can really consider ourselves to have existed in the first place, of course.

Death stars, missiles & threats from space

Science fiction has given us a million stories about marauding alien invaders with death-ray-equipped flying saucers. But we could meet our doom from much less exotic cosmic phenomena: massive lumps of rock hurtling through space; bursts of solar energy; all-devouring black holes; galaxies colliding with each other; and geomagnetic reversals. The more you discover about our little planet's place in the universe, the more it seems we're merely dust on a ball on a giant snooker table.

Target Earth
asteroid impacts and comet collisions

There is a hidden menace stalking our solar system, in the form of enormous chunks of rock and ice – some the size of mountains. Now and again, one of these cosmic behemoths will slam into the Earth, falling from the sky and exploding with enormous consequences. Just such an impact event, 65 million years ago, is thought to have been the cause of the mass extinction in which the dinosaurs were wiped from the face of the planet.

Rocks in space
Asteroids are relics from the birth of the solar system, over four and a half billion years ago. When the solar system first formed it was just

a swirling cloud of gas and dust. But gradually, dust grains started sticking together to form larger clumps. When the clumps grew big enough, they began to exert a gravitational force on other nearby matter, causing the clumps to grow even faster. A small number of these clumps became very big indeed, forming the planets. The rest remained smaller agglomerations of rock and dust: these are the asteroids.

They typically formed in the inner portion of the solar system, where the sun's scorching heat stripped away all volatile materials such as water, as well as gases including methane and carbon dioxide. But in the outer solar system these substances were able to condense into chunks of ice.

Occasionally, gravitational disturbances – caused by interactions between the pieces of ice, or even by other stars passing close to the solar system – dislodged some of these icy chunks, causing them to fall inwards. As they reached the inner solar system, the sun's heat began evaporating the volatile material to form a bright tail of gas and dust. Such objects are known as comets. A comet striking the Earth can be as calamitous as the impact of an asteroid.

Both comets and asteroids have been battering our planet from the year dot. A glance at the pockmarked and cratered surface of the moon gives a hint of the ferocity of the barrage. The Earth has escaped a similar fate because of its atmosphere, which has absorbed the impacts of the smaller objects and eroded the craters left by the larger ones.

The impacts can be unimaginably devastating. A space rock measuring 250m across, travelling at a typical speed of 20km per second, lands with the explosive force of five hundred megatons of TNT. That's over thirty thousand times the power of the bomb that destroyed Hiroshima in 1945. And it's over twice the energy of the volcanic blast that ripped apart Krakatoa in 1883, making a bang so loud it was heard in Australia, over 3000km away.

Impact winters

In Part 2, we explained how volcanic outbursts can have a drastic long-term cooling effect on the climate. However, the impacts of large comets and asteroids upon the planet's surface also fling mate-

A sunrise view of the moon's Tycho crater, captured by NASA's Lunar Reconnaissance Orbiter. Were it not for the Earth's atmosphere, our home planet might regularly suffer the kind of bombardments of asteroids and comets to those which have left the moon with its pockmarked and cratered surface.

rial up into the atmosphere, leading to what are known as impact winters. An asteroid might be as small as a few tens of metres across, but it can create an explosion equivalent to the detonation of a ten-megaton nuclear bomb. This is quite sufficient to send aloft asteroid fragments as well as rock, soil and anything else excavated in the process of forming a crater on Earth.

The second effect – unsurprising, given a blast of such magnitude – is fire. Smoke from the multitude of fires ignited by the blast then billows high up into the atmosphere. It's generally the most problematic of the two effects, because smoke particles are much lighter than denser physical detritus (soil et al.), and so they are easily blown around the planet. Smoke particles take much longer to fall out of the atmosphere so the sky can clear.

There is evidence that a severe impact winter followed the asteroid strike that wiped out the dinosaurs 65 million years ago. Indeed, it was probably a major contributor to their demise. A study published in the journal *Geology* in 2004 by a team of US and Dutch palae-ontologists examined the fossil record near the K-Pg boundary, the layer above which dinosaur fossils abruptly disappear. The team was studying an exposed region of the K-Pg layer in Tunisia – a warm region of the planet. However, they discovered microscopic fossils of sea creatures normally only found at colder, more northerly latitudes – the implication being that warm climes had become chillier than normal.

Their findings suggest that debris from that dinosaur-killing impact may have reduced the amount of sunlight reaching the ground by as much as ninety percent. This period of darkness could have lasted for anything up to a decade; however, the cooling it caused may have persisted for as long as two thousand years.

Dino devastation

The event that wiped out the dinosaurs – and, indeed, seventy percent of all life on Earth at the time – is thought to have been caused by a 12km-wide comet or asteroid slamming into what's now the Yucatán peninsula, in Mexico. This much was discovered when geologists studied the layer in the fossil record where the dinosaurs disappeared, finding it to be rich in iridium, a rare-Earth element. There was so much iridium that it must have arrived in one large consignment from space. An asteroid was the most likely mechanism by which this happened, and this theory was confirmed in 1990 when scientists re-examined 1970s rock-bed surveys of the Mexican coast, revealing the ring-shaped remnant of a giant impact crater 180km across.

This impact ignited firestorms around the planet and unleashed devastating tidal waves. That would have been followed by a freezing impact winter as ash and debris flung into the air enshrouded the Earth, blotting out the sun for up to a year.

Impact hazard

Impacts of the magnitude that clobbered the dinosaurs are gratifyingly rare – they happen on average once every one hundred million years. But smaller strikes, still capable of causing localized devastation, occur with much greater frequency. In 1908, a 45m-wide object exploded in the sky over the Tunguska River in Siberia. The blast – estimated to have been between three and five megatons –

Trees were flattened and burned over hundreds of square kilometres in the Tunguska area of Siberia in June 1908. It was the largest impact event in recorded history – believed to be the result of a meteor or comet that burst prior to hitting the Earth's surface. The force of impact was the equivalent 10–20 megatons of TNT (one thousand times more powerful than the nuclear detonation at Hiroshima).

would have been enough to incinerate a modern city. In fact, if a similar object landed on Westminster everything within London's M25 motorway would be toast. The Earth is thought to be strafed by a Tunguska-like impact once every few hundred years.

The biggest comet and asteroid impacts are low-frequency, high-consequence events: they don't happen very often but, when they do, a large proportion of life on Earth dies. That means that during the time between these extinction-level impacts it's easy to forget how destructive they really are. To make the danger plain, astronomers David Morrison and Clark Chapman have carried out an actuarial (statistical) analysis of the asteroid risk. They calculated the average number of fatalities per year – by taking the annual probability of an impact occurring and multiplying that by the number of people likely to be killed in such an event. They found that, on average, asteroids claim nearly seven hundred lives per year, every year – meaning that your individual risk is about one in ten million.

That said, asteroids are still buzzing past the Earth today. On 3 November 2008, an asteroid missed us by just 38,500km, about an eighth of the distance to the moon – that's a hair's breadth in astronomical terms. The asteroid was detected mere hours before its closest approach. A month earlier, another small space rock actually hit, exploding high in the skies over Sudan with just a couple of days' warning.

Defenders of the Earth

If we were to stand any chance of defending the planet against this threat, the first thing we'd need is an early warning system that can spot hazardous comets and asteroids years, and preferably decades, ahead of any potential impact. It will be the astronomers who save our skins.

The days when astronomers worked in person at their telescopes scouring the night sky for asteroids are long gone. Nowadays, the grunt work is done by robotic instruments, which take regular images of the night sky and automatically compare them with reference images of known star fields, looking for new objects that are changing their position from night to night.

It's now thought that around eighty percent of the most dangerous comets and asteroids – those more than 1km across – have been discovered and catalogued by these surveys. Now astronomers

An illustration of the Large Synoptic Survey Telescope, currently in its development stage. When operational, the telescope will survey the entire sky every three nights, detecting any Earth-bound asteroids.

are trying to log all of the material in the next bracket down – smaller objects between around 140m and 1km across which, despite being smaller, are still capable of causing regional devastation.

NASA has been given a congressional mandate to log ninety percent of asteroids bigger than 140m by 2020. That will require even more sophisticated robotic instruments, such as the Large Synoptic Survey Telescope (LSST), with its giant 8m mirror, now being built in Chile. This instrument is due to begin operations in 2015.

Then attention is likely to turn to the even smaller asteroids – those ranging in size from 140m right down to about 30m. There could be over a million of these out there – and any one of them would be capable of unleashing an explosion with enough force to take out a city. There is concern that – while asteroids can be catalogued and then tracked – some comets are extremely hard to see in telescopic surveys. Known as dark comets, all of their surface ice has evaporated away during previous passes near the sun, meaning that they don't develop the bright tails that normally give them away.

Comet 19P/Borrelly, visited by NASA's *Deep Space 1* probe in 2001, was found to have areas on its surface blacker than anything previously known (other than nanomaterials specially engineered by mankind). In 1983, another dark comet, IRAS-Araki-Alcock, brushed by the Earth at a distance of 5 million km, the nearest pass of any comet in two hundred years. Yet it was discovered only two weeks ahead of its closest approach. They don't give us much breathing space. Astronomer Clark Chapman, at Southwest Research Institute, in Boulder, Colorado, has suggested that such dark comets could be detected by the infrared heat radiation they give off, rather than by their visible light – a little like the space-telescope equivalent of night vision goggles.

Scramble!

If an astronomer spots a new comet or asteroid, they can track its path across the sky. This data enables them to get a good idea of the object's precise orbit around the sun. And as soon as they know that, then they're in a position to estimate whether it might ever come near the Earth, the orbit of which is well established.

The probability of an impact taking place, together with the level of destruction that would result, gives the asteroid a threat rating from zero to ten on what's called the Torino scale – named after a 1999 scientific conference in Torino, Italy, at which it was introduced. A zero on this scale corresponds to no threat, while a ten spells a certainty of global devastation.

The highest that any astronomical object has ever scored on the Torino scale so far is a four. This was the asteroid 99942 Apophis which, for a time, had a small probability of striking the Earth in 2029. It was later downgraded to a one on the scale as there remained some concern that, during its 2029 flyby, Apophis may yet pass through a so-called gravitational keyhole. An asteroid passing through one of these regions of near-Earth space would be pulled by the planet's gravity onto a new trajectory that would lead to an Earth impact at a later date. Were it to happen in this case, it would be in 2036. However, the probability of this occurring was judged to be one in 250,000, so small that the risk was again downgraded, to a zero.

When the alarm is sounded, the good news is that astronomers and other scientists have come up with a number of feasible strategies for batting away an inbound comet or asteroid. Most of these require a few years' warning – preferably decades. So we'll have enough time to try again, should our first attempt at deflection fail. Big asteroids and comets will eventually collide with the Earth again, as surely as night follows day. We just need to ensure that we are as prepared as we can be.

Taking out asteroids (when Bruce Willis is busy)

The dinosaurs were woefully lacking in the ballistic missile department. Not so with us humans. If, tonight, our astronomers detected a killer space rock heading our way, there's a range of firepower – and solid scientific strategies – that we might hope to use in order to deflect or destroy the asteroid before it reaches us.

Nuclear assault

The Bruce Willis approach, of wheeling out the atomic hardware at the first sign of an incoming space rock, probably isn't our best option. The trouble is that nuclear blasts unleash a vast amount of energy in a

In the sci-fi disaster movie *Deep Impact* (1998), the world takes the nuclear route in asteroid disposal. A spacecraft named *Messiah* attempts to blow up the world-threatening space bolide with nukes. The plan has mixed results…

largely uncontrolled manner, which would tend to shatter a comet or asteroid into very many small pieces. The pieces would still crash into our planet but, instead of a single chunk, which we might have hoped to deflect by other means, we would have a hail of fragments – and it'll be practically impossible to deflect all of them.

That woudn't be a problem if we could guarantee that the fragments were small enough to burn up in the atmosphere. But if they're bigger than about 30m across then all Bruce and colleagues would have achieved is to turn a big rock into lots of little ones, or a rifle bullet into a shotgun blast.

Kinetic impact

Very few of the schemes that have been proposed for deflecting a comet or asteroid on a collision course with the Earth have actually been tried out. In 2005, NASA's *Deep Impact* space probe

This photograph of comet 9P/Tempel (also known as Tempel 1) was taken one minute after the impactor section of the *Deep Impact* spacecraft collided with it.

was deliberately steered to collide with the comet 9P/Tempel. The purpose was to excavate a hole in the comet's side, into which scientists could then peer, in order to see what comets are actually made of. The mission was virtually the same as the process of guiding a "kinetic impactor" to a comet. This refers to a heavy, solid object that can collide with the comet to alter its orbit ever so slightly – hopefully by enough to miss the Earth. The European Space Agency is now planning a mission to try out a full-scale test of a kinetic impact attack on an asteroid. Called *Don Quijote*, the mission is planned to fly by 2015.

Space mirrors

Our sun is a formidable source of energy. Now some enterprising physicists have figured out how this power could be harnessed to save us from space rocks. It's all done with mirrors, as the saying goes. Professor Massimiliano Vasile at the University of Glasgow, in Scotland, says that a flotilla of reflective surfaces launched into space could work in concert to focus so much light onto the surface of an asteroid that parts of its surface would begin to vaporize. The gases produced by the vaporization venting away from the asteroid's surface then act rather like a rocket engine – a jet that would propel the asteroid onto a new orbit around the sun which, fingers crossed, would take it wide of the Earth.

Getting large mirrors into space is no mean feat. But Professor Vasile has come up with a solution – using inflatable mirrors that can be packed into the limited cargo space on board a rocket and then deployed once in orbit. He's calculated that ten 20m wide inflatable mirrors could, given about six months' warning, deflect an asteroid up to 150m across – three times bigger than the Tunguska asteroid that struck Earth in 1908.

Gravity tractor

It's something we're all familiar with – gravity has the power to make heavy things move. In 2005, scientists Edward Lu and Stanley Love realized that because asteroids are so heavy it might be possible to alter their course using their gravitational attraction towards a space-craft flying alongside. As the spacecraft fires its engines to move away, gravity would pull the asteroid after it – as if the two were con-nected by a rope. The idea is known as a gravity tractor. Its advantage is that it requires no special technology – this could, in principle, be done using the robotic spacecraft that are already in existence today. The downside is that gravity is the weakest of the forces in nature,

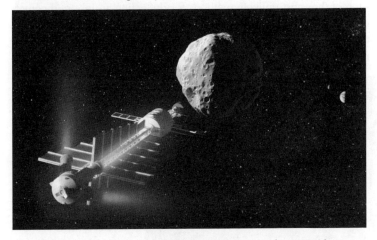

An artist's impression of a gravity tractor altering the course of an asteroid.

meaning that it would take a long time to work any appreciable deflection into the asteroid's course – typically several years.

Rocket motor

If the mountain won't come to Muhammad, then try strapping a Space Shuttle Main Engine to it. A more efficient version of the gravity tractor idea is to simply attach a rocket motor to the asteroid directly – though, of course, this strategy is riskier because it involves landing on the asteroid's surface.

Spacecraft engines don't have to rely on those archetypal jets of flame spewing out the back. Other options have been considered, including solar sails, which are giant silver sheets that hitch a ride on the light streaming out from the sun. Ion engines are another possibility: space drives that accelerate a jet of exhaust gas using electricity rather than combustion. There's also the mass driver. This consists, essentially, of a robot that sits on the surface of the asteroid digging chunks out of it and firing them off into space. Just as a rifle kicks back against your shoulder each time it fires a bullet, every chunk leaving the asteroid's surface creates a recoil that pushes the space rock in the opposite direction – and, over time, this pushing effect produces a change in its trajectory.

Paint job

One of the most unlikely methods for deflecting an inbound comet or asteroid is to paint its surface. As was shown by the pioneers of quantum physics in the early twentieth century, radiation carries momentum. And so, in just the same way that a mass driver can

A four-quadrant solar sail system, measuring 66 feet on each side, being tested in the world's largest vacuum chamber. Solar sails rely on sunlight to propel vehicles through space: the sail captures constantly streaming solar particles, called photons, which, over time, provides enough thrust for a small spacecraft to travel in space.

impart momentum to an asteroid, particles of heat radiation (called photons) also give sizeable kicks to the asteroid as they leave its surface. In general, asteroids rotate as they move through space and so their surfaces are periodically heated and cooled as they spin in and out of the sun's light. This means that the dusk hemisphere of the asteroid is warmer than the dawn hemisphere – making that hemisphere give out more heat radiation, which in turn gives the asteroid a net shove in the opposite direction.

It's called the Yarkovsky effect, after the Russian engineer Ivan Yarkovsky, who first did the maths. Different colours absorb and emit radiation more efficiently (for example, black objects absorb more heat than white ones). And so painting the asteroid is a way to vary the strength of the Yarkovsky effect, in turn moving the asteroid's future orbit closer to, or further away, from the sun.

The death star

Most planetary scientists believe that the biggest rock-related threat from space comes from asteroids – because in the inner solar system, where we live, asteroids are by far the most numerous. Comets, on the other hand, tend to lurk in the solar system's chilly outer reaches, only occasionally heading in towards the sun, which is when we see them as spectacular objects in the night sky, sporting tails of gas boiled off from their surfaces by the solar heat.

Some astronomers, however, believe that now and again something happens in the outer solar system that sends a blizzard of comets raining inwards – like apples being shaken from a tree – leading to death and devastation on Earth. The question is: what's doing the shaking?

One of the most popular theories is that our sun isn't a lone star in space, but actually forms a binary system with another star. This star's orbit, so the theory goes, is highly oval, taking it alternately close to and then far away from the sun. During the close passes, its gravity is thought to yank comets out of their established orbits and hurl them in towards the Earth. For this reason, our sun's companion has been given the name Nemesis – the death star.

The theory has its origins in the work of two palaeontologists at the University of Chicago, David Raup and Jack Sepkoski. In the early 1980s they carried out a study into mass extinctions – points in the fossil record where the numbers of fossilized species abruptly drops. They looked at the record for the last 250 million years, finding evidence for twelve widespread extinction events. But the really interesting fact was the spacing between each event – roughly the same period, thirty million years.

Shortly after, two teams of astronomers independently put forward the Nemesis theory: that a star on a thirty-million-year orbit around the sun was responsible. The theory called for the star to be very faint, otherwise telescopic surveys of the night sky would have detected it already. Such small, dim stars – just a few times the size of the planet Jupiter – are already well known to astronomers, who call them brown dwarfs and red dwarfs. Brown dwarfs are failed stars that never quite gain enough mass to light up the nuclear reactions in their cores needed to make them shine. Red dwarfs are extremely cool, dim stars that – although they have managed to ignite nuclear reactions – still only give out as little as 0.01 percent as much light as the sun.

From the timing of past extinctions, the astronomers calculate that the star should currently be a little over a light year away from Earth. By comparison, the nearest known star – Proxima Centauri – is 4.2 light years distant. Roughly half of all the stars that we observe in the night sky are members of binary systems (they have a partner), so it wouldn't be at all anomalous for our sun to be in one as well.

Seeking Nemesis

Comets swarm around the outer solar system, forming what's known as the Oort cloud – named after Dutch astronomer Jan Oort, who first postulated its existence in 1950. In 2003, astronomer Mike Brown, at the California Institute of Technology, discovered an icy body plying the outer solar system, known as Sedna. This comet-like object was found to be on a highly elliptical orbit – with no obvious explanation for how it got there. Comets are normally thrown onto elliptical orbits by interactions with giant planets, such as Jupiter. But the closest Sedna's orbit brings it to the sun is still fifteen times further out than Jupiter – much too far away. This suggests something else was responsible for flinging Sedna onto its elongated orbit. Could that something have been Nemesis?

WISE eyes on the skies: an artist's impression of the Wide-field Infrared Survey Explorer at work, relaying images of the entire sky back to Earth.

Although it'll be very hard to see any visible light from Nemesis, the star is expected to shine quite brightly in infrared. A NASA infrared space telescope, called the Wide-field Infrared Survey Explorer (WISE), was operational between 2009 and 2011, and could have caught any such star in the act. As well as locating faint objects, the telescope was able to take measurements of their motion, allowing astronomers to potentially identify stars that are on an orbit matching that predicted for Nemesis. Scientists are currently analyzing the WISE survey's data.

The threat from beyond

Even if it turns out that there is no death star in orbit around the sun, we might not be in the clear just yet. Between 1989 and 1993, the European Space Agency operated a space telescope called *Hipparcos*. Its job was to gather ultra-precise data on the positions and speeds of one hundred thousand stars in our neighbourhood of the Milky Way. But when, in 1997, scientists finished analysing the mass of data the probe had gathered they were in for a shock. It revealed that one star in particular – called Gliese 710 – is heading pretty much straight for us.

The star, which currently resides 63 light years away in the constellation of Serpens Cauda is heading our way at nearly 14 kilometres per second. It's very unlikely to score a direct hit. But astronomers say that approximately 1.4 million years from now, Gliese 710 will brush past us – with an 86 percent chance of smashing through the Oort cloud, knocking comets this way and that.

Meanwhile, other astronomers have suggested that it's not stars drawing a bead on us that's the problem, but rather our own solar system's haphazard motion through the galactic maelstrom that threatens to disrupt the Oort cloud. One theory in particular puts this down to the regular passage of the sun and solar system through the dense midplane of our galaxy. As the sun orbits around the galaxy it also bobs up and down, rather like a carousel horse, punching through the galactic midplane twice on each cycle.

The midplane is the densest part of the galaxy's disc, filled not only with stars but also massive clouds of hydrogen gas – any of which would be quite capable of triggering a fall of Oort cloud comets if the sun passed near them. This idea is called the Shiva hypothesis – after the Hindu god of destruction.

Whether they're caused by rogue stars or our cosmic meanderings through the galaxy, showers of comets from the outer solar system have the power to explain some of the most calamitous mass extinctions of life on Earth. If the theory is correct, these strafe the planet every thirty million years. The last one was five million years ago, meaning that the dinosaurs (who vanished 65 million years ago) may number among its victims.

When galaxies collide
galactic-scale prangs

Look overhead on a clear winter's evening and there's a chance that you could see something amazing. In between the famous square of the night sky that houses Pegasus and the "W" of Cassiopeia, if there's not too much light pollution, you might just catch sight of what looks like a faintly glowing cloud. This is the Andromeda galaxy. At 2.5 million light years from Earth, it's the most distant object that you can see with the naked eye. And yet some astronomers say it's not going to remain that way forever. Because Andromeda is heading our way. As if having to worry about stars crashing into our solar system wasn't bad enough, now it seems Andromeda and our own galaxy, the Milky Way, could be destined for one monumental pile-up in a few billion years' time.

The Andromeda galaxy is similar in form to the Milky Way: a flattened disc of stars with spiral arms sweeping through it, where new generations of stars are bursting into life. Our Milky Way is home to between two hundred and four hundred billion stars. Andromeda is believed to be even bigger, packing in around a trillion suns. To the naked eye, Andromeda appears as an oval about as long as the width of the full moon. But in fact, all you're seeing here is the galaxy's bright core – look through a telescope and you'll see its full extent, which is some seven times the moon's width.

The galaxy was first recorded in the year 964 by the Islamic astronomer al-Sufi, who called it a "small cloud". The first telescopic observations were made in 1612, just three years after Galileo first turned a telescope on the heavens. Even as recently as the late nineteenth century, scientists were baffled by Andromeda – and other objects like it that were gradually being discovered. One view was that these swirling maelstroms were new solar systems in the process of forming. But those ideas were dashed in the mid-1920s when American astronomer Edwin Hubble made the first reliable distance measurements, showing that galaxies were hundreds of thousands of light years away. A solar system at this distance would be too faint to see. Instead, these were enormous swirling systems made up of billions of stars, each like our own sun.

Galactic dodgems

Despite their size, galaxies are almost entirely empty space. That is, the average separation of the stars in a galaxy is very much more than the stars' size. For example, the nearest star to the sun is 4.2 light years away – nearly seven million times the sun's diameter. And this means that direct collisions between stars are very rare (although close approaches, where stars pass close enough to be influenced by one another's gravity, do take place). On the other hand, the separation between galaxies, measured in terms of their size, is a lot smaller. The distance from the Milky Way to Andromeda (2.5 million light years) divided by the size of the Milky Way (around one hundred thousand light years) comes out at just 25. And so collisions between galaxies are a lot more common.

Indeed, there's plenty of evidence for this in the night sky. Powerful instruments, such as the Hubble Space Telescope, have returned spectacular imagery of galaxies ploughing into one another. These galaxies show massive distortions to their delicate spiral structures, with bright streamers of stars and gaseous debris being cast off into space.

The end state of such a cosmic smash depends how fast the galaxies are slammed together and whether the collision is head-on or just a scrape. If the galaxies just brush past each other then they might experience nothing more than a little distortion in shape from the pull of each other's gravity. On the other hand, if they bash together directly then, if the impact speed is relatively slow, it's possible for the two galaxies to merge into one. The new galaxy could be an "elliptical", where the stars from each galaxy are mixed to form a smooth ellipsoidal mass. Though a more likely form is a so-called irregular galaxy – where the collision produces a weird new shape that defies classification. A classic irregular galaxy is the Antennae, two spiral galaxies in the constellation Corvus which have almost torn each other apart. The new galaxy will almost never be a spiral: the collision always destroys any such delicate structure.

If the collision between two galaxies is head-on and fast, it's

The Antennae galaxies are the nearest and youngest examples of a pair of colliding galaxies. They give us a preview of what may happen when our Milky Way collides with the neighboring Andromeda galaxy in several billion years' time.

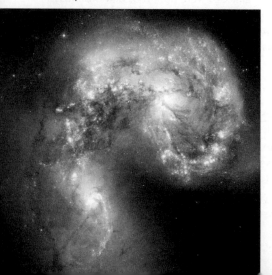

possible for both galaxies to pass straight through one another. (It's possible because stars themselves hardly ever collide.) When a small galaxy passes through a bigger galaxy the ripple created by the passage can sometimes convert the bigger galaxy into a bright ring of stars, called a ring galaxy. A classic example of a ring galaxy is Hoag's object, in the constellation of Serpens.

Andromeda rising

Astronomical observations show that the Andromeda galaxy is heading towards the Milky Way at somewhere between 100 and 140 kilometres per second. This means that the two will collide in two to five billion years' time. However, while Andromeda's speed towards us has been accurately determined, the speed in the perpendicular direction, across the plane of the sky, is poorly known. This makes it hard to say whether the two galaxies will meet in a direct collision, or whether it'll be more of a gentle brush.

Astronomers Thomas Cox and Avi Loeb, at the Harvard-Smithsonian Center for Astrophysics, have run computer simulations of the collision to try and find out more details. Their models suggest that the two galaxies are most likely to merge to form a new elliptical galaxy. They found that there would probably be an initial collision around two billion years from now, spitting stars and debris in all directions, before gravity pulled all the material back inwards to form the new galaxy, which they have christened Milkomeda.

What will happen to the sun and the solar system? The models give a 67 percent chance to the prediction that the sun will end up more than 65,000 light years from Milkomeda's centre (it's currently 26,000 light years from the core of the Milky Way). The good news, they say, is that the sun will hang on to the planets and there will be little disruption to the overall structure of the solar system. The bad news, however, is that by this time, the sun will have already inflated to become a red giant star, engulfing the Earth.

Human beings, if we are to exist as a race beyond the incineration of the Earth when the sun expands, will have necessarily become a space-faring race. Indeed, it's likely that we'll have colonized our corner of the galaxy by this time, perhaps forging an empire spread across a number of star systems. However, the potential disruption to

The sun and solar system will be hurled into deep space when the Milky Way collides with Andromeda in a few billion years. This artist's conception shows a future Earth, its oceans having boiled away due to the sun's increasing heat, exiled to the outskirts of the new merged galaxy dubbed "Milkomeda".

the relative positions of the stars caused by a galactic collision could set back such a civilization by many millennia.

Cox and Loeb have calculated that there's a twelve percent chance the sun might even get ejected from the new galaxy altogether when the Milky Way and Andromeda meet. Presumably the same fate could befall any star system in the galaxy. This brings the terrifying possibility that a human colony in the far future could find itself adrift lost and alone in the cold, dark gulf of intergalactic space.

The day space exploded

nature does not abhor a vacuum decay

Empty space looks harmless enough. Yet research suggests it could be anything but. Some scientists say it isn't empty at all, but is actually loaded with energy, which – like the proverbial coiled spring – could snap back in our faces at any moment.

The phenomenon is known as vacuum decay. It's one of the reasons why particle accelerators have received such bad press over recent years. There are a multitude of ill-advised scare stories about how the Large Hadron Collider, a machine that smashes together subatomic particles to probe the physics of the quantum world, could destroy the Earth. Triggering vacuum decay is just one of these. However, the consensus amongst the sane is that none of them is likely to pose a serious risk.

At least, not from a particle accelerator, that is. There are far more violent processes going on out in deep space than can be mustered in any accelerator ring, and now the fear is that one of these could potentially trigger the vacuum of space to cave in on itself, with devastating consequences not just for the Earth but for the entire cosmos.

False vacuum

The idea that energy can be locked away in empty space was first predicted by physicists trying to do quantum theory in the early universe – during the hot fires shortly after the Big Bang in which the universe was created. They found some very appealing models of particle physics in which the energy of the vacuum actually drops as the universe expands and cools.

These models were attractive because they allowed different forces of nature – such as gravity, electromagnetism and the forces inside the nuclei of atoms – to have been elegantly unified into a single superforce when the universe was born. This then split apart to form the forces we're familiar with today, as space gradually cooled down.

However, in some of these models it's possible for the universe to remain in the old high-energy vacuum state, while the true energy of the vacuum falls to become much lower. A universe in this state is said to be trapped in a false vacuum, the energy of which can be very much higher than the new true vacuum state.

A universe getting trapped in a false vacuum is very similar to the way a glass of water placed in a microwave oven can then become superheated, absorbing far more energy than is needed to make the water boil but without turning any of it into steam. As soon as the water is disturbed, for example by stirring it or adding coffee powder, it abruptly converts to steam – sometimes dangerously.

Why does water get superheated like this? The reason is that water boils by the nucleation of tiny steam bubbles which then expand and rise to the surface. This nucleation tends to take place around impurities in the water, or bumps and scratches on the inside of the glass, which encourage the transition from water to steam. This means the water is more likely to get trapped in a superheated state if it's very pure, or if it's been poured into a very new or otherwise unblemished glass.

And this is the root of the concern over vacuum decay in our universe. Because if space has become superheated into a false vacuum state then the concentrations of energy generated during high-speed particle collisions – either inside an accelerator or, more likely, in or around dense objects in space such as neutron stars and black holes – could serve as the equivalent of the impurities in the water, or the chips and scratches on the inside of the glass.

They could nucleate a bubble of true vacuum, the expansion speed of which rapidly approaches light speed. The bubble then grows until it gradually envelops the whole universe.

True vacuum apocalypse

Why is vacuum decay such a bad thing? The problem is that, as we alluded to earlier, switching to a new vacuum regime radically alters the laws of particle physics. These laws determine the laws of chemistry, and that set of laws in turn govern all the processes in biology. The long and the short of it is that the delicate balance in chemistry which allows life to exist in our universe would be shattered, meaning life – all life – that came into contact with the true vacuum would be instantly obliterated.

That's probably why scientists have dubbed vacuum decay "the ultimate ecological catastrophe". Its adverse effects were first calculated in 1980 by American physicists Sidney Coleman and Frank de Luccia. In their paper, published in the journal *Physical Review D*, they starkly commented: "One could always draw stoic comfort from the possibility that perhaps in the course of time the new vacuum would sustain, if not life as we know it, at least some structures capable of knowing joy. This possibility has now been eliminated."

In addition, the bubble walls – travelling within a whisker of light speed – are packing an enormous quantity of energy. So anything that might stand a chance of enduring the new physics of the true vacuum would probably be blasted to smithereens by the collision.

There is, however, one way we might hope to postpone our demise in the event of a vacuum decay bubble being nucleated: by legging it. Or rather, relocating our entire civilization onto a huge spacecraft that's travelling faster than the advancing bubble wall. The speed of light is fast but, compared to the immensity of the universe, it will still take billions of years for the bubble to engulf the whole of space. And that's assuming the universe is finite – it may well be infinite in extent. A civilization that's able to outrun the approaching bubble could therefore enjoy aeons of continued existence.

But how could you do this? After all, you'd have to travel faster than light. This could be possible via a scheme that was put forward in 1994 by a physicist called Miguel Alcubierre, working at the University of Cardiff. Although travelling faster than light is prohibited by Albert Einstein's special theory of relativity, it is permitted within the more widely reaching general theory.

The basic idea of Alcubierre's scheme is to make the space in front of the ship contract, shrinking the distance between the spaceship and its destination, while at the same time the space behind expands at the same rate. The net effect is to sweep the ship along arbitrarily quickly.

Of course, it's not as simple as that. Calculations have since shown that implementing the plan requires vast amounts of a weird kind of negative-mass material, dubbed "exotic matter" by physicists. It's exactly the same stuff that you'd need to fuel up a working time machine (see p.279). So perhaps travelling faster than light would just be a temporary solution to the problem of vacuum decay, while other scientists head back in time to try and prevent the calamity occurring in the first place.

Into the heart of darkness
down the galactic plughole

Black holes are one of the eeriest and most perplexing concepts in science. They are usually stars which have become so dense that their gravitational field won't even permit light to escape. Black holes have enjoyed many an outing in science fiction: they usually play the bad guys, variously devouring people, spacecraft and planets. The question is, are black holes getting a bad rap at the hands of Hollywood directors, or is the defamation well deserved? Is it ever possible that a black hole could saunter into the solar system and unleash gravitational pandemonium on planet Earth? And, if so, is there anything we can do about it?

What's a black hole?

Scientists and philosophers have long appreciated the thinking behind black holes. Ever since Isaac Newton and his theory of gravity in the seventeenth century, physicists have known about the concept of escape velocity: the speed that needs to be imparted to an object in order for it to sail off into space and never get pulled back down by gravity. For the Earth, this is just over 11 kilometres per second. Fire a cannon ball upwards at this speed or quicker and you won't see it again. The value for escape velocity varies, depending on the mass and density of the gravitating body. For the moon it's just 2.4 kilometres per second while for the giant planet Jupiter it's nearly 60 kilometres per second.

But what if you could make an object so heavy and dense that the escape velocity was faster than the speed of light? Not even a light ray could leave the surface of this dark foreboding place. That is a black hole.

The detailed physics of black holes had to wait for a better theory of gravity than Newton's. This arrived in 1915 in the form of Albert Einstein's general theory of relativity. The theory ascribed gravity to the structure of space and time. In Newton's theory, space is like a flat tabletop across which the force of gravity acts. Einstein's great insight was to realize that the effects of gravity could be produced

How to survive falling into a black hole

As anyone who's read the textbooks knows, falling into a black hole is a one-way ticket to oblivion. Or is it? It turns out there could actually be a way to stave off the inevitable and survive a headlong plunge into the heart of darkness. Once you poke a head or a limb over the event horizon – the outer surface of a black hole – standard application of the general theory of relativity says you're done for. You are, from that moment on, doomed to intercept the infinite-density singularity at the black hole's centre and, in so doing, meet a particularly nasty fate as your body is stretched out by gravitational forces into human string.

But two physicists in the US – Deborah Freedman, of Harvard University, and Richard Gott, at Princeton – have shown that it's actually possible to delay your demise as you fall in. The Gott-Freedman life preserver, as it's become known, is a theoretical scheme that works by placing a massive ring of material around the hapless traveller's waist. The ring is conjectured to weigh roughly the same as a large asteroid. The gravity of this mass of material would then pull back against the forces trying to stretch the traveller as they fall in, preventing their body from being torn apart. Far away from the black hole, where only a weak corrective force is required, the ring would be about the size of the rings of Saturn. But as the traveller got closer, and an increasingly stronger corrective force is needed, so the ring would have to shrink down.

The delay this buys you is tiny, amounting to just a tenth of a second, but it could be enough to save you from certain doom – if you're falling into a black hole that's rotating or electrically charged (as most objects in nature are). Whereas ordinary black holes have a point-like singularity at their centres – which it's impossible to avoid – a hole with spin or charge actually has a ring-shaped singularity, which our traveller could pass through the middle of, unscathed.

Calculations using Einstein's theory of relativity then suggest that the traveller could emerge on the other side of the ring, into a new region of space. It's as if they've passed through a wormhole – a tunnel through space and time – that ferries them safely away from the mayhem of a black hole eating the solar system. Though quite where it is that they come out – in our universe, or beyond – is anyone's guess.

by bending that flat tabletop, as if it were a rubber sheet. Massive objects, like stars, bend space according to precise mathematical laws. Other objects then move within this curved space to trace out the curved paths that we see when, for example, we throw a ball in the air and watch it drop back to Earth – or when the planets orbit around the sun.

According to Einstein's theory, the space of the solar system has been distorted by the gravity of the sun into a shape rather like a great big pudding basin. The planets roll around the inside of the basin like marbles. If we could make the sun magically denser then this basin would get deeper, changing from a gentle depression in space into a long, deep funnel. And this bottomless pit in space is how general relativity describes a black hole. At the hole's centre is a point of infinite density known as a singularity – anything encountering a singularity will be crushed out of existence in an instant.

Do they really exist?

Black holes sound like such a fantastic concept, you might rightly wonder whether there's any solid evidence for their existence in the real world. And there is. Black holes have been detected at the centres of many galaxies. We haven't seen them directly, but stars have been measured circling close to the galaxies' cores on orbits so tight, and travelling so fast, that the massive object at the centre, whose gravity is shaping their paths, can only be a black hole.

There's also a compelling theoretical argument why black holes should be a real feature of our universe – because there's no known force of nature capable of supporting the densest objects in space against the force of their own gravity. An ordinary star, for example, is held up by its thermal pressure. Heat generated by nuclear reactions in the star's interior creates an outward pressure that balances the inward tug of its gravity.

But the end of a massive star's life is often marked by a violent explosion called a supernova (see p.225). This not only throws off the star's outer layers but also compresses its core to unimaginably high densities. Thermal pressure cannot support the core against the high gravity a supernova creates. There are quantum mechanical pressures that can step in to support the core in some cases, and these can lead to the creation of stable remnants, known as white dwarfs and neutron stars. But the death throes of the biggest stars produce densities that must overwhelm even quantum forces. And these stars are destined to end their days as black holes.

This artist's impression depicts a supermassive black hole "eating up" a doomed star that has got a little too close to the gravitational field of a black hole. Beginning left and following the arrow, the star is shown being stretched by the tidal forces until finally it is torn apart.

Who's afraid of the big black hole?

What would happen if a stellar-mass black hole strayed into our cosmic neighbourhood? Before we even start to fret over the Earth or the sun being devoured, we should worry first about the danger posed as the black hole bowls through the comet clouds in the outer solar system. This would be just like a renegade star passing too close to the sun and it would throw comets inwards towards it, some of which would inevitably strike the Earth – with nasty consequences for us.

It could be that the black hole passes straight through the comet clouds and on into the domain of the planets. This would be a recipe for even more chaos. Even though the black hole may not pass close enough to any planets to actually swallow them (although this is possible), its gravitational influence at a distance is still equivalent to, or greater than, the sun's. This will rip the planets from their orbits and fling them onto new trajectories, passing either closer to the sun or further away from it.

Which of these fates befalls the Earth is a matter of pure chance. But neither of them is good news. Even a marginal shift towards or away from the sun would be disastrous for the delicate tempera-

Cosmic thunderbolts

In 1974, Cambridge University physicist Stephen Hawking stunned the scientific community when he published a mathematical proof that black holes are not simply one-way funnels that hoover up matter from our universe. Hawking used quantum theory to show that black holes also emit radiation back into space.

But there was a sinister side to this "black hole evaporation", as it was termed. In research published in 1993 with Cambridge colleague John Stewart, Hawking showed that when a black hole evaporates away entirely, the result can sometimes be a "naked singularity".

Ordinarily, a black hole has an infinite density point called a singularity at its centre. But this is shrouded behind the black hole's outer surface – the event horizon (the sphere surrounding the black hole from which light cannot escape). It's impossible to see inside the event horizon without crossing it, and if you do cross it then you are doomed to get pulled into the singularity and be crushed to death.

But in a naked singularity, the event horizon vanishes revealing the infinite-density point for all to behold. Hawking and Stewart showed that under certain conditions seeing this singularity could be as deadly as poking your head over the horizon of a normal black hole. They found that evaporation of a black hole could leave behind something they named a thunderbolt – a type of naked singularity that spreads out across space at the speed of light, or faster. Anything the thunderbolt runs into would be ripped apart, as if it had fallen into a black hole.

Given the number of black holes there must be in the universe, and the fact that some of these must have evaporated away to nothing by now, Hawking may have got his sums wrong this time – given that we are still here. Then again, the universe is big – and maybe, out there somewhere, there's a thunderbolt hurtling through space towards us right now.

ture balance upon which the planet's climate relies. Some planets may be cast directly into the sun's fires, others may be lobbed out of the solar system altogether – and some may even collide with each other.

If the Earth does actually get eaten by the black hole, it'll be an especially unpleasant experience. Objects closer to a gravitational source experience a stronger force than those further away. This is why the moon and sun are able to raise ocean tides on the surface of the Earth: because the water, which is fractionally nearer to them than the ground below, experiences a stronger force. But near a black hole this effect goes mad. The force that normally raises a gentle tide in the ocean tears the whole planet apart, stretching it out into a long stream of rubble that's then sucked into the black hole like a strand of spaghetti.

The hole truth

The big difference, of course, between an ordinary star and a black hole encroaching upon the solar system is that we'll be able to see an ordinary star coming and prepare for it. Seeing a black hole coming will be much harder. Because it's black.

One method we might employ to monitor the skies for rogue black holes is known as microlensing. Astronomers use this technique for detecting small, dark objects in space such as brown dwarfs – failed stars that are too small to shine. It works using the theory of general relativity and the fact that even small objects can bend space by a noticeable amount. This bending effect curves the light from any stars behind, rather like a lens, magnifying the background stars and causing a brief flash as the black hole passes.

Once the black hole has reached the outer solar system, it will begin feeding on comets and maybe the odd planet. This celestial snack will first spiral around the black hole, forming a disc that glows brightly as the material is compressed before it gets sucked in.

Even if we fail to detect this strangely bright object getting nearer, the penny should finally drop when astronomers notice odd perturbations to the orbits of the planets. Planetary orbits in the solar system are very well understood. A black hole marching in would soon throw these delicate paths out of kilter. It wouldn't be long before telescopic sky surveys, of the sort already keeping watch for hazardous asteroids, would notice that the sun's planetary retinue isn't where it should be.

The good news is that computers running sophisticated mathematical models of the solar system would soon be able to collate all the data on the planets' new positions and use it to pinpoint the position and trajectory of the gravitational source – the black hole – that's been pulling the planets off course.

And then what?

Quite what we do about an incoming black hole is, most likely, a problem to be addressed when our technology is several centuries more sophisticated. There are theoretical ideas about how you might survive falling into a black hole, using a ring of matter to counter the hole's destructive forces (see box on p.215). However, as we saw above, getting eaten by the black hole seems to be the least of our worries. The more pressing problem is to alter its course before it trashes the solar system. For this, we might consider upscaling some of the asteroid deflection strategies outlined on p.198. However, the only one of these that could practically be applied to a black hole (which doesn't have any kind of solid surface) is the gravity tractor option. And quite how we could make this work – manoeuvring a large enough mass into place to alter the course of a stellar-mass black hole – isn't clear at all.

It may be that our only possible course of action is to evacuate the Earth, but even that will require technology considerably more advanced than we currently have at our disposal. Perhaps it's just as well that astronomers say a black hole turning up in our solar system is an extremely unlikely eventuality.

The angry sun

the sun has got his hate on

At 2.44am on 13 March 1989, a massive outburst of fast-moving electrically charged particles from the sun slammed into the Earth. The particles caused brilliant displays of the Northern Lights, which on this occasion extended as far south as Texas. And they played havoc with electrical systems. In Canada, the magnetic fluctuations they induced caused large electrical currents that overloaded power grids across Quebec – leaving six million people without electricity for nine hours.

Today, the world is even more reliant on sensitive electronics than it was in 1989. These systems now govern defence, communications, air traffic control and financial networks, to name just a few. The problem isn't confined to the Earth: in April 2010 a solar storm caused the shutdown of the *Galaxy 15* telecom satellite. What would happen if a storm knocked out the GPS satellites that the world relies on for accurate navigation? Or irradiated the crew of a manned space mission? And could the sun ever unleash an outburst powerful enough to cause loss of life on the planet's surface?

Sun bursts

Solar storms are triggered by natural shifts in the sun's magnetic field. They come in various forms. Solar flares, for example, are caused when magnetic fields near the solar surface become tangled together and then suddenly snap apart, releasing the pent-up energy (often equivalent to millions of times the yield of the most powerful nuclear weapons). Another type of solar eruption is known as a coronal mass ejection (CME), where billions of tons of particles are disgorged from the sun's ghostly outer atmosphere and flung towards Earth at up to eighty percent light speed. CMEs are often associated with solar flares, but they can occur on their own as well.

Both CMEs and solar flares are more common when there are cool patches known as sunspots visible on the solar surface. Sunspots are a sign of growing magnetic anomalies on the sun. They work to force apart the sun's blisteringly hot outer surface – called the photosphere – to reveal a patch of the cooler convective layer below. Sunspot numbers rise and fall over an eleven-year cycle – and the current cycle is due to reach its peak in May 2013.

The particle showers caused by solar activity are responsible for aurorae – the spectacular northern and southern light shows seen near Earth's polar regions. These are produced as electrically charged solar particles are drawn down onto the planet's magnetic poles where they collide with particles of gas in the atmosphere, giving off flashes of light in the process. Astronomers have witnessed similar auroral light shows on the planets Jupiter and Saturn.

Electric overload

The first solar storm observed was a CME recorded by English astronomer Richard Carrington in 1859. Eighteen hours later the night sky lit up with a bright aurora. Telegraph operators received electric shocks and in some cases were even able to operate their systems with the batteries disconnected – relying entirely on the current induced in the telegraph wires by the barrage of electrically charged solar particles.

This is the big concern over such outbursts from the sun. Although our planet's thick atmosphere and magnetic field generally keep us shielded from the solar radiation, the magnetic disturbance created can wreak havoc with sensitive electronics. This happens because of a phenomenon called electromagnetic induction. It was discovered in 1831 by English physicist Michael Faraday, who noticed that moving a wire through a magnetic field generates a current in the wire

Lucky Apollo: a narrow brush with a solar storm

Violent outbursts from the sun already take their toll on unmanned satellites in Earth orbit. But space weather is also a deadly hazard to astronauts. So much so that the crew of the Earth-orbiting International Space Station (ISS) must take cover in specially shielded areas during times of high solar activity.

The Apollo astronauts travelling to the moon and back were simply lucky. The *Apollo 16* mission returned to Earth in April 1972 and *Apollo 17*, the final mission in the program, blasted off in December that year. Right in between, in August, the sun unleashed an enormous coronal mass ejection – a shower of high-energy particles that strafed the Earth, and the moon.

It's likely an astronaut walking on the moon's surface when this CME hit would have been exposed to a radiation blast of 400–1000rem. That's a potentially deadly dose. One rem (short for Röntgen equivalent in man) is about what you would receive from a medical CT scan. It doesn't pose any long-term risk. Even 50rem will only induce temporary minor changes to your body. However, 400rem will make you quite seriously ill, with a significant risk of death. While at the upper end, 1000rem is invariably fatal. With no atmosphere or magnetic field to guard against radiation, the moon is an extremely exposed place. Paper-thin spacesuits offer little protection either. Any moonwalkers caught in the solar blast of August 1972 would have been in urgent need of medical attention.

Astronauts remaining aboard the spacecraft would have been better protected by its aluminium hull, which would cut the dose to around 40-100rem. The shielded modules of the ISS have hulls that are twice as thick again, reducing the dose to just a few rem – which is relatively harmless. Fittingly, studies of particles from solar flares and CMEs lodged in moon rocks returned by the Apollo astronauts has contributed greatly to our understanding of these violent yet enigmatic storms in space.

– and, conversely, passing a current through a moving wire gives rise to a magnetic field. This would form the basis for how dynamo generators and electric motors work.

During a solar storm, the Earth's magnetic field is pummelled by charged solar particles, causing it to reel this way and that. These large magnetic variations then set up, via induction, geomagnetically induced currents (GICs) in any conducting materials at the Earth's surface. Large GICs can have the power to fry computer chips, trip circuit breakers and scramble communications: a large solar flare in 1972 brought down telephone networks in Illinois. GICs measuring from tens to hundreds of amps have been recorded at high latitudes, where the Earth's magnetic field is at its strongest.

Astronaut Charles M. Duke Jr., *Apollo 16* Lunar Module pilot, collecting samples at Station No. 1 at the Descartes landing site. Duke is standing at the rim of Plum crater. The lunar rover can be seen in the background.

Spacecraft in Earth orbit can also get their systems cooked by GICs, and can even be sent hurtling back to Earth by the associated solar storm. That's because the storm's heating effect causes the atmosphere to expand, introducing a drag force that pulls the spacecraft down. This was the case with the *Skylab* space station, which fell back to Earth in 1979 following unexpectedly high levels of solar activity.

Hot in the shade

A NASA report compiled in 2009 concluded that the damage caused by solar storms to ground-based electrical systems has the potential to cost the American economy alone $2 trillion, just during the first year of recovery – and that full repairs could take as long as ten years.

Mitigation strategies are inherently limited in their scope. It's not for lack of warning. Astronomers usually detect a CME or solar flare hours and even days in advance of the particles striking the planet. And the raft of solar-observing spacecraft stationed between the Earth and the sun give us a final heads-up as much as an hour before impact. The trouble is that whereas people can dive into a shelter, our vulnerable systems and infrastructure cannot. And shielding every kilometre of cable, and every building that houses electronic equipment, is simply not practical. The only option that remains is to install safeguards that make it possible to shield sensitive systems and isolate them at the flick of a switch, thus containing the damage. Such safeguards are being implemented.

And not a moment too soon. As the modern world becomes increasingly reliant on electronic technology, the potential damage caused by solar storms is only going to increase. Looking to the far future, it's difficult to tell how far this trend may continue. But to give an extreme example, we should hope that a civilization which, for example, chooses to upload the mind of all its citizens into a computer (see p.272), would first come up with a reliable solution to the solar storm problem before placing its very existence at the mercy of the capricious sun.

Killer sun?

We can at least take comfort in one fact. It's very unlikely a solar storm could ever deliver a radiation dose that's lethal to biological life on Earth. Our star is presently going through a very stable period of its life, when its overall output is at its most predictable – a fact reinforced by the existence of the regular eleven-year solar cycle. The outbursts we've seen already are probably the worst that our sun is capable of. Given we have lived to tell the tale so far, we should be safe enough (that is, assuming a storm doesn't strike during a geomagnetic field reversal – see p.231).

But not all stars are so well behaved. In 2006, NASA's *Swift* probe – a spacecraft that monitors high-energy radiation from space – detected a colossal flare from the star II Pegasi, 135 light years away in the constellation of Pegasus. The flare emitted X-rays, far more intense than those used in any hospital or ever given off by our own sun. Indeed, if the sun had sent a similar outburst in our direction, it would almost certainly have led to a mass extinction of life on Earth.

That might not be something we need to worry about now. But it's a reminder that when the human race eventually becomes a space-faring civilization, we should probably exercise some caution when selecting the star systems in which we choose to set up camp.

Death rays from the stars

the savageness of supernovae

Stars are the powerhouses of outer space, churning out almost unimaginable quantities of energy. In the last section, we saw what a threat the tempestuous outbursts from the sun can pose to the Earth – even though the sun is normally regarded as the giver of life on our planet. But the sun isn't the only star that can cause us problems. When massive stars in deep space reach the end of their lives, they detonate in colossal explosions known as supernovae. And if one of these ever went off within a few hundred light years of the solar system, it could be curtains for us all.

Live fast, die young

Supernova explosions are the fates that await stars heavier than ten times the mass of our own sun. With so much extra weight compressing them and heating their interiors, these stars can burn up all their fuel in as little as a million years – one ten-thousandth of the sun's life expectancy.

When there's nothing left to burn, the centre of the star abruptly cools and contracts, collapsing inwards. The layers above soon follow, piling down on the compressed mass at the core until the density there becomes so great that the material falling in momentarily jams solid and then bounces violently back outwards. The result is a monumental explosion, filling nearby space with high-speed debris and deadly radiation.

Meanwhile, at the heart of the dying star the terrific pressure can create superdense remnant objects which survive the explosion. These include white dwarfs (stars that pack the mass of the sun into an object the size of the Earth), neutron stars (which condense a solar mass down into a sphere just 15km across) and black holes (in which the core becomes so dense that not even light can escape its gravity).

Supernovae do actually serve a good purpose too. In fact, if it wasn't for these savage cosmic blasts neither you nor I would be here right now. As various musicians have pointed out, we are all made of star dust. That's because all the chemical elements heavier than hydrogen and helium, upon which biochemistry depends, were forged in the nuclear fires at the centres of massive stars. Supernovae scatter these elements across space. Without them, life on Earth – or anywhere else in the universe – could never have arisen.

Danger zone

In 1987, a supernova went off in the Large Magellanic Cloud (LMC) – a satellite galaxy of our Milky Way. This nearby detonation at a known distance allowed astronomers to calculate the intensity of the radiation supernovae typically kick out. And this in turn permitted estimates of the range within which the explosions are likely to pose a lethal threat to life. This is now generally accepted at several hundred light years.

Happily, there are no big bright stars – obvious supernova candidates – within this distance of the Earth. However, some dimmer stars are also thought to be capable of going supernova. If a dim white dwarf is in a binary star system, where one star is orbiting around another, then the white dwarf's gravity can pull matter from its companion star and compress it sufficiently to detonate a supernova. Astronomers have warned that the binary star IK Pegasi, 150 light years from Earth, might be just such a system. And there could be others that we've yet to detect – making these potentially the most dangerous kind of supernova explosion.

Stellar snipers

There could also be danger from further afield. Bright stars destined to go supernova typically weigh no more than about a hundred times the mass of the sun. But there is an even bigger, fiercer kind of supernova – unleashed by the death of Wolf-Rayet stars (which can weigh up to three hundred solar masses). It's known as a hypernova.

Hypernovae are thought to give out intense blasts of gamma rays – extremely high-energy electromagnetic radiation. These gamma-ray bursts have been detected by space-based gamma-ray detectors since the 1960s. In the 1990s, their origin was traced to stars in dis-

Stellar exterminators

When big stars reach the ends of their lives they have an annoying habit of exploding and, in the process, ruining things for anyone who happens to be on a planet nearby. Here are the top five (in terms of proximity to us) stellar explosions waiting to happen:

Star	Constellation	Distance (ly)	Type of star
IK Pegasi	Pegasus	150	Binary
Betelgeuse	Orion	640	Red supergiant
RS Ophiuchi	Ophiuchus	5000	Recurrent nova
Eta Carinae	Carina	7500	Wolf-Rayet
WR104	Sagittarius	8000	Wolf-Rayet

tant galaxies, meaning that their energy output – in order to cross the gulf of intergalactic space – must be off the chart.

The bursts are created by gravitational energy released during a hypernova by the in-falling matter at the star's centre. But instead of being given off evenly in all directions, the radiation is concentrated into two beams emitted from the poles of the star. This happens because the star's rotation generally pulls in-falling material into a disc around its equator. The disc is incredibly dense, making it impossible for any radiation to pass through it. The only escape route is through the more rarefied material at the polar regions.

Hypernovae, and their associated gamma-ray bursts, are rare events: the Milky Way is thought to host one roughly once every two hundred million years. The plus side is that the polar beaming effect means there's a chance that even if one does go off it will miss us. The minus side is that the same effect boosts the lethality range of the resulting gamma burst to many thousands of light years.

Radiation hazard

If a gamma-ray burst, or a supernova blast wave, were to strike the Earth, what would the effects be? Studies suggest the most destructive aspect would be decimation of the ozone layer which serves to absorb harmful radiation from space. The gamma rays would split apart nitrogen in the atmosphere, which would then combine with oxygen to form nitric oxides – compounds that are highly destructive to ozone. Ice cores recovered from Antarctica show supporting evidence for this, in the form of enhanced nitrate content corresponding to the times of known supernova explosions: in AD 1006 and AD 1054.

With the ozone layer stripped away, intense UV rays from the sun would now stream through to the ground below, causing a massive extinction of life on the planet's surface and in the upper layers of the oceans. Other effects would include acid rain and global cooling as chemical changes in the atmosphere created murky gases, obscuring the sun's light.

Bruce Lieberman, a palaeontologist at the University of Kansas, has suggested that a supernova or gamma burst could have been responsible for a mass extinction that took place 440 million years ago, at the end of the Ordovician period of Earth's prehistory, in which sixty percent of life in the planet's oceans died. This mass extinction is normally blamed on an ice age. However, Lieberman argues that the duration of the ice age was unusually short, suggesting some freak effect may have caused it – such as global cooling resulting from irradiation of the planet's atmosphere.

Neutrino warning

So how might humans survive such an event? The only hope we'd have is to pile into pre-built radiation shelters with enough supplies to see us through while either the planet's ozone layer repairs itself or we patch it up ourselves, using some hypothetical future tech. The trouble, of course, is knowing when a nearby star is about to pop so we can all take cover in time. After all, spending your entire life underground as a precautionary measure could make for a rather dismal existence.

But there could be a solution. Roughly three hours before the 1987 supernova in the LMC showed up in optical telescopes, a number of physics experiments detected a seemingly inexplicable rush of ghostly subatomic particles called neutrinos. These particles are thought to be given off as a by-product of particle physics reactions deep inside supernovae and hypernovae, as the terrific pressures squash protons and electrons together to form neutrons.

Neutrinos pass through almost all intervening matter, allowing them to stream out from the core of the dying star before the deadly radiation is released. This could be our advance warning. Currently there are at least three astronomical neutrino detectors in service around the world. And we should probably keep a close eye on their findings – the next stellar explosion may not be for millions of years, but it could happen tomorrow.

The geomagnetic yo-yo

Our planet is one great big magnet. Stretching from the Arctic to the Antarctic is a huge magnetic field that threads through the planet's centre and then arches tens of thousands of kilometres out into space. Earth's magnetic field is still used for navigation by humans –

and some animal species. It also protects our planet against some of the hazardous radiation that batters it from space.

But there's evidence in the fossil record that the Earth's magnetic field can spontaneously flip, with north and south literally changing places. Studies suggest that, during these geomagnetic reversals, the overall strength of the planet's magnetic field drops. And this has fuelled speculation that these events may allow harmful radiation from space to rain down on the planet's surface, with dire consequences for terrestrial life.

Our dipole field

Much of the radiation that strikes planet Earth isn't really radiation at all – at least, not in the strictest sense. So-called cosmic rays are usually made of high-energy particles that have been accelerated to high speed by the shock waves from supernova explosions, or belched out from the raging cores of bright galaxies. The radiation showers that follow solar flares and coronal mass ejections from the sun are also made of particles.

The thing all these particles have in common is that they are electrically charged. As British physicist Michael Faraday proved in the early nineteenth century, electric and magnetic fields interact with one another to influence their respective movements. Put simply, the path of an electrically charged particle is deflected by the presence of a magnetic field. A charged radiation particle from space will then be slowed down and even deflected away entirely by its interaction with the Earth's magnetic field. And this, combined with the cushioning effect of the atmosphere, has helped create a safe environment in which life on Earth has been able to evolve.

The Earth is thought to have had a magnetic field all of its life. It's what's called a dipole field, which means it has two poles – labelled north and south. Other magnetic dipoles, such as an ordinary bar magnet, will try to align themselves with the field. And this is how a navigational compass works, using a needle-shaped bar magnet that's free to swivel: thus pointing the way to magnetic north. Research has shown that some animals, such as bats, are also able to sense their orientation to the Earth's magnetic field and thus use it to get their bearings. One theory says that they do this thanks to particles of magnetically sensitive iron oxide within special cells in their bodies.

Nevertheless, this ability is all the more amazing when you consider how weak the Earth's field actually is. At the planet's surface, it measures between thirty and sixty microteslas – which is about one-thousandth the strength of a typical fridge magnet.

The field itself is generated in the bowels of the planet. Swirling currents of molten conducting metals, such as iron and nickel, in the Earth's outer core generate magnetism through the dynamo effect. The magnetic field then feeds back, creating more electric currents, which in turn generate even stronger magnetic fields – making the system highly non-linear.

It's all gone south

The first evidence that the Earth's magnetic poles can swap places turned up in studies of the ocean floor. Magnetic measurements of the rock that the ocean floor is made of revealed "stripes" of different magnetic orientation. This was later interpreted in terms of sea-floor spreading sites – long ridges at the bottom of the ocean, where new sea floor is being created as molten magma bubbles up from below. Atoms and molecules in the magma align their magnetic axes in the direction of the prevailing magnetic field, and this orientation then gets locked in as the magma solidifies and moves away from the ridge, leaving a distinct magnetic stripe in the ocean floor. The discovery of these stripes was then a clear signal that the planet's magnetic field has been reversing over time. Studies of the stripes also showed that during a reversal the overall strength of the Earth's field weakens.

There appear to have been tens of thousands of geomagnetic field reversals since the planet formed. And yet there is no obvious rhyme or reason to their timing. During some periods of the planet's prehistory, the magnetic polarity has remained unchanged for tens of millions of years. However, at other times reversals have been separated by as little as fifty thousand years – a heartbeat in geological terms. The last reversal took place 780,000 years ago.

The non-linearity governing the production of the Earth's magnetic field in the planet's core could offer a clue to the cause of geomagnetic reversals. Non-linear systems in physics are often

Cosmic radiation let in by a weakening magnetic field (bad science of the silliest kind) destroys San Francisco's Golden Gate Bridge in *The Core* (2003), a sci-fi disaster movie wondering what would happen if the Earth's molten core ceased to rotate.

prone to "chaotic" behaviour, in which the future state of a system is extremely sensitive to its initial conditions. The weather is another example. Computer simulations of the motion of conducting fluids in the Earth's core support this view: reversals have even taken place in some computer models that have been run. However, like the weather, if chaos is the cause then predicting reversals far in advance is virtually impossible.

That hasn't stopped people from trying. It's been noted that, over the last 150 years, the strength of the Earth's field has declined by ten to fifteen percent. Extrapolations from this trend suggest that the field could drop to zero in the next 1500–1600 years, leading to concerns that a reversal could be imminent. The truth is that we cannot say when the next one will be. Humans have yet to measure the build-up to a field reversal (we were at the *Homo erectus* stage of our evolution when the last one struck), so we simply don't know what to look for. Most geologists agree that the present downtrend is probably a blip that will turn around again before long.

Shields down?

Would a magnetic field reversal, when it finally happens, really expose the Earth to a potential mass extinction of life? The magnetic

Core control: a radical solution

What if the Earth's magnetic field did suddenly die on us, due to a geomagnetic reversal? Chances are we could survive thanks to the protection afforded by the atmosphere. But what if the reversal coincided with an imminent outburst of cosmic radiation – such as the collision of two neutron stars just a few light years away, or a solar maximum the likes of which we've never seen before?

Perhaps the most realistic course of action is to build physical shielding – thick layers of lead and concrete that we could shelter under, and which would also serve to protect critical elements of our infrastructure that are prone to radiation attack, such as computer systems and communication networks. Another, more futuristic, option might be to try and generate an artificial magnetic field around the Earth, perhaps using the world's biggest ever superconducting magnet.

A third, somewhat more fanciful strategy, was explored in the sci-fi movie *The Core* (2003). In this story, the Earth's core has stopped spinning, switching off the planet's magnetic field and exposing us to killer cosmic radiation. The solution, it's decided, is to send a team of geologists down to the core to start it spinning again. The temperature at the centre of the planet is 7000°C: hotter than the surface of the sun. So, in the real world at least, sending people there is almost certainly out of the question. However, it might be possible to send a robot. In a paper published in the science journal *Nature* in 2003 David Stevenson, of the California Institute of Technology, put forward a scheme by which we could send a robotic probe down to the core.

He proposed using a nuclear bomb to open a crack in the planet's crust. Into this would be poured 100,000 tonnes of molten iron (roughly equal to the amount produced by the world's foundries every week). The robot would be dropped in with the iron which, owing to its weight, would then sink down to the core over the space of a week or so. Stevenson proposed communicating with the probe using seismic waves – sound vibrations transmitted through the Earth.

All well and good, though quite what we could do with the robot once it got there isn't clear. In *The Core*, a nuclear detonation was used to restart the planet's heart. However, the core is nearly 7000km across – twice the size of the moon. Making this spin is going to take a lot more than a nuclear blast – or probably anything else we can muster in the immediate future.

imprints left in volcanic rocks and on the ocean floor suggest that the reversals don't happen overnight, but can take thousands to tens of thousands of years. So could life on Earth really survive a lowering of its magnetic shield for such an extended period?

The plain fact is that it already has. Terrestrial life has endured many thousands of these reversals – and is still here to tell the tale. It could be that the Earth's atmosphere is able to take up the slack in fending off radiation particles while the magnetic field recovers its strength. The atmosphere is, after all, equivalent to several metres of concrete in its radiation screening ability. Alternatively, say scientists, the solar wind – the steady stream of charged particles blowing out from the sun – may be able to set up its own protective magnetic shield as it billows around the planet.

Then again, perhaps we shouldn't just assume that things will necessarily turn out okay. As we have seen, radiation from space can, now and again, pose a lethal threat to Earth – and that's when the magnetic field is working as advertised. It may be that in the past Earth has simply been lucky, and a field reversal has never coincided with one of the universe's deadliest radiation outbursts.

As with crossing the road, making a transatlantic flight or being struck by lightning, the odds are against you losing your life this way – but the risk is nevertheless there.

Planetary billiards

wandering stars (and planets)

The planets go around the sun as regularly as clockwork. And yet sometimes, of course, clocks can go wrong. Humanity's long-term existence on planet Earth relies on the behaviour of the solar system remaining stable for many years into the future. But some recent studies by astronomers suggest this is by no means guaranteed. They have run computer simulations of planetary orbits that extend for billions of years into the future, which seem to show a small probability that Mercury and Mars could wander from their regular paths and careen around the inner solar system like billiard balls on a baize table. Needless to say, this would be very bad news indeed.

Orbital migration

One of the first clues that planets don't always stay where they're put came not from our solar system but from the first planets found in orbit around other stars beyond. These planets weren't seen directly through a telescope, but rather their presence was inferred by making precise measurements of their host star's position. Just as a star's massive gravity has a massive effect on the position of a planet, so a planet's relatively small gravity has a small – but measurable – effect on the position of a star. This makes the star wobble slightly, and the size and frequency of the wobbles can be used to infer the mass of the planet and its orbital radius.

But when the astronomers calculated these quantities in the late 1990s, they were in for a surprise. The masses of the first planets around other stars tended to be comparable with our own gas giant planet Jupiter. And yet their orbital radii were just a tenth the radius of Mercury's orbit around the sun. This was totally at odds with the theory of planet formation – that gas-giant worlds must form far from their stars, otherwise their gaseous outer layers get stripped away by the star's radiation. The only way these so-called "hot Jupiters" could exist was if they had formed far away from their stars and then somehow migrated inwards to their present positions. Planets, it seemed, can shift their orbits.

How to move a planet

This led astrophysicists to investigate theoretical schemes by which this could happen. And they soon came up with several of them. The favourite one for explaining the hot Jupiters involves a "drag effect" from gas and dust in the disc of material surrounding the star. This gas and dust is the material from which the planets originally formed. It has long since gone from our solar system – having either condensed into planets and asteroids or been blasted away by the sun. But it's still there in the new solar systems being discovered. The drag effect that the gas and dust exerts on a planet moving through it saps the planet's momentum, causing it to spiral inwards towards the star. Although there's no way this particular mechanism can lead to migration in our own solar system, it inspired astrophysicists to investigate other theories that might do so. And, sure enough, they found one.

In fact, it was a phenomenon that physicists had known about since the days of Isaac Newton, but which could only really be investigated with the help of powerful computers. It's called the "n-body problem" – that is, how to describe the motion of "n" (a number of) celestial objects all moving under the influence of each other's gravity. It's an easy matter to do this when n equals two. Accordingly, the most simplistic models for the solar system work by plotting each planet's motion according to the gravitational interaction between just that planet and the sun.

In reality though, every planet is experiencing some degree of gravitational force from all the other planets, which means that "n=2" is only an approximation to the true picture. This approximation presumes a solar system that's indefinitely stable: usually the extra contribution from the other planets is very small, meaning that in the short term we can expect the planets to be well-behaved. But will this always be the case? Finding the answer to that means solving mathematical equations when n equals three or more. And because this is so much harder, for years no one knew whether the solar system would be stable in the long run.

Number crunching

In 2008, two independent groups of astrophysicists decided to bring powerful computers to bear on the problem. Although the equations when n is greater than 2 cannot be solved exactly, in theory it's possible for a computer to get the answer by brute force, as it were: plugging in numbers and tweaking them until all the sums add up correctly. Of course, a human could do this too, but it would take them decades. A computer can get the answer overnight.

Jacques Laskar, of the Observatoire de Paris, in France, ran 1001 simulations of the future evolution of the solar system, each with ever-so-slightly different initial conditions. He found that in a very small number of the simulations – around one to two percent of them – the orbit of the planet Mercury becomes stretched out by the gravity of Jupiter. Compared to the other planets of the solar system,

Mercury already has quite an oval orbit. But in Laskar's model, the planet's path becomes so elongated that it strays dangerously close to the orbit of Venus.

Laskar's findings are backed up by similar work, carried out by Gregory Laughlin and Konstantin Batygin, at the University of California in Santa Cruz. Their simulations turned up one scenario in which the planet Mercury was cast into the sun 1.3 billion years from now, and another in which Mars gets ejected into interstellar space in 820 million years, followed 40 million years after that by a head-on smash between Mercury and Venus.

Earth's gyroscope: the moon

Not all big collisions with planet-sized objects are bad news. Shortly after the Earth formed it is believed to have undergone an enormous smash-up with a body comparable in size to the planet Mars. The debris from this impact later coalesced to form the moon. And just as well for us – the moon has acted as a set of stabilizer wheels for the Earth, preventing the planet from tilting too far towards or away from the sun, and has thus kept the long-term climate stable enough for life to evolve.

Violent events on Earth, such as the collision of giant asteroids, and even major seismic events, like the shifting patterns of the continents, have the potential to alter the planet's tilt. It's currently tipped over by 23.5 degrees, relative to the plane in which the planets orbit the sun – and this is responsible for the planet's seasons. When the Earth's tilt makes it lean towards the sun, the sun's light is concentrated over a small area of the Earth's surface. This is summer. But when it's leaning away, the light is spread over a larger area – and this corresponds to winter. Disruptions to this steady cycle would be catastrophic and can even trigger the onset of ice ages.

Of course, the Earth has endured ice ages in the past. But these would probably have been more frequent and more severe were it not for the influence of the moon. Why? The centrifugal effect of Earth's rotation causes it to bulge outwards around its equator so that its shape is an oblate spheroid (resembling an M&M) rather than a perfect sphere. Because the Earth is tilted to the orbital plane of the moon, the moon's gravity is able to pull on these two equatorial bulges. It's rather like the bulges are attached to the moon by a pair of reins. These then stop the planet's tilt from undergoing any radical changes.

And just as well. Or the Earth could have ended up like the outer world Uranus, which is tilted by over 90 degrees, and rolls around its orbit on its side. Needless to say, this is not a recipe for climatic stability.

In the limited number of simulation runs that each team carried out there were no collisions explicitly involving the Earth. But with the inner solar system thrown into chaos it certainly couldn't be ruled out. A collision between Earth and another planet – even the relatively lightweight Mercury – would be a catastrophe many times worse than the impact of the largest asteroid. The energy of the smash would be so great that the Earth's surface would be entirely melted, and would remain in a molten state – an ocean of lava at a temperature of several thousand degrees – for at least a thousand years.

Such an event would be an instant game over for anyone foolish enough to have hung around on the planet. This would definitely be one instance in which fortune does not favour the brave, but rather those who proceeded directly to the lifeboats.

There goes the sun

it won't be around forever

In 6.5 billion years' time the sun will die. The path to that end is a turbulent one, and it will render the Earth a lifeless cinder. Today, the sun is what astronomers call a main sequence dwarf. It measures 1.4 million km across and weighs 2 billion billion billion tons. The sun is currently 4.5 billion years old and its power source is nuclear fusion – binding together nuclei of hydrogen in its high-temperature core to produce helium and a lot of energy. The sun converts roughly 600 million tons of hydrogen into helium every second, maintaining its surface at a temperature of about 5500°C.

The sun has already burned up fifty percent of its hydrogen fuel. As it slowly converts its core from hydrogen to helium, it grows bigger and brighter – at a rate of about ten percent every billion years. By the time the sun is eight billion years old (3.5 billion years from now), it will be about forty percent brighter than it is today. Indeed, in the past the sun was much dimmer – and this may have slowed the development of life on Earth. At present, although climate-change headlines may suggest otherwise, we are enjoying the golden age of the sun's relationship with life on Earth. In the future, solar brightening will make life here once again more difficult – until ultimately it becomes impossible.

Welcome to hell

In 3.5 billion years' time, assuming the human race is still around, the temperature on the Earth's surface will get so hot that the oceans will boil. Snow and ice will become the stuff of legend as the planet's surface bakes. All natural life will become extinct – even the hardiest extremophile organisms. Humans might just about be able survive for a time in specially protected and cooled shelters underground. It's possible some die-hards might remain in such accommodation, preferring to live out the rest of their days on the planet they've called home all their lives. At the end, just a few bold scientists might remain, carefully monitoring Earth's final hours.

But eventually, evacuation will be the only option for everyone. Remember, this will be billions of years in the future and we should hope that, in the time between now and then, we will have perfected space travel to the point that transporting the population of the entire planet is feasible. If we are still around it's likely we will have already colonized other worlds – providing an interstellar infrastructure that's able to provide new homes for the exodus of refugees fleeing from humanity's place of origin. Interestingly, given how it has tradi-tionally been treated in sci-fi novels, Mars may become habitable for a time, and so could be a temporary sanctuary for us.

We might also hope that the zoologists and botanists of the future Earth will have taken a leaf from Noah's book, and gathered samples of Earth's fauna and flora before the planet is incinerated. These might not be physical plants and animals, but gene sequences stored on computer – which could later be synthesized into DNA and implanted into biological cells to re-animate these species into living, breathing organisms.

The swelling sun

The sun's core will finally run out of hydrogen fuel about six billion years from now. Nuclear reactions in the core will then stop and the centre of the sun, with no nuclear fire to sustain it, will begin to cool down and slowly contract. But this compression will warm up the helium gas in the core, and its intense radiation will then puff up the sun's outer envelope.

By the time our star is ten billion years old, this process will inflate the sun to as much as two hundred times its size today. The expansion, however, will cool the surface down to around 2800°C – a temperature that will radiate mainly red light. For this reason, the sun would then be described as a red giant star. This growth phase will be bad news for the inner planets. Mercury will be the first to go, then Venus. These planets will disappear beneath the sun's surface and their orbits will then decay rapidly as "gas drag" from the sun's envelope saps their energy, causing them to spiral into its fiery heart.

Earth's ultimate fate is uncertain. Because gravity is inversely proportional to size, as the aging sun swells its gravity will diminish. And this will allow its powerful radiation to blow material away from its surface, diminishing its gravity still further. This process will

Danny Boyle's movie *Sunshine* (2007) tells of a desperate deep-space mission to re-ignite our dying sun using, surprise surprise, nuclear bombs. The spacecraft is equipped with specially designed mirrors and filters to protect the crew from the sun's searing heat and glaring light. Still, not nearly enough of them take the sensible advice of "never looking directly at the sun" anything like as seriously as they should...

reduce the sun's mass to just 68 percent of what it is today. And the overall reduction in gravity means that the sun will loosen its grip on the planets, causing their orbits to widen.

A study in 2001 by astronomers at the University of Sussex had suggested that this orbital migration effect would save the Earth from being devoured by the expanding sun. However, revisions to their calculations published in 2008, now suggest that the Earth may slip beneath the sun's surface after all. Its fate will be on a knife edge.

Final fling

The sun itself will begin the final stage of its life around 6.5 billion years from now. With no hydrogen left in its core for nuclear fusion, the core will contract until the temperature is hot enough to ignite helium instead. This will sustain it for a hundred million years or so before helium supplies run low too. Next on the list of possible nuclear fuels that would sustain it are carbon and oxygen, but a low-mass star like the sun could never generate the temperatures needed in its core to ignite these heavier chemical elements. Instead it will burn the remaining dregs of its helium in fits and starts, which will cause the outer layers of the star to pulsate violently.

The pulsations will last for around four hundred thousand years and gradually blow the sun's outer layers of gas away into space. And so we reach the end of the sun's life, aged eleven billion years old. It will leave a beautiful corpse, called a planetary nebula. This is a cloud of gas, formerly the sun's outer envelope, gloriously illuminated by a pinprick of intense light at its centre. The pinprick is a white dwarf star, the remnant of the sun's core. The white dwarf will weigh about half the mass of the present-day sun and be roughly the same size as the Earth. Although it will have no energy source of its own, its temperature will be enormous – over 100,000°C. That, coupled with its small size, means it will keep shining for many billions of years.

It's possible some of the planets of the solar system will survive the cataclysm – including Earth, if it can escape falling into the sun. Astronomers have found evidence for planets orbiting known white dwarf stars. It may be that the remnant cinder of the Earth could continue to circle the final glowing ember of the sun. Perhaps the system will serve as an interstellar monument to the birthplace of humanity – somewhere our spacefaring descendents might come to visit, and pay their respects, for many millions of generations to come.

The end of the universe
it's time to face the final curtain

In his novel *The Restaurant At the End of the Universe* (1980), the late science-fiction author Douglas Adams imagined a fictional eatery where diners could relax over a meal and watch the ultimate demise of the cosmos unfold in front of them. Most astronomers would no doubt welcome the opportunity to visit such an establishment in the real world. At the moment, there are numerous ideas as to how our universe will ultimately end its days, but – while certain theories seem more likely than others – there is as yet no absolutely conclusive evidence of exactly how it will end.

Two ultimate fates

There are essentially two principle fates for our universe. Space has been expanding ever since the universe popped into existence in the Big Bang, a little under fourteen billion years ago. This was discovered in the 1920s by American astronomer Edwin Hubble. He found that distant galaxies are all receding away from us and that the speed of recession is directly proportional to each galaxy's distance – a finding which has since become known as Hubble's law.

This is exactly what you'd expect if the universe is expanding at a constant rate. Try this simple experiment: draw dots on the surface of a balloon. Now inflate the balloon, and you will see every dot move away from every other dot.

Albert Einstein, when he initially applied the general theory of relativity to the universe at large, thought space would be static and unchanging – meaning the universe had no beginning and will have no end. But the realization that space expands meant that the universe is changing with time. Astrophysicists soon realized this meant that the universe must have had a beginning – which we now call the Big Bang – and that sooner or later (hopefully later), it will very

Countdown to extinction

▶ One billion years from now

The sun's output has increased by ten percent, making the surface of the Earth too hot for liquid water to exist. Humans may be able to live on in shielded bunkers. But for all natural life on the planet, the final great mass extinction begins.

▶ 3.5 billion years

The sun is now 40 percent brighter and has made the Earth a hot trap, locked in an extreme greenhouse effect similar to that which bakes the surface of Venus today. No life remains on the surface. And even the most intrepid or foolhardy humans will have fled.

▶ Six billion years

The sun runs out of hydrogen fuel in its core and begins burning helium instead. This causes it to swell up, becoming a 'red giant' star – engulfing Mercury, Venus, and possibly the Earth too.

▶ 6.5 billion years

The sun's supply of helium fuel begins to run low. This makes the sun unstable, leading to waves of pulsation in its outer layers.

▶ Over 6.5 billion years

The sun's pulsations soon become violent enough to slough off its outer layers, creating a glorious 'planetary nebula' with a hot, dense white dwarf star at its centre.

▶ One million billion years

The sun's white dwarf remnant has cooled to become the same temperature as the background universe. The light at the centre of the solar system finally goes out.

likely come to an end.

The two possibilities for how that end might transpire became clear. Either the universe will continue to expand forever, gradually diluting its contents away to nothing. Or, at some point in the future, the expansion will be halted by gravity and turn back in on itself – causing the cosmos to recollapse.

Dark future

The first scenario is known as "heat death". Happily, it doesn't really start to bite for another trillion (one thousand billion) years. At this point all the raw materials from which stars are made – primarily hydrogen and helium gas – run out. From here on, no more new stars are born. Gradually, the last generation begins to wink out. The

Will we bounce back – literally?

One recent model of the universe actually suggests that space and time might live forever. Rather than collapsing or expanding indefinitely, the "ekpyrotic" theory (after the Greek word for "conflagration") is an example of a cyclic universe model in which space expands and then contracts. But rather than winking out of existence in a Big Crunch at the end of the contracting phase it bounces back – rising phoenix-like from the ashes to undergo another cycle of expansion. And so on, ad infinitum.

The ekpyrotic theory was put forward by physicists Neil Turok and Paul Steinhardt. It's a consequence of an idea in particle physics known as brane theory, which says that the four-dimensional space and time of our universe is all part of a higher dimensional membrane-like structure.

In the ekpyrotic model two such branes – one of which hosts our universe – oscillate back and forth, periodically colliding. Each time they smash together corresponds to a new Big Bang, as the contracting universe reaches minimum size and bounces back outwards to begin a new phase of expansion.

The time between successive bounces is so long – trillions of years – that it's impossible for us to tell from current observations whether we are in an ever-expanding universe or one that will ultimately recollapse, as required by the ekpyrotic model. Indeed, recent astronomical observations put the average density of matter in the universe at almost exactly the critical value dividing between these two possible eventualities.

Future observations of the "microwave background radiation" could hold the answer though. The microwave background is rather like an echo of the Big Bang that pervades space. It's the residual radiation from the hot fires of the Big Bang, diluted to very low energy by the subsequent expansion of space. Locked away in its structure are all kinds of clues to the birth and early evolution of space. Astronomers believe high-precision measurements of the microwave background's polarisation – the alignment of the electromagnetic waves making up the radiation – could reveal whether we're living in an ekpyrotic universe.

universe steadily gets darker until, as the last stars die, it enters a new age: the Degenerate Era. The name comes from the fact that space is now mainly populated with white dwarfs and neutron stars – objects left behind by stars after they die, which are made from degenerate material (a superdense quantum state of matter).

But they aren't the only inhabitants of this bleak cosmic hinterland. Also plying the darkness are black holes. These gradually eat up the white dwarfs and neutron stars – along with all the dark matter and any remaining gas, dust and planets. A trillion trillion trillion years from now, black holes will be all that's left.

But, as Stephen Hawking has shown, even black holes don't last forever – quantum theory predicts that they slowly evaporate. And so an epic 10^{100} (a one followed by a hundred zeroes) years from now, we enter the final era of our universe as all the black holes finally disappear in a puff of particles and radiation, which are then gradually diluted away to nothing by the never-ending expansion of space.

The Big Crunch

In the heat death scenario, the universe fades away, but the alternative is a dramatic burn-out. If the universe eventually recollapses, astronomers will start to see distant galaxies stop receding away and instead start heading towards us. Space will warm up as the radiation from the Big Bang, which has been cooling for many billions of years, is squashed down and reheated. Galaxy collisions become more common as space starts to shrink down. Eventually all the galaxies will crash into one another and merge. Space soon becomes unbearably hot, as the universe plunges back into the fiery state from which it came. Stars will be ripped apart by the radiation and their dismembered "corpses" devoured by the massive black holes that lurked at the hearts of the galaxies. Planets, including Earth, will suffer a similar fate.

As the density and temperature of the universe rise, particle physics processes that took place shortly after its creation will be reversed. The four forces of nature – gravity, electromagnetism, and the strong and weak nuclear forces – will merge back together into a single unified superforce. Finally, the universe will condense into an infinite density singularity, just like the one that seeded the Big Bang billions of years ago. And then, just as suddenly as it appeared, the universe is gone. This scenario is known as the Big Crunch.

Cosmic weigh-in

Choosing between these two eventualities hangs on one thing: how heavy the universe is. If it's heavier than the critical density (which amounts to just five hydrogen atoms per cubic metre, after averaging the enormous masses of the galaxies with the yawning gulfs of space between them), then the universe will die in the Big Crunch. But if the universe is less than, or equal to, this value then it's destined for a heat death.

Weighing the universe isn't easy. Astronomers began to notice as early as the 1930s that the bright matter we can see only accounts for a tiny proportion of the universe's mass. The movements of stars and galaxies were betraying the presence of far more gravitating matter than was actually visible. This material became known as "dark matter". The situation became further complicated in the 1990s when evidence emerged that space is laced with not just invisible matter but a field of invisible energy too – which was soon christened "dark energy".

The latest measurements made by space probes suggest that the ordinary matter we can see through our telescopes accounts for just 4 percent of the total mass of the universe, while 22 percent is dark matter and the remaining 74 percent is dark energy. Armed with this information, astronomers are now able to deduce that the density of the universe is almost dead on the critical value. This means that space will probably expand forever – and that our universe is destined to meet its maker in a long, protracted heat death trillions of years from now.

Planet Titanic: the final options

Humans have a habit of bouncing back from the worst setbacks imaginable. During the fourteenth century, the Black Death reduced the human population of Europe by as much as sixty percent. Worse still, approximately seventy thousand years ago natural climatic upheaval pushed the human species to the very brink of extinction – researchers estimate that this calamity left as few as two thousand human beings on the planet. But despite this, along with countless other wars, pandemics and general bad stuff, our species has prevailed and, not only that, risen to dominate over all other life on Earth.

Apocalypse on Earth
the mother of all crises

How long can our winning run continue? And how will we as a race react if and when we are ultimately presented with a no-win scenario? If a supervolcano eruption or a large asteroid impact were to strike our planet tomorrow, most of the human race would be eradicated. There would not be enough room in underground shelters for everyone and our space technology is not yet advanced enough to evacuate more than a handful of people to orbit, not to mention the fact that astronauts today are utterly reliant on the ground for resupply and day-to-day support. So how would we cope?

When the end of the world arrives, we might expect human behaviour to quickly revert to its more barbaric roots. Technology and the comforts of modern living have in many ways tamed human society, wrapping it in a veneer of decency. But that veneer is rather thin. When our comforts are taken away and, indeed, our very survival is placed on the line, the human species will be quick to reacquaint itself with the violence and ruthlessness of its past.

So here's the situation: Armageddon is upon us (for any one of many reasons outlined in this book). Governments of all countries have declared a state of emergency, advising all surviving citizens to stay in their homes where possible. What do you do?

The essentials

Staying indoors is all very well, but not if you're going to starve to death there – clearly you're going to need food. Most of us have no more than about a week's worth in the cupboards and freezer, so a trip out will be needed in order to stock the larder. When you go, keep your wits about you and your head down. The instant the crisis kicks off, everyone will begin hoarding food and other resources. Looting will be common, and some people won't think twice about

A surreal scene from the aftermath of Hurricane Katrina's assault on New Orleans in 2005, as looters helped themselves in stores and law and order broke down.

trampling on their fellow human beings in order to secure those things for themselves.

In cities, gangs will quickly take over what resources are available – with little sympathy for those who are forced to go without. In New Orleans, for example, during the approach of Hurricane Katrina, looters stripped supermarkets bare in a few days, while the sound of gunfire was heard ringing out across the city.

If the gangs have already marked their lines by the time you decide to go shopping then you may need to get a little more creative in your search for grub. That will mean scavenging in less obvious places – going to food warehouses rather than shops, and raiding supplies from restaurants, workplace canteens and even homes if you know the owners won't be coming back.

Wherever you get it, make sure you obtain food that has a long shelf life – tinned and dried goods are the best – and if possible a high calorific density. Avoid frozen foods, as you won't be able to rely on the electricity needed to keep your freezer running. A supply of bottled water will also be useful if and when the pumps supplying running water to your home eventually pack up.

When the lights go out

It will only be a matter of time before essential services start falling over. The first to go will be the broadcasting networks. Those responsible for running TV and radio stations will soon decide that their own personal survival is more important than showing up for work. The Internet will be an early casualty too. With no one to provide essential maintenance, the net as a whole will quickly become unusable. Phone lines and networks will fail for the same reason, making communication extremely difficult. The only method of long-range communication by this time might be amateur radio.

After a few days, we can expect power grids to shut down, as nuclear electricity stations and other power plants go into safe mode or malfunction. Now we will be permanently in the dark. With electricity gone, other services that rely on it will also go into decline. The taps will eventually run dry – there'll be no more fresh water on demand. And sewage disposal will shut off, meaning you'll no longer be able to use the toilet, so all effluent will have to be buried instead. Failure to dispose of it safely could lead to the outbreak of diseases such as cholera and typhoid.

Leaving the cities

As the essential utilities become inactive, and gangs control all the resources available in the cities, the pressure will mount on any survivors to flee urban population centres and head out into the countryside.

In the early days of this new age, cities are likely to be gridlocked with traffic, which will make driving difficult. Depending on the nature of the disaster, roads will probably be blocked by debris, or – in the case of a pandemic – people may literally have died behind the wheel of their car. If you must drive, try to take a less obvious route, where the way is less likely to be blocked. It's more likely that walking will be the only option.

This presents a whole new raft of problems, most of them centring around the limited weight of equipment and provisions that it's possible to carry on your back. The most important thing to take is clean drinking water. Water is heavy but, nevertheless, it should make up

The unpleasant business of body disposal

Whatever shape or form Armageddon eventually comes in, one sobering thing is gruesomely certain: there will be an awful lot of dead bodies. Even the localized disasters that generations today have witnessed left more corpses than authorities were able to deal with. The Japanese tsunami in 2011, for example, left around 20,000 people dead or missing. Even though 99.9 percent of Japanese citizens normally opt for cremation rather than burial, mass burial was the only option in many instances. A crematorium is only able to get through a handful of bodies per day.

During a world-threatening apocalyptic scenario, there would come a point where the infrastructure needed to collect and dispose of the dead would simply cease to function. Bodies would begin to pile up in hospitals, homes, in the street – indeed everywhere.

In a major city the death toll could run into the millions. This will present a huge disease risk. For the sake of sanitation, and indeed sanity, survivors will need to get the dead in their immediate vicinity either in the ground or cremated as quickly as possible. That will mean the harrowing possibility of having to deal with deceased loved ones yourself.

at least half the amount you carry. You'll need something waterproof, such as a tarpaulin, to shelter under. Remember to pack a first-aid kit. A flashlight, a sharp knife and a way of making a fire should also be included – and, of course, some food. However, you can last for up to thirty days without eating, so don't make it the top priority. Go without water for just one day, and you'll be in a bad state.

Take a weapon of some form too – a gun, if you've got one. People won't hesitate to kill you for the resources you have: you must therefore be equipped and prepared to defend yourself with deadly force.

Where to go?

Hunting and gathering food in the wild will become a necessity if you are to survive once you have left "civilization" behind. Unless you know your plants, you should stick to a meat diet. Unpleasant as having to kill animals yourself may be, an estimated 75 percent of plant species are toxic to human physiology in one way or another. The real problem will be finding water in the wild. Today, most of us are unused to fending for ourselves: we've never had to deal with the practicalities of finding food or clean water. However, temperate regions such as the UK are at least plentiful in streams and rivers. But in warmer climes, a simple drink may be very hard to come by. Those in the warmer parts of Europe and the US may be reduced to draining water from the radiators of abandoned cars, or boiling water from the hot water tanks of old houses until it's safe to drink.

Your ultimate goal should be to hook up with other survivors: only by forming new communities, in which everyone supports one another, will humanity have any hope for long-term stability. Not all communities will be welcoming. Some will invariably take the view that their food and other resources are theirs alone and that by taking in too many people they risk there being insufficient to go round. The barricades will quickly go up. John Wyndham's novel *Day of the Triffids* (1951) provides a salutary warning about the kind of faction-alism and wrangling for power that we might expect to experience in a post-apocalyptic society: leaders of groups emerging who assume fascistic power over the terrified and bewildered communities who just want to look after their own. Written in much the same spirit,

The *Mad Max* movies imagined a barren, post-apocalyptic, dog-eat-dog world in which gangs of motorbike-riding thugs scrabble for fuel and food. Mel Gibson (above right, in *Mad Max II: The Road Warrior*, (1981) played Max through the series, invariably taking a battering, but always handy with a spanner.

John Christopher's *The Death of Grass* (1956) explores the devastating consequences to society of a terrible plague (one which kills off all grass, as you might expect from the title). It gives plenty of examples of just how quickly ordinary men and women turn to murder in order to protect their loved ones and themselves. Both books seem horribly convincing.

But perhaps a sense of humanity will prevail: maybe the more humane and forward-thinking will realize that people themselves represent the greatest resource in this horror-torn new world – and will thus greet you with open arms. Only by mustering a significant population with a spectrum of abilities will it be possible for us to build houses, restart agriculture and, ultimately, try to bring civilization back to where it was before disaster struck.

Survival tips

▶ Keep your head down

People will want what you have, and combat will certainly have become a brutal reality of everyday life in the new dog-eat-dog world. But remember, every fight you get involved in places you at risk of death or serious injury. Better to avoid combat whenever possible. You can do this by travelling along less obvious routes – avoiding main roads, for example.

▶ Water is more important than food

Bear this in mind when packing your travel bags. Avoid eating unless you have plenty of water to drink with it, as digesting the food will consume water that your body may need elsewhere.

▶ Medicines are worth their weight in gold

We take hospitals and medical care for granted, but after Armageddon there will be no such things. Getting a supply of basic medicines, such as antibiotics, local anaesthetics and antiseptics could save your life.

▶ Best defence

Make sure you have something to defend yourself with. Guns will be harder to get hold of in Europe than in the US – in which case, axes, cricket bats and kitchen knives will all need to be "seconded" for more offensive uses. You're not going to be playing much cricket, or hosting many dinner parties, anyway.

The long game

There was a time when almost everyone on the Earth had some degree of skill at surviving in the wild. Those days are long gone. We are now all too reliant on the luxuries of our modern world to help us through – and without them we are lost. The survivors of Armageddon will thus be on a steep learning curve as they attempt to recover some semblance of civilization, trying to forge communities that can provide the food, shelter and protection that will be essential if the remainder of humanity is to have a shot at long-term stability.

Putting down roots

Civilization is most likely to reboot itself in small communities. Whereas the gangs will exert a stranglehold on the cities, fighting to squeeze the last of the pre-wrapped resources from the rapidly decaying concrete jungle, other groups will start anew, trying to establish a more sustainable existence in the deserted towns and villages that pepper the countryside. Some groups may even found new settlements altogether.

Historically, settlements haven't just grown up anywhere. They've usually been centred around sites that are abundant in natural resources, such as fertile soil and trees that can be cut down and used for building materials and fuel. Not to mention rivers, which can be a source of food, motive power (such as for dams and water wheels), as well as fresh water for drinking and crop irrigation.

The survivors will have to make a living initially by primitive means. And so it won't be scientists, engineers and doctors that possess the most in-demand skills, but rather farmers and builders. A key skill that will need to be mastered swiftly is basic agriculture: the ability to grow food crops, and to grow enough of them to feed a whole community. Almost anyone can make something grow, but growing enough of it to feed yourself and all of your fellow citizens is another matter entirely. And, as any farmer knows, mastering the not inconsiderable art of successful subsistence farming is only one thing: you also need to know how to maximize your crop; and how to store and preserve food. Not all crops will be ready for harvest simultaneously. Most will need to be reaped and stored for use later. This kind of husbandry, this knowledge of the seasons, is wisdom that you don't just pick up overnight.

Food, of course, won't be the only thing we'd cultivate. As supplies of clinical drugs and medicines ran out we'd be likely to see a resurgence in the use of herbal remedies: echinacea for fighting infection during colds; feverfew to treat headaches; and peppermint for stomach upsets, to name a few. Nevertheless, these treatments will not be as effective as modern medicine. Without antibiotics, anaesthetics, antiseptics – or medical facilities in which to receive major treatments, such as surgery – life expectancies will plummet, probably by as much as two decades, in the years immediately following the disaster. To keep our spirits up, however, we will no doubt use some of our crops for that other great application of fruits and grains: namely, the brewing of alcoholic beverages.

Care in the community

For such a settlement to sustain itself will require a good deal of loyalty and trust between its members. The community dynamic might resemble that of the frontier towns in the American West during the latter years of the nineteenth century. Although such post-apocalyptic communities will generally be lawless places, a kind of community order might emerge – whereby the good of the community becomes everyone's overriding priority.

No matter how successful these new communities are, it will soon dawn on their members that they are never going to see civilization as it once was. This will be a stark realization for many. Everyone is going to have to adapt to a new way of life, and it will be those who adapt most readily that will be the most likely to survive. As the years and decades roll by, children will be born for whom this new way of existence will seem relatively normal. They will learn from their elders of the great civilization that once was, and it will be a story that they in turn will pass down to their own children. In the dark science-fiction novel *Riddley Walker* (1980) by Russell Hoban, society has been nuked back to a medieval level of technology. But remnants of history and scientific knowledge survive in the form of a Punch and Judy show, and travelling puppeteers move from village to village, keeping memories of the old ways just about alive.

Brave new world

Could such children of the apocalypse ever hope to restart civilization on the scale that planet Earth once hosted? It depends. As long as there was a large enough group of survivors who had managed to establish a stable way of life, producing their own food and everything else they need to survive, then we might be in with a chance.

The first requirement, that there be a large enough group of survivors, might well be the stumbling block. The Earth is a big place, and it would be easy for very small groups to exist in isolated pockets, unaware of each other's presence. If the Earth had been damaged so badly that there were in total just a few hundred humans alive, then the difficulty of bringing them together could be the greatest obstacle to our continued existence.

How quickly can you repopulate a planet?

The recovery time of the human population following a disaster depends, of course, on the number of survivors. The timescale might be estimated using the table below.

For example, let's say there were three hundred million people left alive (just 4.5 percent of the present-day population). The last time the population was this small was in the year AD 500. So we could then expect the recovery to take no more than 1500 years.

Date	Total human population (millions)
10,000 BC	1
5000 BC	5
2000 BC	27
1000 BC	50
AD 0	200
AD 500	300
AD 1000	400
AD 1500	500
AD 1650	600
AD 1750	750
AD 1800	900
AD 1810	1000
AD 1850	1170
AD 1900	1600
AD 1920	1830
AD 1930	2010
AD 1940	2220
AD 1950	2410
AD 1960	2970
AD 1970	3700
AD 1980	4400
AD 1990	5100
AD 2000	6080
AD 2005	6450

How long would it take to repopulate the Earth to 2012 levels? That depends on the number of survivors. An upper estimate figure would be the same amount of time it took to get the planet's population to current levels the first time around (see box opposite). That would be an upper bound because humans have evolved and become more intelligent since then – and should in theory be able to rebuild society at a faster rate, already possessing much of the knowledge they need.

However, restoring our high-tech society probably wouldn't be possible until the population has reached at least hundreds of millions. By this point there would be enough workers to provide the basics of food and shelter, allowing others to begin the task of resurrecting human science and technology. Only then could we seriously begin to think about getting civilization back to where it was when disaster struck. It would be a long and difficult road. But human tenacity might just see us through.

Bunkered: humanity lives on underground

In the 1998 movie *Deep Impact*, a giant comet is detected on a collision course with the Earth. After attempts to destroy the comet with nuclear weapons fail, the president of the United States declares the limestone caves of Missouri to be a national refuge. The underground complex is large enough to accommodate a million people – two hundred thousand of whom are pre-selected according to their profession or status, while the remaining eight hundred thousand are drawn on a lottery basis from all Americans under the age of fifty.

This is quite a likely course of action for world leaders to take in the face of an unstoppable global threat. The world is riddled with underground bunkers from the Cold War – into which a country's essential personnel were all due to file in the event of World War III. One such example is the Burlington Bunker near Corsham, in the southwest United Kingdom. Spanning a total area of 240 acres, it encompasses 60 miles of road and a railway station, and it even has its own pub. This underground city was built in the 1950s and was capable of housing over four thousand key staff in the event of a full-scale nuclear exchange. These bunkers could be adapted as impromptu Armageddon shelters, at minimal expense.

However, not all Armageddon scenarios come with a warning that they're about to happen. In the case of a deadly pandemic, everyone could be infected by the time we realize there's a problem. The insurance plan would be to keep these bunkers permanently staffed. Crews could be sealed in with all the provisions they need for a nominal time period – say, a year – after which a new detail would take over. If a disaster were to strike, while a large number of people would probably still perish, humanity as a species would at least have secured its future. For the time being.

The post-human Earth

Neville Shute's novel *On the Beach* (1957) describes a world suffering from the aftermath of a large-scale nuclear war. In the southern hemisphere, citizens are issued with suicide pills so that they can take their own lives quickly and painlessly, rather than suffer the prolonged and unpleasant fate of death by radiation sickness. Generally speaking, one of humanity's great strengths has been its irrepressible spirit. We don't give up easily – and certainly not without a fight. But, one way or another, there will inevitably come a moment when the last human left above ground will draw his or her terminal breath. Then what?

Buildings are generally constructed to last between about sixty and a few hundred years. And without maintenance these figures will probably be much reduced. Moisture in concrete that has expanded during frozen winter nights will open cracks that soon trap airborne plant seeds. The seeds will germinate and, like tree roots undermining roads and pavements, the plants will reclaim their territory as they split the buildings asunder.

Once humans have left the Earth for good, the planet will begin the slow process of recovery from man-made pollution – and from whatever environmental damage may have been caused by the calamity that killed us. Chemicals will gradually be washed out of the atmosphere, and be either carried below ground, chemically degraded or broken down biologically. Assuming the Earth hasn't passed a tipping point already, carbon dioxide levels will eventually fall, allowing the planet's climate to stabilize.

The damage wrought by human beings is nowhere more evident

A stiff upper lip: facing the world's end with dignity

In Nevil Shute's 1957 novel *On the Beach*, the northern hemisphere of the Earth has been turned into a radioactive wasteland by World War III – with the US and Russia having exchanged thousands of nuclear warheads. Vestiges of humanity cling on in the southern hemisphere, in refuges such as Australia and New Zealand. But, gradually, the radioactive pollution is spreading to encompass the whole planet. Humanity is doomed. Those human beings who remain know that the deaths of both themselves and their species is fast approaching. And yet many of them continue going about their day-to-day lives – even planning for the future – right up until the moment the fatal radioactive cloud arrives.

Nick Bostrom, the director of the University of Oxford's Future of Humanity Institute – a think-tank tasked with analysing the big problems facing our planet and our species – believes this may well be how humanity reacts to its own impending extinction. Bostrom has concluded, judging from the response of humans in real disaster situations, that it won't be panic that hampers our survival, but rather denial and complacency, driven by a failure to fully comprehend the seriousness of the situation.

He also wonders whether some people might start living their lives as perhaps they should have done all along – with greater awareness and sincerity, and focusing more on the things that really matter, such as authentic relationships. Indeed, in 2009, a study by a team of British psychologists uncovered considerable evidence for crowd solidarity in interviews with survivors of major disasters and mass emergencies ranging from terrorist bombings to crowd stampedes. Many of these people reported feelings of a shared fate that united them with others in the same predicament. Many reported strangers selflessly helping others, and order prevailing over panic – with people, for example, calmly queuing to use emergency escape routes.

than at Pripyat – the city nearest to the Chernobyl nuclear power plant that exploded in 1986. Evacuated by all humans long ago, the city has been overrun by plants and animals. Indeed, nature here is thriving. Clearly, the after-effects of a full-scale nuclear meltdown are less detrimental to the local environment than the day-to-day damage caused by human activity.

Human traffic

where to put three hundred million refugees

We would all like to think that the human species is resourceful enough to weather an Earth-shattering calamity without going totally extinct. Even so, no matter how much we plan for Judgement Day, there will always be a terrible human cost to bear. Death and suffering are inevitable in disaster scenarios, and the carnage is likely to reach horrendous scales when the fate of the very world is at stake.

The impact of a 2km-wide asteroid is thought to be capable of wiping out around a quarter of the population – some 1.5–2 billion people. A supervolcano eruption could be even worse, able to reduce the number of people on Earth to just a few thousand. And other disasters, such as pandemics, have demonstrated their terrifying ability to exterminate up to half the population from regions of the planet's surface.

Evacuation options

One way we can hope to minimize casualties is by evacuating the hardest-hit areas (or those likely to be hardest hit) as quickly and efficiently as possible. In 1955, a mayoral panel in New York concluded that it was possible to get one million people out of the very worst danger zones within an hour, if ever NYC needed to be evacuated. That would leave some three million people behind.

That figure squares with the number of people who commute in and out of city centres every day for work – and who do so in the space of a few short hours. This kind of evacuation would certainly reduce the casualties from a Hiroshima-sized atomic bomb (based on nuclear fission), but would be much less effective in the face of a much more destructive hydrogen bomb (based on nuclear fusion). Evacuating people at this rate would also allow the path of a major hurricane to be cleared, given notice of about two days – which is feasible.

But could we ever hope to evacuate a whole continent, as might well be required in the event of an asteroid impact or a supervolcanic blast? The key consideration, of course, is how much warning time we are given. In the case of a supersized asteroid or comet heading our way, it's likely that astronomers would have detected the ominous missile months or even years in advance. If possible, attempts would first be made to avert catastrophe. But if these failed then evacuation would be the only option.

It's possible we'll know the area that must be evacuated. In the event of an asteroid impact, for example, astronomers would be able to predict the impact zone on the Earth's surface with pinpoint accuracy – in much the same way that eclipse paths can be predicted years in advance. If the asteroid was due for an impact on land, this would allow the immediate vicinity to be cleared with plenty of time to spare. That would save some lives, but not all, as the global impact winter following the strike would lead to mass food shortages. More likely is that the impact would occur at sea – ocean does after all cover seventy percent of the planet's surface. This would send meg-atsunamis racing around the planet, from which no one except those

In the disaster movie *Deep Impact* (1998), the world is threatened by comets. The movie shows just how difficult it would be to get you and your family somewhere safe, when everybody else has exactly the same idea.

evacuated to the highest ground would be safe.

For events such as asteroid impacts, the time of Armageddon would be predictable almost to the second. Not so for many other catastrophes. For example, the location of a supervolcano is obviously fixed. But volcanologists are only able to give vague likelihoods – timescales of hundreds to thousands of years – as to when it will erupt. The lack of a hard deadline for evacuation in these cases might remove some of the urgency, making it likely that some residents will opt to remain. This was the case during the evacuation of New Orleans in the face of Hurricane Katrina in 2005. A mandatory evacuation order was imposed but, despite hard-and-fast predictions of the storm's imminent arrival and the damage it would cause, many people stayed in the city – seven hundred of whom perished.

Everybody out!

If we had short notice – say a week – to clear everybody out of a continent-size region, would there be time for the evacuation? Could we clear the danger zone before disaster strikes? The last mass evacuation that has been anywhere near this scale was World War II's Dunkirk rescue of 1940, when three hundred thousand retreating Allied troops were evacuated from the French coast to England over the space of about a week. The rescue was conducted by British Navy ships assisted by a flotilla of commercial vessels: passenger ships, fishing boats and practically anything that would float. The craft were hindered further by German bombardment.

Given the benefit of modern transport technology, global cooperation (most of the developed world would likely assist in the operation), not to mention the absence of Nazi-led soldiers, it seems reasonable to speculate that hundreds of millions could be evacuated from the disaster zone in time. And thus the evacuation of a large land mass, such as North America, in a week or two might just be feasible.

The question then is: where would all the evacuees go? Despite all the fears about population overcrowding on the Earth, there are large areas of the planet's surface that are only sparsely populated – such as the outback of Australia, areas of Russia and Central Africa.

Let's take Australia, for example. There are presently almost 23 million Australian citizens spread across a land area of 7.6 million square kilometres, giving a mean population density of just three people per square kilometre. This could be brought in line with that seen in more densely populated nations, such as the UK – which has a mean density of 255 inhabitants per square kilometre, and yet is hardly bursting at the seams. Raising Australia's density to this level means that, given its total land area, it could accommodate an additional 1.9 billion people. This is a truly vast capacity – more than twice the total population of South America, the United States and Canada combined. If all the people from these nations were evacuated to Australia, it would still only take the population density up to a relatively sparse 123 people per square kilometre.

To start with, the outback would be little more than a refugee camp, with very basic accommodation and facilities. A great deal of development would be needed to give Armageddon's survivors a new life that even faintly resembled the one they'd fled from. And, of course, there's the small issue of persuading Australia to relax its stern immigration policy, and allow hundreds of millions of asylum seekers across its borders. Not to mention the amount of water (and other resources) that would be needed for all these refugees. Then again, crises such as this may be just what's needed to foster some unity and cooperation between the nations of our rather disjointed world.

Noah's Ark 2.0

It's one thing to evacuate people, but what about other forms of life? Preserving biodiversity is crucial to the environmental stability of our planet – and will thus play an essential role in the recovery of the climate following a major upheaval. And so a prudent civilization would be well advised to take account of flora and fauna, as well as humans, in any emergency evacuation scheme.

Plans to preserve plant seeds are already underway. The Millennium Seed Bank Project, at London's Kew Gardens, stores 24,000 seed species (representing ten percent of the world's land plants). Naturally, this isn't the most secure location in the world, and so at the Svalbard Global Seed Vault, on the Norwegian island of Spitsbergen, 250 million seeds are kept in a secure cavern, situated 120m inside a mountain. The seed bank is 130m above sea level – guarded against the ravages of rising oceans and climate change, in a location that's volcanically inert. The idea is that in the event of a plant species going extinct, either naturally or through a global catastrophe, seeds from the vault could be used to recultivate it in the wild.

Meanwhile, at San Diego Zoo, in California, a similar project is underway to conserve animal species. The Frozen Zoo houses a collection of biological material from more than eight hundred different animal species. The material takes various forms, including female eggs, male sperm and whole fertilized embryos – as well as raw DNA. The latter, it's hoped, might eventually enable animals to be brought back from extinction even when there isn't a single specimen of the species left alive. This would be achieved via techniques developed for cloning and synthetic biology, whereby DNA can be inserted into an egg cell of a related species and the cell then implanted into a mother animal of that species and brought to term.

There is already research underway, led by Akira Iritani, a professor at Kyoto University, to resurrect the woolly mammoth using this technique – using DNA from mammoths found preserved in polar ice, and implanting it into a modern elephant. So far, these attempts have been unsuccessful because of frost damage sustained during the DNA's eight thousand-year freeze. But now scientists are hoping they might be able to use samples recovered from many mammoths to reconstruct the creature's genetic sequence in a computer, and then synthesize the corresponding DNA artificially. The work continues.

Cryonics

If we can freeze animal and plant species in order to preserve the world's biodiversity then could we freeze human beings too? This might be an appealing option following an Armageddon scenario that leaves the world in a polluted or otherwise uninhabitable state for many years – such as a nuclear war. In these cases, food and clean water could be in very short supply, and it would thus be useful if humans (or at least most of them) could be placed in suspended animation until the world has had time to detoxify itself.

Such a procedure already exists. Known as cryonics, it involves freezing subjects in supercold liquid nitrogen, thus preserving their body tissue and, it's hoped, all of their memories and psychology, as encoded in the cellular structure of the brain. At present, cryonics is used for people who die from conditions that are untreatable with modern-day medical science. Proponents believe that, one day, medicine will advance to the point that these patients' conditions will be treatable – and that it will also be possible to revive a cryonically suspended patient (which, at present, it's not).

The procedure doesn't come cheap. American cryonics firm Alcor charges $200,000 for whole-body preservation (plus a $500 per year membership fee during life) or, as a cheaper alternative, so-called neuropreservation (where just the head is frozen) for $80,000. Neuropreservation is dependent upon it one day becoming possible to transplant the revived brain into a new body – or perhaps to upload the patient's consciousness into a computer, as the transhumanists fervently expect to be able to do one day.

Perhaps the biggest obstacle that cryonics faces is that of reviving patients at the end of the process. Freezing biological material can cause it a great deal of damage, due to the formation of ice crystals. In an effort to minimize the damage, cryonics organizations pump so-called cryoprotectants into patients' bodies prior to cooling. These prevent the formation of ice at low temperature, inducing instead a state known as vitrification.

There are currently around two hundred cryopreserved patients being maintained by various organizations around the world. Walt Disney, however, is not one of them – contrary to the common urban myth.

Space arks and cosmic colonies
the final frontier

The last section examined how we might go about evacuating large areas of the Earth in the face of extinction-level events. But what if an event was so destructive that it threatened every square inch of the Earth's surface? There's one evacuation route we haven't yet considered – up. Escaping into orbit and beyond may well become viable over the coming centuries as space launch technology improves.

Planet Earth won't be here forever. Even if we're exceptionally careful with our world, and manage to avert climate change, habitat destruction and overpopulation – as well as dodging the bullets nature sends our way, such as supervolcano eruptions, asteroids and ice ages – humanity can only exist on this planet's surface for a finite number of days.

The sun – like all other stars – is not immortal. It will end its days in around 6.5 billion years' time, and when it does it'll take the Earth down with it, scorching the planet's surface to a crisp. If humans, or our transhuman descendants, are still around at this time then clearly, if they want to survive, they will need to leave the Earth behind and migrate out into space. We can only hope that 6.5 billion years from now, travelling into space will be a lot easier than it is today. Not to mention cheaper. At present, getting into orbit can cost as much as $20,000 per kilogram of payload: that works out at around $1.7m to transport a single average human being from the surface of the Earth into space. The high cost is indicative of the fact that the resources needed to get into space are not plentiful. When crunch time arrives then, if our technology has not improved, we will be hard-pushed to get the planet evacuated.

Going up!

One idea is to station a platform in Earth orbit from which a cable can be lowered to the ground and then used to haul payloads up into space. Called a "space elevator", this idea was first hinted at in 1895: a Russian space technology pioneer named Konstantin Tsiolkovsky, proposed a tower that could be built as high as space. His idea was developed more fully in the 1950s by another Russian, Yuri Artsutanov. Tsiolkovsky envisaged an elevator supporting its weight from below; later models relied on tensile principles, wherein the space lift supports itself from above.

It's believed that a functioning space elevator could lower the cost of getting into space to as little as $50 per kilogram. The main stumbling block to building one is finding a material tough enough and light enough to build the cable from. Ordinary steel would break under its own weight. However, there is hope in the form of new materials known as carbon nanotubes. These are a phenomenally strong form of carbon that could be used to make a cable that can

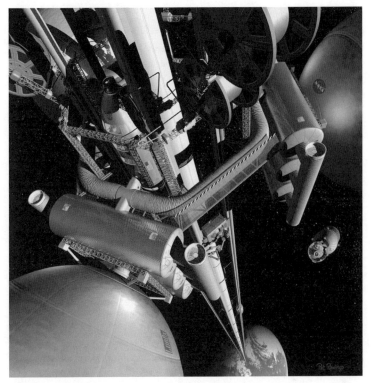

An artist's impression of what a space elevator might look like. For now, these are science fiction, but carbon nanotubes may make them scientific fact.

support itself even when thousands of kilometres in length.

There would be a few other constraints. For example, the platform would need to orbit at exactly the same rate as the Earth spins – so it appeared to hover in the sky. And this is only possible for orbits that lie in the plane of the planet's equator. A counterweight would be reeled out on the opposite side of the orbiting platform, to prevent the payload from pulling the platform down towards the Earth. As the payload is winched up, so the counterweight would be reeled in, keeping the platform's centre of gravity on its designated orbit.

There's also the consideration that humans wishing to ascend using an elevator would require adequate protection against radiation, depending on how long it would take to get through the Van Allen belts. These are a ring of high-energy charged particles around Earth,

Force fields and space radiation

The biggest hazard facing human explorers in space is radiation. Our sun is continually spewing subatomic particles into the interplanetary environment, and occasionally spits out a very-high-energy burst of them. These outbursts come in different forms, known as solar flares and coronal mass ejections, and they are capable of causing fatal radiation sickness to anyone caught in the blast without adequate protective shielding. If the human race is hoping to use space as a potential escape route by which to flee calamities on Earth, then we'd better first make sure that we won't be leaping from the frying pan and into the fire.

The Earth-orbiting International Space Station (ISS) has special radiation-shielded modules, in which the hull is much thicker than normal, enabling the metal to block incoming radiation particles. Astronauts on the station take cover in these modules during times of high solar activity. But boosting into orbit the vast amount of metal needed to shield a large spacecraft – large enough, that is, to carry a significant portion of the human race – will take vast amounts of rocket fuel, maybe more than we can lay our hands on at short notice.

Luckily for us, there is an alternative. Part of the reason why we on Earth don't get zapped with radiation sickness every time the sun throws out a coronal mass ejection is that our planet has a magnetic field. Most radiation particles are electrically charged, which means that magnetism alters their paths – and the particles are thus deflected harmlessly away into space.

Early studies suggested that to place such an artificial magnetic shield around a spacecraft would require a field tens of kilometres across – demanding vast, heavy magnets and many megawatts of electrical power. But new research in 2008, by Dr Ruth Bamford and colleagues at Rutherford Appleton Laboratories in England, has shown that a working magnetic deflector could be built using a much smaller field, just 100m across. And this would mean much less equipment having to be boosted into space. Magnetism could well be the force to protect our interplanetary lifeboats, enabling them to ferry humanity safely away from the ailing Earth.

held in place by Earth's magnetic field. At the times currently imagined, radiation from the Van Allen belts would, if unshielded, dish out a potentially fatal dose.

Island Three

So let's say we're all up in space. Then what? We might be destined to stay up there for good. In the 1970s, American physicist Gerard O'Neill came up with a number of designs for giant space stations which human beings could colonize as the Earth became overcrowded or uninhabitable. Perhaps his most famous design was known as Island Three. It consisted of two giant cylinders, each 8km in diameter and 30km long, side by side and counter-rotating.

The cylinders spin on their axes at a rate of forty times per hour, creating a centrifugal force roughly equal to Earth's gravity, which would stick objects to the cylinder's inside surface. This inner surface is where the space colonists could set up their homes. This living space is divided into three giant "stripes" of land stretching the length of each cylinder, separated by three equally sized window stripes. An arrangement of mirrors, placed outside the cylinder, reflects sunlight in through these windows. The mirrors can be tilted to simulate the motion of the sun across the sky, and then reflect the sun away entirely to simulate night-time – just like a real day on Earth.

The cylinders would be filled with oxygen and nitrogen to create an Earth-like atmosphere. Photosynthesizing plants would cover much of the virtual land, converting our exhaled carbon dioxide back into oxygen, and maintaining a stable environment. Each of these orbital colonies, it has been estimated, could provide a home in space for over a million people.

The colonies would most likely be stationed at the Lagrange points, where the gravity of the Earth and sun, roughly speaking, cancel out – allowing objects to orbit the sun in step with the Earth. There are two Lagrange points in particular, called L4 and L5, that are situated 60° ahead of and behind the Earth in its orbit. This means they are stable, so colonies floating at these points wouldn't need to expend any energy to maintain their course through space.

One of the designs for a space colony that the American physicist Gerard O'Neill came up with in the 1970s – and looking very much of its time.

A new home?

Of course, if the Earth and the sun are no more, an O'Neill colony will probably be unfeasible – at least in our solar system. We may have to look at colonizing another world, perhaps orbiting another star altogether. Some space scientists have suggested that we might be able to colonize asteroids, perhaps burrowing into their surfaces to create vast underground living spaces. The big benefit of setting up on a natural body in this way would be that all the raw materials we'd ever need would be right under our feet – greatly reducing the amount of luggage we'd have to bring with us when abandoning the Earth. Asteroids all formed from the same cloud of gas, dust and debris as the other planets, and are thus rich in elements such as iron, oxygen and carbon.

Another, slightly more radical, option might be to adopt a new planet. The odds of us finding somewhere precisely suited to our biology are, admittedly, slim. However, we may not have to. If we can find a barren world of about the same size and gravity as the

Moonbase: our first home away from home

Plans for a permanent human base on the moon stretch back to the 1960s – both as a research station, and as a military platform from which the Cold War superpowers could lob down missiles with impunity. US plans called for a subsurface base, using the lunar soil as a natural shield against radiation. It was to be powered by nuclear reactors, which were at the time a more efficient and continuous energy solution than solar panels.

However, the political will for such an outpost dried up following the end of the space race, when the United States became the first to plant those all-important flags and footprints in the lunar soil. In 2004, President George W. Bush pledged to send humans back to moon, with the goal being to establish a base there, as a practice run for the real Big Enchilada: a crewed landing on Mars. However, following the financial crisis of 2007–10, the new US president, Barack Obama, cancelled the programme.

There may well be a change of heart in the not too distant future though. The moon is believed to be an abundant source of helium-3. Helium is the second-lightest chemical element in the universe. Helium-3 is an isotope of this element that's even lighter still, having had a neutron particle removed from its atomic nucleus. It could turn out to be important for nuclear fusion reactors: devices that generate energy by bonding together the nuclei of light atoms. Fusion could offer us a rich source of energy in the future. Physicists say that helium-3 would be preferable as a fusion fuel because it can undergo fusion reactions without giving off harmful "neutron radiation" – which is a difficult kind of radiation to block. And so, rather like California in the mid-nineteenth century, colonization of the Moon may be driven by enterprise rather than exploration.

The first lunar colonists will undoubtedly be helped by the discovery in 2009 of significant quantities of water on the moon. This could be mined not only for settlers to drink, but – through application of an electric current – split into its components of hydrogen and oxygen and used as rocket fuel.

Earth, we may be able to engineer ourselves a hospitable climate. After all, that's what ultimately happened on the Earth. Our planet began with an atmosphere rich in carbon dioxide. Plants were the first life forms to evolve in this environment, and they then converted the carbon dioxide to oxygen – through photosynthesis. This flood of oxygen into the atmosphere is what paved the way for the emergence, later, of animal life. Perhaps we could arrange for the same thing to happen again, by seeding our new planet with photosynthetic plants. Scientists refer to this kind of planetary engineering as terraforming – literally shaping a world to make it Earth-like.

Once there's enough oxygen, we could even populate our new home with earthly animal species. We might not need to play Noah, taking living specimens of these creatures with us, though. The emerging science of synthetic biology means that all we may need are the genetic sequences of these life forms, stored on computer. By using this information to programme host cells, we could hope to reanimate these creatures and thus create for ourselves a true home from home.

Escape to cyberspace
Second Life becomes first life

The one problem with migrating into space is that it could all be rather miserable. After the initial thrill of blasting into orbit, the eternal black sky and the cold technological surroundings of a spacecraft or space station could make for a somewhat dull existence as the days and years roll by. Even if we managed to relocate to another natural body in the solar system, this would likely be an asteroid or rocky moon – neither of which are especially known for their scenic vistas.

Keeping the human race going is one thing, but if our quality of life is going to be so poor then you have to wonder whether it would really be worth all the effort. Technology, according to some people, might offer a solution of sorts. Futurologists and science-fiction writers have long mused over the idea of uploading human consciousness into a computer. The human brain, where consciousness currently resides, is essentially just a biological information processor. If it were possible to extract all of the information about "you" from the cells making up your grey matter and then upload it into an electronic computer, then it might be a way for your consciousness to be safely stored.

Moreover, you could then choose what environment you wanted to exist in. After all, our everyday experiences ultimately boil down to a large number of nerve impulses relayed to the brain from our senses – and from which the brain then stitches together our picture of reality. If the brain was transferred to a computer then all of those nerve impulses could be generated artificially, like a kind of all-immersing virtual reality simulation. Indeed, this is all quite similar to the "simulation argument" put forward by philosopher Nick Bostrom at the University of Oxford, in which he argues that our universe may already be an elaborate computer program.

Could it really be done?

Some scientists and researchers think uploading your mind into a computer will one day be possible. Ian Pearson, a futurologist at the Futurizon consultancy in Switzerland, believes the technology could be here as soon as 2050. So what would be required? The first thing, obviously, is a computer that's powerful enough. The human brain consists of a large number of brain cells, called neurons, with an even larger number of connections between them. These connections encode the "state" of the brain – everything about your personality and psychology, as well as all your memories. There are around one thousand trillion of these connections (a one followed by fifteen zeroes). Encoding the precise configuration of all of them would require a computer with a vast memory – about twenty thousand terabytes (TB). By comparison, IBM's state-of-the-art Sequoia supercomputer has a memory of 1600TB. So in the memory stakes, computers are getting there, but still have some way to go.

In terms of sheer processing power, a desktop PC is already much quicker than the human brain. A neuron can send several hundred signals per second – perhaps one thousand at full stretch. However, a 2GHz computer processor is two million times quicker than this. That means that someone uploading their consciousness into a computer would be able to think at extraordinary speed. In fact, the figures above imply that every single thought a human brain can process in the space of a year could be run through a computer in about fifteen seconds. Subjective time for such an electronic consciousness would pass very quickly.

You 2.0

Another big problem at the moment is how you would read off the configuration of someone's brain in order to create an electronic data file which could be fed into a computer in the first place. There has been considerable progress towards doing this non-invasively. For example, fMRI scanners have been used to detect what someone is thinking. This has been used in everything from lie detection to the design of advertising. But resolving the detail needed to describe the complete state of every neuron in a person's head is still a very long way off indeed.

The only way to do this in the foreseeable future would be to remove the brain, freeze it, slice it into wafer-thin sections and then scan it section by section using an electron microscope: a device that uses electron particles in place of light to produce highly detailed images. Naturally, the brain is completely destroyed in the process, and so you'd need to be fairly confident that uploading yourself into a computer would work – and that this computer version of your brain would actually like it once it was there.

Once "you" are safely uploaded into a computer, there could be numerous benefits in addition to being able to select your scenery. For a start, there's immortality. So long as you have a means to manufacture new computers to replace old ones as they wear out – say, through robotic interfaces – then this "you" will never die. Placing your consciousness in a computer that is part of a robot will, in addition, give you some mobility – just in case you ever did get a wistful hankering to explore the real world once more.

A small digi-world

Over recent decades, technology has made computers ever smaller. But how small could a computer become and still be powerful

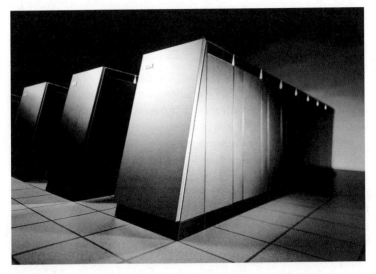

The most powerful computer in the world? The massed drives of IBM's 1600-terabyte Sequoia supercomputer. One day, virtual versions of our brains could be residing inside a swish address such as this.

enough to host human consciousness? Physicist Jacob Bekenstein, at the Hebrew University of Jerusalem, has worked out the smallest physical volume that a given quantity of information can be compressed down into. His calculation was actually based on the physics of black holes. He showed that if information could be squashed down smaller than the so-called "Bekenstein bound" then dropping it into a black hole would violate the laws of thermodynamics, which govern the physics of energy and heat.

Bekenstein's formula depends on the density of the matter used to encode the information – and the size of the Bekenstein bound decreases as the density gets larger. Taking, as a conservative estimate, the density of matter attained in particle accelerators today implies a minimum dimension for the information in the human brain that's about the size of an atom. Using denser matter may be possible in the future, which would allow it to be even smaller.

And so we're led towards an unusual scenario for the ultimate fate of our species – a swarm of human souls, fleeing from the stricken Earth, each living inside a computer the size of an atom and adrift in the great gulf of outer space.

The ultimate escape plan
surviving the end of the universe

The demise of an ecosystem is bad. The death of a whole planet is a catastrophe. But both these scenarios pale into insignificance next to the end of the entire universe. That means not just the end of the Earth and the sun, but of every planet, star and galaxy in the whole of space. It's the ultimate Armageddon scenario. No one gets out alive – not even the colony four light years away on Alpha Centauri – because there is, quite literally, nowhere to run.

Or is there? If you believe some physicists then it might be possible to escape into "hyperspace" – space which exists beyond the three dimensions that we experience day to day. No one knows what we might find in this higher plane, whether there will be stars and planets or whether the laws of physics there will even permit life as we know it. But when our universe begins its death throes, a headlong dash into the unknown might well be our only hope.

There are two principal routes by which the universe could bow out. It could either undergo a "heat death", in which space expands forever, gradually getting colder and darker as all the galaxies rush apart, or it could fall in on itself in a "Big Crunch" – a violent antithesis of the Big Bang in which the universe was born. Determining which of these two scenarios actually plays out depends how much mass the universe contains. If the universe is above a certain critical density then it will collapse in a Big Crunch; otherwise it'll end in a heat death.

The day the sky fell in

Let's look at the Big Crunch first. How could we escape if we discovered that our universe was imploding? How would we even know if our universe was imploding? The second part's easy. Astronomers can see that the universe is safely expanding for the time being by using powerful telescopes to study the light from distant galaxies. They look for characteristic features in the light's spectrum – peaks and dips in the graph you get by plotting its brightness against wavelength. These features are usually found at wavelengths longer than they should be, which means that the galaxies are moving away from us and the universe is expanding. It's similar to the effect that stretches out the sound from an ambulance siren to longer wavelength (lower pitch) as it moves away from you.

The moment astronomers start seeing these features in the light from galaxies shifting to shorter wavelengths, it's time to worry – that would be a sign that the Big Crunch has begun. If that ever happened, what could we do about it?

One option might be to exploit an idea in subatomic particle physics, known as string theory. This essentially says that all fundamental particles of matter, such as protons and electrons, are ultimately made up of tiny, one-dimensional vibrating "strings" of energy. The mathematics describing the theory is incredibly complex, but one of its consequences is that in order for string theory to work space must have six extra dimensions, in addition to the three that we can see.

These extra dimensions are "compactified" – curled up very tightly – which is why they are invisible to us. It's rather like looking at a garden hosepipe. When viewed from a distance the pipe looks one-dimensional, even though we know its surface is actually two-dimensional: one of the two dimensions is curled up and hidden.

If this is the case then, when the universe was born in the Big Bang, fourteen billion years ago, six of the nine space dimensions were compactified while the other three expanded to form our universe. However, many theoretical models of string theory suggest that during the Big Crunch, the reverse will happen: as the three dimensions that we live in shrink down, so the other six will start to expand. Better still, it seems that there would be a transition point – where our home three dimensions and the expanding six dimensions would both be about the same size and, crucially, large enough for us to survive in. And this would make it possible for humans to jump across into these new dimensions at the last minute. It would be like an emergency exit through space opened up for a brief few moments, through which humanity could make the greatest of great escapes.

Parallel worlds

That's encouraging, but it does of course require that the universe obligingly ends its days in a Big Crunch. Lately, however, that scenario has been looking rather improbable. In the 1990s, astronomers discovered that the expansion rate of our universe actually seems to be accelerating, making it unlikely (although not impossible) that

Do parallel universes exist?

They've been floating round in science fiction for decades. Now scientists are coming around to the astonishing idea that parallel universes – regions of space completely dislocated from the space and time of our own universe – might actually exist for real.

Parallel universes could be rather like mirror images of our own universe – albeit slightly distorted. That's because they allow history to unfold differently. There may be Universes out there in which you are the president of the United States, others where you were the first person to land on Mars and others in which you do not exist at all.

This wholesale shift in our understanding of physics began in 1957, with the work of Hugh Everett. He came up with a new interpretation of quantum physics, the branch of science describing the behaviour of tiny subatomic particles. In his theory, called the "many worlds interpretation", he was able to explain some of the more bizarre behaviours of subatomic particles – such as appearing to be in several different places at the same time – in terms of interference between versions of the particle in different parallel universes. The gamut of parallel universes that the many worlds interpretation suggests exist has become known as the "multiverse".

In the 1980s, physicist David Deutsch at the University of Oxford figured out how it might be possible to exploit the laws of quantum physics to build quantum computers – the processing power of which vastly outstrips that of any desktop PC – or even a university supercomputer. But Deutsch backed up his calculations with an interesting corollary. He worked out that in the course of carrying out a computation, a quantum computer would need to store more bits (binary digits) of information than there are atoms in our universe. If the information in its memory can't be stored in our universe, then where exactly?

According to Everett's many worlds theory, it's being stored in parallel universes: a quantum computer derives its power by harnessing the processing and storage capabilities of the many copies of itself out there across the multiverse.

space could ever slow down and recollapse – our cosmos, it seems, is destined instead for the dark, chilly fade-out of a heat death. So what can we do in that case?

One option would be to try to tunnel, not into higher dimensions of our own universe, but to other universes entirely. Scientists are becoming increasingly convinced that such parallel universes really exist. They think that if our universe is like a sheet of paper, and we exist on its surface rather like ants, then there could be other sheets of paper all stacked up in a big sheaf (literally, in parallel) between which it's possible for the ants to hop.

How? Physicists now think that space is nothing like the fixed stage that it was once imagined to be. Albert Einstein's theory of relativity, for example, revealed just how mutable space can be – bending this way and that in response to the matter that it contains. Now scientists believe that just as subatomic particles can be split apart if subjected to high enough energy, so space can be made to bubble and seethe on the tiniest scales.

What if we could develop the technology to grab such a tendril of boiling space? Could we then stretch it out to form a bridge linking parallel universes – a so-called wormhole? It's certainly feasible in principle. Physicists have already discovered a kind of material, known as exotic matter, which is capable of expanding such a tiny wormhole to macroscopic size and holding it open long enough for someone to travel through.

So far, exotic matter has only been manufactured in minuscule quantities. And, although particle accelerators such as the Large Hadron Collider are able to generate immense particle collision energies, these are still nowhere near powerful enough to enable us to create wormholes to other universes. But the important thing is we know roughly how it could be done and, it appears, we have plenty of time – the cosmic heat death won't start to bite for another 10^{100} years – a one with one hundred zeroes after it. This is one disaster scenario where, for a change, time is on our side.

Resources

The end of days is a popular subject, not just as a field of scientific enquiry and cultural research but as the inspiring idea behind an array of novels and movies. People, it seems, are fascinated by the concept of Armageddon, what will cause it and what, if anything, we can do to prevent it. If you've got the bug, as it were, then here is a selection of books, films and websites to feed your fever.

Books

Non-fiction

How to Build a Nuclear Bomb Frank Barnaby (2003)
Nuclear physicist Frank Barnaby gives a scarily simple account of how nuclear weapons – from ICBMs to the terrorist's dirty bombs – actually work and what their effects are. Barnaby should know, having worked at the UK's Atomic Weapons Research Establishment during its bomb-test heyday in the 1950s.

The Zombie Survival Guide: Complete Protection from the Living Dead Max Brooks (2004)
Whether this really belongs in a non-fiction section is debatable. But everything you never wanted to know about fending off the undead hordes can be found inside this guide to zombie Armageddon. If you enjoy this one, you'll be pleased to learn Brooks (who is, incidentally, the son of the comedy king Mel) has written umpteen sequels, including the somewhat unfeasibly titled *Recorded Attacks*.

Engines of Creation Eric Drexler (1986)
When asked to name the book that started the nanotech revolution, many experts cite Drexler's account of the ultimate end-state of miniaturization – electromechanical devices built from individual atoms. It is in this book that the dreaded "grey goo" scenario, in which self-replicating nanomachines devour the world, gets its first outing.

The Rough Guide to Climate Change Robert Henson (2008)
If you're still somewhat baffled as to what climate change is really all about, then this is one book that has pretty much everything you need to know. What causes it, what the effects are, why we need to worry – and, most importantly, what we can do about it – are all addressed.

Physics of the Impossible Michio Kaku (2006)
Invisibility, teleportation, skipping back and forth through time, and faster-than-light travel – it's all in here. Physicist and science communicator Kaku has written the ultimate guide to the outer limits of modern physics.

The Singularity Is Near Ray Kurzweil (2006)
The machines are coming to get us, warns renowned US inventor Ray Kurzweil. He extrapolates from the observation that the power of computers is doubling every few years to predict a point at which computing power exceeds human intelligence, becomes conscious and develops the capability of improving itself. This leads to a feedback loop and infinitely fast machine development – a state Kurzweil dubs the "singularity".

Frozen Earth Doug Macdougall (2006)
What is it exactly that causes ice ages, and do we need to worry about one gripping the planet tomorrow? Doug Macdougall explains the ice ages of the past – from the first known example, three billion years ago, up to the Little Ice Age that chilled medieval Europe.

Global Catastrophes: A Very Short Introduction Bill McGuire (2006)
Known in the media as "Disasterman", Professor Bill McGuire is an expert in the field of volcanology and seismology, as well as impact hazards, tsunamis, hurricanes and any other kind of natural catastrophe you can think of. He has condensed his expertise into this easily digestible volume.

When the Rivers Run Dry Fred Pearce (2006)
In an age when everyone seems to be worrying about rising sea levels, environmental journalist Fred Pearce focuses on the problem that, while sea-water levels are rising, the fresh water available to us is steadily diminishing as a result of our water-thirsty food manufacturing processes.

Target Earth Duncan Steel (2003)
An account of the threat posed to Earth by comet and asteroid impacts, written by a scientist who has made seminal contributions to modern understanding of the field. Steel also surveys the possible technology we might use to deflect an inbound space rock – which might just prevent humanity going the same way as the dinosaurs.

The Rough Guide to the Future Jon Turney (2010)

What's in store for the human race? Science writer Jon Turney has the answers in this guide to the years and decades yet to come. Turney covers some big, disaster-rich topics including nanotech, food supply and war. Not recommended as bedtime reading.

Fiction

Flood Stephen Baxter (2008)

Seismic activity has cracked open the ocean floor, causing subterranean reservoirs to release their vast loads of water, swelling the oceans to the point where the entire planet becomes submerged (Everest slips below the waves in 2052). A smattering of survivors keep humanity's flame alive, living on a fleet of arks.

The Postman David Brin (1985)

Sci-fi author David Brin's foray into post-apocalyptic fiction revolves around a survivor who finds a postman's uniform and keeps it, purely to stay warm. However, his appearance as a messenger inadvertently gives hope to the communities of survivors he encounters. The cause of the apocalypse is never made entirely clear, though it seems to be man-made.

Prey Michael Crichton (2002)

Swarms of self-reproducing nanobots escape from a lab and begin devouring the world – it's that dreaded "grey goo" scenario. The robots' programming gives them a degree of intelligence and they are able to evolve, developing and exploiting technologies such as solar electricity.

The Black Cloud Fred Hoyle (1957)

A dense cloud of gas from beyond the solar system drifts inwards to engulf the Earth, blocking out the sun and causing massive loss of life. It transpires, however, that the cloud isn't just inanimate gas but is actually alive – and this turns out to be the fact that saves humanity from extinction.

The Stand Stephen King (1978)

A military-engineered superflu bug escapes from the lab, leading to a pandemic that eradicates virtually all of the human race. Two principal groups of survivors – one good, the other evil – clash, leading to the conflict that gives this epic novel its title.

I Am Legend Richard Matheson (1954)

Adapted for the screen as *The Omega Man* (starring Charlton Heston) and again under its proper name (starring Will Smith), this is a perverse tale of how the sole survivor of a global disease (which leaves its hosts in a vampire-like state) himself becomes renowned as a monster of legend.

The Road Cormac McCarthy (2006)
A very bleak vision of the future is offered up in this novel about a father's efforts to protect his young son amidst the dying embers of civilization, following an unnamed global apocalypse that has reduced the world to a savage wasteland in which cannibalism is rife.

Lucifer's Hammer Larry Niven and Jerry Pournelle (1977)
A thoughtful yet highly dramatic account of how humankind might respond to the impact of a massive comet with planet Earth. The science is excellent, although the novel's prognosis isn't optimistic, forecasting the use of nuclear strikes by nations against each other to stem the flux of refugees from comet-struck regions.

On the Beach Neville Shute (1957)
Neville Shute's post-apocalyptic novel tells the tale of World War III and how the nuclear fires have left the planet awash with clouds of radioactive fallout. The novel tells the story of a group of survivors in Australia, as they gradually realize that fate has inevitably caught up with them.

Earth Abides George R. Stewart (1949)
This novel is regarded by many critics and sci-fi connoisseurs as the definitive fictional account of humanity struggling on after the impact of a global disaster; in this case, a disease pandemic. Central to the plot is the realization that the high culture of Earth's former civilization is of no use to a hunter-gatherer society – much to the dismay of the book's protagonist.

War of the Worlds H.G. Wells (1898)
This remains the mother of all alien invasion stories, and has been adapted for the screen on several occasions. Wells's novel tells of desperate Martians leaving their dying world behind to conquer Earth. Encased in metal "fighting machines", they almost succeed. But in the end they are defeated by Earth's most humble inhabitants – bacteria.

Day of the Triffids John Wyndham (1951)
What would happen if intelligent, mobile and deadly plants decided they'd had enough of relying on human beings to do the watering and would like to claim the Earth for themselves? That's the premise of this novel, in which plants brandishing deadly stingers push mankind to the brink of extinction.

Movies

Armageddon (1998)

A giant asteroid is on collision course with the Earth and it takes a spacecraft armed with nuclear warheads on a suicide mission to destroy it. Sound familiar? Luckily we have Bruce Willis (and his vest) on board, scotching any hopes the asteroid might have had of restaging a dino-Armageddon.

2012 (2009)

Director Roland Emmerich's take on the idea that the world will end when the Mayan Long Count Calendar reaches the end of its longest cycle – in December 2012. It's a good yarn, albeit one with no basis in science, ascribing the Earth's ultimate demise to neutrino particles from the sun that melt the planet's core.

28 Days Later (2002)

Forget the sluggish, lumbering zombies of George A. Romero's films – the undead beasties in Danny Boyle's *28 Days Later* would give Usain Bolt cause to break sweat. The film paints a bleak picture of life in England after a disease epidemic has turned most of the population into lightning-fast flesh eaters. There are just a few pockets of human survivors – many of whom have become equally vicious.

Children of Men (2006)

Welcome to a world where the youngest person alive is aged nineteen. Dwindling fertility means the human race probably has just a few decades left. The realization that this is the end has sapped the world of hope and brought civilization to its knees. The UK is the only place where any hint of normality remains but, deluged with refugees and rife with epidemics, its grip is quickly slipping.

The Day After (1983)

This movie shocked millions when it first aired on network TV in 1983. A confrontation between the two Cold War alliances – NATO and the Communist Warsaw Pact – escalates into all-out nuclear conflict. Terrible levels of devastation are sustained by both sides before a ceasefire is finally called. A bleak ending leaves the viewer uncertain whether the Herculean task of rebuilding civilization is even possible.

The Day After Tomorrow (2004)

More scientifically squiffy doom from Roland Emmerich, this time centred around the hazards of natural climate change – only somewhat accelerated, so that the next ice age begins practically overnight.

Deep Impact (1998)

A giant comet is on collision course with the Earth and it takes a spacecraft armed with nuclear warheads to destroy it. The movie is based on Spielberg's optioning of the Arthur C. Clarke novel *The Hammer of God* (1993) although, to its detriment, none of Clarke's novel made it to the screen.

Dr Strangelove or How I Learned to Stop Worrying and Love the Bomb (1964)

Stanley Kubrick's satirical masterpiece takes a tongue-in-cheek look at how a nuclear first strike by the US against the Communist USSR during the Cold War might have unfolded, thanks to a renegade mad general. The movie is based on Peter George's novel *Red Alert* (1958), and was originally intended to be serious – until Kubrick saw the funny side of it all.

Independence Day (1996)

The basic *War of the Worlds* premise went super big-budget with this blockbuster, starring Will Smith. Aliens launch an all-out assault on planet Earth. They seem to be impervious to bacteria and viruses – except, that is, those of the computer variety.

Mad Max II (1981)

One of the definitive post-apocalypse movies, *Mad Max II* shifts attention away from the cause of the apocalypse, focusing instead on life in the aftermath, a barbaric wasteland ruled by gangs, not entirely unlike the early American West.

Night of the Living Dead (1968)

In 1968, George A. Romero made the archetypal zombie film. Shot in black and white, it was a terrifying film for its time, featuring scenes of cannibalism, insanity and violent death. It has become the blueprint for a number of sequels and remakes, and has earned Romero the epithet "Godfather of all zombies".

The Terminator (1984)

Now we're talking. Arnold Schwarzenegger stars as the eponymous robot from the future, sent back from an age in which machines have already conquered the planet. Well, almost. One young man called John Connor is disrupting digital tyranny, and Arnie has come back to 1980s Los Angeles to remove his mother, thus erasing John from existence.

Waterworld (1995)

Imagine the worst-case global warming scenario possible: the poles have totally melted, raising sea levels by 100m or more. Now suppose an awful lot more water gets released from somewhere (perhaps underground reservoirs), so that the entire planet becomes an ocean. That's the planet portrayed in the Kevin Costner movie *Waterworld*. The result is, more or less, *Mad Max II* in boats.

Websites

AON Benfield UCL Hazard Research Centre www.abuhc.org
There are very few academic centres around the world that deal with nothing but volcanoes, earthquakes, asteroid impacts, hurricanes, tsunamis and other capricious acts of nature – and which do so solely because these phenomena are dangerous. The ABUHRC is one. Go here for news, information, research reports and a disaster image library.

Armageddon Online www.armageddononline.org
A daily update of disaster events around the world, plus detailed information on pretty much every catastrophe that could ever befall our hapless planet. If that's not enough there's also a handy guide to preparing for disasters, extolling the merits of "duck and cover" and listing the essential items that every household's disaster kit should include.

Centres for Disease Control and Prevention www.cdc.gov
Whether it's bird flu, swine flu or man flu, this is probably the first website you should check upon learning that a pandemic may be afoot. It provides updates on disease outbreaks around the world, as well as expert advice on how to protect yourself from the nastiest of lurgies.

Cosmic Ancestry www.panspermia.org
Forget Stig of the Dump. According to these guys, human forebears were a lot greener, slimier and otherworldly than the Neanderthal children's book hero. Here you'll find everything you ever wanted to know, and probably a lot more besides, about the scientific theory that life on Earth began in space.

Death Rays from Space www.astrobio.net/exclusive/3227/death-rays-from-space
We are very, very lucky that the Earth has both an atmosphere and a magnetic field. Both bat away the torrent of high energy particles raining down on the planet from cosmic phenomena such as supernovae, galaxy cores and mass ejections from the sun. Long may they continue.

RESOURCES

Future of Humanity Institute www.fhi.ox.ac.uk
How will human beings survive the hazards presented by climate change or asteroid impacts, not to mention the perils thrown up by our own technology? These are some of the questions grappled with by the scientists and philosophers at the University of Oxford's Future of Humanity Institute. Details of their work are presented on this site.

Intergovernmental Panel on Climate Change www.ipcc.ch
Established by the United Nations, the IPCC gathers and interprets research on global warming and climate change from around the world, using its findings to advise governments on the action they should take. Their website offers updates, information and advice.

Pacific Tsunami Warning Centre ptwc.weather.gov/ptwc/index.php
A network of buoys across the Pacific Ocean, known as DART (Deep Ocean Assessment and Reporting of Tsunamis), monitors for the tell-tale disturbance caused by the passing of a tsunami wave – and raises the alarm. Current alerts are posted on this website, as are details of how the system works.

The Safety of the LHC public.web.cern.ch/public/en/lhc/safety-en.html
In the succinct words of pop-star-turned-physicist Brian Cox: "Anyone who thinks the Large Hadron Collider will destroy the world is a twat." This website explains why we have nothing to worry about from black holes, strangelets, vacuum instability or any other high-energy phenomena cooked up in the world's hottest particle accelerator.

Space Weather spaceweather.com
The sun is the giver of life on Earth, but it also has a foul temper – it's prone to chucking clouds of high-energy subatomic particles our way. These create pretty aurorae in the sky, but at their worst they cause mayhem on Earth – disrupting power grids as well as communication and navigation equipment.

Svalbard Global Seed Vault regjeringen.no/en/dep/lmd/campain/svalbard-global-seed-vault.html
Okay, so you won't be able to hide yourself in this particular underground bunker, no matter how bad the risk of asteroid impact, nuclear war or global pandemic might get. But take heart from the fact that post-apocalyptic man will still be able to enjoy gladioli, thanks to this bomb-proof seed repository. This website has all its details.

Index

Picture credits

Inside front cover: Corbis/Mike Agliolo
Corbis: 6 (PBNJ Productions), 53 (US coast guards), 88 (Paul Souders), 93 (Jeremy Horner), 98 (Qilai Shen), 153 (Karen Kasmauski)
Dorling Kindersley: 18 (Jon Hughes), 65
Getty Images: 15 (Michael Ochs Archives), 29 (Exclusive/Hammer Film Productions), 46 (Arlan Naeg), 248 (Marko Georgiev)
Greenpeace/Bernd Roemmelt 126
Moviestore Collection: 5 (Columbia Pictures), 20 (Tim Burton Productions/Warner Bros), 26 (Universal Pictures/Atmosphere Entertainment MM), 35 (Allied Artists Pictures/Security Pictures), 80 (Universal Pictures), 104 (MGM), 108 (Universal Pictures/Strike Entertainment), 164 (Universal Pictures/Atlas Entertainment), 176 (Hemdale Film/Pacific Western), 181 (Orion Pictures Corporation), 183 (Universal Pictures), 199 (Paramount Pictures/Dreamworks SKG), 232 (David Foster Productions/Paramount Pictures), 240 (DNA Films/Ingenious Film Partners), 252 (Kennedy Miller Entertainment), 261 (Paramount Pictures/Dreamworks SKG)
NASA: 193, 200, 202, 205, 208, 210, 217, 223, 270
Smithsonian Institute: 195